D0276708

GREAT SCOTTISH SPEECHES

VOLUME II

By the same Author

Great Scottish Speeches, Vol. 1 (ed.)

As Scotland embarks on a new process of discussion and debate about our constitutional future, it is timely to celebrate the different voices and strands of opinion which have taken the nation to our present place – and to encourage new voices for our future progress. Let the discourse begin!
ALEX SALMOND

From politicians such as Keir Hardie, through Lions coach Jim Telfer, to fictional characters like Miss Jean Brodie, their words still resonate – powerful, lyrical, moving.
THE SCOTSMAN

The Scottish Secretaries (Birlinn, 2006)

George Younger: A Life Well Lived (Birlinn, 2008)

'We in Scotland': Thatcherism in a Cold Climate (Birlinn, 2009)

Noel Skelton and the Property-Owning Democracy (Biteback, 2010)

Inside Edinburgh: Discovering the Classic Interiors of Edinburgh (Birlinn, 2010)

Salmond: Against the Odds (Birlinn, 2011)

David Steel: Rising Hope to Elder Statesman (Biteback, 2012)

Whatever Happened to Tory Scotland? (ed.) (Edinburgh University Press, 2012)

The Battle for Britain: Scotland and the Independence Referendum (Biteback, 2013)

GREAT SCOTTISH SPEECHES

VOLUME II

INTRODUCED AND EDITED BY DAVID TORRANCE

❧

Luath Press Limited

EDINBURGH

www.luath.co.uk

For my brother Michael, who's always complaining I haven't dedicated a book to him.

First published 2013

ISBN: 978-1-908373-63-2

The publishers acknowledge the support of

towards the publication of this volume.

The paper used in this book is recyclable. It is made from low-chlorine pulps produced in a low-energy, low-emissions manner from renewable forests.

Printed and bound by
ScandBook, Sweden

Typeset in 10.5 point Gill and 10.5 point Quadraat
by 3btype.com

Contents

Introduction

I WROTE THIS introduction in the midst of celebrations to mark five decades since the delivery of a speech. It is not every day the President of the United States (and indeed two of his predecessors) marks the anniversary of a piece of oratory, but it was a testament to the enduring influence of Dr Martin Luther King's searing 'I have a dream' oration.

Large crowds gathered at Washington DC's Lincoln Memorial, where Obama spoke just after 7 p.m., the exact moment Dr King delivered his spellbinding speech to around 250,000 people. Not only did he and others remember the fine words spoken that day, but also the speech's legislative impact – within two years the Civil Rights Act and Voting Rights Act had been signed into law.

It was a moment rich with history and symbolism, with the first black President, himself a fine orator, standing where Dr King first sketched out his dream. 'We rightly and best remember Dr King's soaring oratory that day – how he gave mighty voice to the quiet hopes of millions,' Obama said. 'His words belong to the ages, possessing a power and prophecy unmatched in our time.' 'This march,' declared President Clinton, 'and that speech, changed America.'

Few speeches have such an impact, and indeed those gathered in this volume are much more modest – though still important – in scope. Indeed, when I began gathering material for *Great Scottish Speeches* in early 2011, I was concerned I would not find enough speeches to fill a book. But I need not have worried. Not only did around 70 speeches make it into the first volume, but I also had a couple of dozen spare.

Given my ongoing appeal for new speeches, that two dozen became three, then four, and carried on growing; so by the time Gavin MacDougall at Luath suggested a second volume, I only had to source about half the speeches that follow this introduction. Again I used social media (although twitter rather than facebook) to gather suggestions, and that yielded yet another dozen, most of them by women.

The criteria remained much the same. First, a speech had to be 'Scottish', although as before I have interpreted this fairly loosely to mean speeches delivered by anyone (Scots and non-Scots) *in Scotland* or speeches made *by Scots* anywhere else in the world. Next, anything worthy of inclusion had to be demonstrably a 'speech' (a lot of potentially promising material fell on this point), and finally each piece of oratory had to be 'great', not necessarily heart stopping in its eloquence (although obviously that helped), but notable, memorable beyond its original delivery.

Again, most of the speeches herein have been edited – I hope sympathetically – for reasons of brevity, and as before, I have not limited myself to the realms of reality, so there are fictional speeches from Schiller, Armando Iannucci, Lewis Grassic Gibbon and Sir David Lindsay to complement those in volume one. As before, I can only apologise for the dominance of political speeches, although I have consciously tried to include a good spread of Left and Right, Nationalist and Unionist, and everything in between.

The former governor of New York (state) Mario Cuomo coined the famous aphorism that you 'campaign in poetry and govern in prose', and indeed I am struck that more than a few of the speeches included in this volume date from the past three years. This mini renaissance has probably arisen as a consequence of Scotland's pending independence referendum in September 2014; naturally politicians on both sides of the argument are conscious that such historical moments are shaped by words, so they are endeavouring to make them good ones.

Texts for these were easy to locate, for these days transcripts of speeches are available online moments after they have been delivered and carried live on television news channels. Those predating the internet era again required a bit of digging, which was both challenging and fun, time consuming and occasionally frustrating. There are more female voices in this volume, though tracking down original speeches – particularly the older ones – still proved incredibly difficult. There are also a few more cultural examples, which I was conscious were under-represented in volume one.

Events during the compilation of this volume reassured me that reports of the death of speechmaking are greatly exaggerated. At the London Olympic opening ceremony last summer Kenneth Branagh declaimed the 'Be not afeared: the isle is full of noises' speech from *The Tempest*; a few months later the Labour leader Ed Miliband (briefly) turned his political fortunes around with an oratorical *tour de force* at his party's annual conference in Manchester, while at around the same time Australian PM Julia Gillard's verbal filleting of opposition leader Tony Abbott became an unlikely YouTube sensation.

Finally, this volume – like the first – would not have been possible without suggestions and helpful pointers from the following: James Bailey, Sean Bye, Ellen Cheshire, Kirsty Connell, Ian Duncan, Andrew Keenan, Carole McCallum, Blair McDougall, Harry McGrath, Alasdair McKillop, John MacLeod, Angus Millar, @Nuestory, Ian Rankin, Larry Smith, Michael Torrance and Timothy Neat. Special thanks should go to Professor Norman Macdonald for transcribing (in Gaelic) the speech from Sheriff Nicholson and providing useful background information. I am quite proud that *Great Scottish Speeches Volume II* includes speeches in Gaelic *and* Scots.

David Torrance
Edinburgh, August 2013
www.davidtorrance.com
Follow @davidtorrance on twitter

I know that many have complained, and do yet loudly complain, of my too great severity.

John Knox
c.1514–72

FINAL SERMON · EDINBURGH

9 NOVEMBER 1572

By the early 1570s, John Knox's health had deteriorated to such an extent that walking unaided was difficult and he could not even travel to the Church of Scotland's annual General Assembly. Knox also had to be helped into the pulpit, although as his sermons progressed he became more vigorous, beating the pulpit and instilling a certain amount of fear in his congregation.

When he resumed preaching at St Giles's Cathedral on 31 August 1572 Knox's voice was so weak he was moved to the smaller Tolbooth section of the building, where he could be more easily heard. This is his final sermon, delivered with grim determination on 9 November at the admission of James Lawson, his successor. Thereafter he was too sick to leave his house, suffering from a violent cough that indicated the onset of bronchopneumonia.

Many of his supporters visited over the next few weeks and, on 24 November, Knox died at 11 p.m. surrounded by his wife and friends. Two days later he was buried at St Giles's, where the newly-appointed regent, the 4th Earl of Morton, made his famous tribute: 'Here lyeth a man who in his life never feared the face of man; who hath beene often threatned with dagge and dagger, but yet hath ended his dayes in peace and honour.'

John Knox was born in 1514 near Haddington. Probably educated at St Andrews University, he was influenced by early church reformers such as George Wishart and spent his early career in the Church of England, rising to become King Edward VI's royal chaplain. When Mary Tudor re-established Roman Catholicism he resigned and moved to Geneva, where he met John Calvin. On returning to Scotland Knox led its Protestant Reformation, helping to establish the ecclesiastical order for the newly created Church of Scotland.

THE DAY APPROACHES and is now before the door, for which I have frequently and vehemently thirsted, when I shall be released from my great labours and innumerable sorrows, and shall be with Christ. And now God is my witness, whom I have served in spirit, in the Gospel of His Son, that I have taught nothing but the true and solid doctrine of the Gospel of the Son of God; and have had it for my own object, to instruct the ignorant, to confirm the faithful; to comfort the weak, the fearful, and the distressed, by the promises of grace; and to fight against the proud and rebellious, by the divine threatenings. I know that many have complained, and do yet loudly complain, of my too great severity; but God knows that my mind was always void of hatred to the persons of those against whom I thundered the severest judgements.

I know that many have complained, and do yet loudly complain, of my too great severity; but God knows that my mind was always void of hatred to the persons of those against whom I thundered the severest judgements.

I cannot deny but that I felt the greatest abhorrence at the sins in which they indulged; but I still kept this one thing in view, that, if possible, I might gain them to the Lord. What influenced me to utter whatever the Lord put into my mouth so boldly, without respect of persons, was a reverential fear of God, who called, and out of his grace appointed me to be a steward of divine mysteries, and a belief that He will demand an account of my discharge of the trust committed unto me, when I shall stand before His tribunal.

I profess, therefore, before God, and before His holy angels, that I never made merchandise of the sacred word of God, never studied to please men, never indulged my own private passions, or those of others, but faithfully distributed the talent entrusted to me, for the edification of the church over which I watched. Whatever obloquy wicked men may cast on me respecting this point, I rejoice in the testimony of a good conscience. In the meantime, my dearest brethren, do you persevere in the eternal truth of the Gospel; wait diligently on the flock over which the Lord hath set you, and which He redeemed by the blood of His only begotten Son. And thou, my dear brother Lawson, fight the good fight, and do the work of the Lord joyfully and resolutely. The Lord from on high bless you and the whole church of Edinburgh, against whom, as long as they persevere in the word of truth, which they have heard of me, the gates of hell shall not prevail.[1]

Sum seiks to warldlie dignities /
And sum to sensuall vanities.

Folly

SERMON FROM *The Satire of the Three Estates*

1602

A *Satire of the Three Estates* was a satirical morality play written by makar Sir David Lyndsay (or Lindsay). It was first performed in Cupar, Fife, in June 1552, and subsequently in Edinburgh a couple of years later. An attack on the 'three estates' represented in the old Scottish Parliament – the clergy, lords and burgh representatives, symbolised by the characters Spiritualitie, Temporalitie and Merchant.

Sir David Lyndsay of the Mount was born in c1490 and believed to have been educated at St Andrews University. He first worked in the Royal Court as an equerry, then an usher to the future King James V of Scotland, and in 1529 he was appointed Lord Lyon King of Arms and knighted. Later a diplomat, after the death of James V, Sir David continued to represent Cupar in the old Scottish Parliament. He is believed to have died around 1555.

The second part of the play sees the three estates greet the king as Parliament is opened. The failures of the estates are aired and Temporalitie gets punished while the three vices, Deceit, Falsehood and Flatterie, are allowed to speak before they are hanged. After their execution comes this rousing speech from the character Folly (also styled Folie).

As Jamie Reid-Baxter, an expert in early theatre and Scottish literature, has written, the character of Folly was cut out of the famous Edinburgh University productions. He suggested 'both Diligence and Folly are David Lindsay's alter egos'. Reid-Baxter also enthused about the Middle Scots tongue in which the play is written, talking about the 'roughness of Scots…the clods of earth, the earthiness of it…but also the grandeur of those harsher consonants and pure vowel sounds'.[1]

Salamon, the maist sapient king,
In Israeli quhen he did ring,
Thir word[i]s, in effect did write:
The number of fuillis ar infinite.
I think na schame, sa Christ me saife,
To be ane fuill, amang the laife,

Howbeit ane hundreth stands heir-by
Perventure als great fuillis as I

I have of my genelogie
Dwelland in everie cuntrie:

Earles, duiks, kings, and empriours,
With mony guckit conquerours,
Quhilk dois in folie perseveir
And hes done sa this many yeir.
Sum seiks to warldlie dignities
And sum to sensuall vanities.
Quhat vails all thir vaine honours,
Nocht being sure to leife twa houris?
Sum greidie fuill dois fill ane box;
Ane uther fuill cummis and breaks the lox
And spends that uther fuillis hes spaird,
Quhilk never thocht on them to wairde.
Sum dois as thay sould never die:
Is nocht this folie, quhat say ye?

Becaus thair is sa many fuillis
Rydand on hors, and sum, on muillis,
Heir I have [brocht] gude chafery
Till ony fuill that lists to by;
And speciallie for the Thrie Estaits,
Quhair I haue mony tender maits,
Quhilk causit them, as ye may see,
Gang backwart throw the haill cuntrie.
Gif with my merchandise ye list to mell,
Heir I have folie hattis to sell.
Quhairfoir is this hat, wald je ken?
Marie, for insatiabill merchant-men.

Sum dois as thay sould never die:
Is nocht this folie, quhat say ye?

Quhen God hes send them abundance
Ar nocht content with sufficiance,
Bot saillis into the stormy blastis
In winter, to get greater castis,
In mony terribill great torment,
Against the Acts of Parliament:
Sum tynis thair geir, and sum ar drounde-
With this sic merchants sould be crounde...

This hude to sell richt faine I wald
Till him that is baith auld and cald,
Reddie till pas to Hell or Heavin,
And hes fair bairn[i]s sax or seavin,
And is of age fourscoir of yeir,
And taks ane lasse to be his peir
Quhilk is nocht fourteine yeir of age,
And ioynis with hir in mariage,
Geifand hir traist that scho nocht wald
Rycht haistelie mak him cuckold–
Quha maryes beand sa neir their dead,
Set on this hat upon his head!

... This is ane haly hude, I say the:
This hude is ordanit, I the assure,
For spirituall fuillis that taks in cure
The saullis of great diocies
And regiment of great abesies
For gredines of wardlie pelfe,

To win them warldlie gloir and gude
Thay cure nocht schedding of saikles blude.

That can nocht justlie gyde them-selfe;
Uthers sauls to saife it settis them weill,
Syne sell thair awin saullis to the Devil–
Quha-ever dois sa, this I conclude,
Upon his heid set on this hude!

... Gie I lie, God nor thou be hangit!
For I have heir, I to the tell,
Ane nobill cap imperiell,
Quhilk is nocht ordanit bot for doings
Of empreours, of duiks and kings,
For princelie and imperiall fuillis:
Thay sould have luggis al slang as muillis.
The pryde of princes, withoutin faill,
Gars all the warld rin top ovir tail:
To win them warldlie gloir and gude
Thay cure nocht schedding of saikles blude.
Quhat cummer have ye had in Scotland
Be our auld enemies of Ingland?
Had nocht bene the support of France,

We had bene brocht to great mischance.
Now I heir tell the Empreour
Schaippis for to be ane conquerour,
And is muifing his ordinance
Against the nobill King of France;
Bot I knaw nocht his just querrell
That he hes, for till mak battell.
All the princes of Almanie,
Spainye, Flanders and Italie
This present year ar in ane flocht:
Sum sall thair wages find deir bocht!
The Paip with bombard, speir and scheild
Hes send his armie to the field:
Sanct Peter, Sanct Paull nor Sanct Androw
Raisit never sic ane oist, I trow!
Is this fraternall charitie
Or furious foly, quhat say ye?
Thay leird nocht this at Christis scuillis;
Thairfor I think them verie fuillis.
I think it folie, be Gods mother,
Ilk Christian prince to ding doun uther–
Because that this hat sould belang them!
The Prophesie, withouttin weir.
Of Merling beis compleit this year;
For my gudame, the Gyre Carling,
Leirnde me the Prophesie of Marling,
Quhairof I sall schwa the sentence,
Gif ye will gif me audience...
Sa be this Prophesie plainlie appears
That mortall weirs salbe amang freirs:
Thay sall nocht knaw weill in thair closters
To quhorn thay sall say thair Pater nesters.
Wald thay fall to and fecht with speir and shield,
The Feind mak cuir quhilk of them win the feild!
Now of my sermon have I maid ane end:
To Gilly-moubrand I yow all commend,
And I you all beseik richt hartfullie,
Pray for the saull of gude Cacaphatie,
Quhilk laitlie drownit himself into Lochleavin,
That his sweit saull may be above the Heavin.[2]

Solomon, the wisest King of Israel, has said that fools are innumerable; and I am not ashamed to be one, since there are so many. I have kindred in every land, Earls, Dukes, Kings, &c., – fools now, as they have long been. They aim after unsubstantial things, though life is quite uncertain. One fool hoards gold; and another fool steals and spends it. Others are so foolish as to act as if they were never to die. There being many wealthy fools, I have bought goods for them, and, especially, for the three Estates, in which I have many mates, as appears from their acts. I have fools-caps to sell. This one is for the merchants. Not content with abundance, they run risks in winter-time, in the teeth of the Acts of Parliament, with various results. This cap suits such... I would sell it to some one old and cold, ready to die, with a family of children, and who, yet, weds a mere girl, trusting that she will not make him a cuckold. For the like of him this cap is suited... This cap is holy and ordained, and is for spiritual fools who, unfit,

*One fool hoards gold;
and another fool steals and spends it.
Others are so foolish as to act as if they were never to die.*

undertake cures from mere motives of gain, and sell themselves to Satan. This cap is proper for such... Not so. For I have, here, a noble cap, suited for royal fools of every sort and description. Princes confuse the world by their pride, and, to satisfy it, slay the innocent. England would have troubled us sorely, but for the aid of France. And now the Emperor is going to blows with France. His reason I know not. Princes in general are, this year, in a commotion, which some will regret. The Pope has sent his army into the field, outdoing the old Saints. Is this charity? Or is it folly? Christ taught not this foolishness; for such it is, among Christians. For them is this cap. Fulfilled, now, is Merlin's prophecy, which I learnt from my grandmother; and thus it runs... So, friars are to wrangle; their religion being disordered. Would that they fought with spear and shield! Finally I commend you to Gilly-mouband. Pray, too, for the sould of Cacaphatie, who was drowned.[3]

As also we...do declare a war with such a tyrant and usurper, and all the men of his practices, as enemies to our Lord Jesus Christ.

Michael Cameron

'THE SANQUHAR DECLARATION' · SANQUHAR

22 JUNE 1680

Sanquhar is a small town in Dumfries and Galloway in the south-west of Scotland. Despite its size and location, it has been the scene for no fewer than six declarations. The first was on 22 June 1680. On that day the townspeople of Sanquhar watched as around 20 horsemen rode up the main street with swords drawn and pistols at the ready.

The Cameronians were a band of Scottish Covenanters who followed the teachings of Richard Cameron and composed largely of those who signed the Sanquhar Declaration in 1680. They became a separate church after the religious settlement of 1690, taking the official title of Reformed Presbyterians in 1743. Essentially, they wished to restore the religious order that existed between 1638 and 1649. The Cameronians objected strongly to the Union of Scotland and England in 1707.

The group halted at the market cross and two dismounted, Richard Cameron and his brother Michael. After singing a psalm and offering a prayer to the assembled throng, Michael Cameron read aloud the Sanquhar Declaration. It disavowed allegiance to King Charles II and the government of Scotland, in the name of the 'true Protestant and Presbyterian interest', opposition to government interference in religious affairs, and anti-Catholicism.

This symbolic demonstration, essentially a declaration of war, was among the first of a series of events that led to the Glorious Revolution and the end of the reign of the House of Stuart. When Cameron had finished reading the declaration it was nailed to the town cross and the horsemen rode off. Regarded as highly treasonous, it led to a proclamation that Richard Cameron and his associates were 'Rebels and Traitors', with a reward offered for their capture, dead or alive.

It is not amongst the smallest of the Lord's mercies to this poor land, that there have been always some who have given their testimony against every cause of defection that many are guilty of; which is a token for good, that He doth not, as yet, intend to cast us off altogether, but that He will leave a remnant in whom

He will be glorious, if they, through His grace, keep themselves clean still, and walk in His way and method as it has been walked in, and owned by Him in our predecessors of truly worthy memory; in their carrying on of our noble work of reformation, in the several steps thereof, from Popery, Prelacy, and likewise Erastian supremacy—so much usurped by him who, it is true, so far as we know, is descended from the race of our kings; yet he hath so far debased from what he ought to have been, by his perjury and usurpation in Church matters, and tyranny in matters civil, as is known by the whole land, that we have just reason to account it one of the Lord's great controversies against us, that we have not disowned him, and the men of his practices, whether inferior magistrates or any other, as enemies to our Lord and His Crown, and the true Protestant and Presbyterian interest in this land—our Lord's espoused bride and Church. Therefore, although we be for government and governors, such as the Word of God and our covenant allows; yet we, for ourselves, and all that will adhere to us as the representative of the true Presbyterian Kirk and covenanted nation of Scotland, considering the great hazard of lying under such a sin any longer, do by these presents, disown

For which reason we declare, that several years since he should have been denuded of being king, ruler, or magistrate, or of having any power to act or to be obeyed as such.

Charles Stuart, that has been reigning, or rather tyrannising, as we may say, on the throne of Britain these years bygone, as having any right, title to, or interest in, the said Crown of Scotland for government, as forfeited, several years since, by his perjury and breach of covenant both to God and His Kirk, and usurpation of His Crown and royal prerogatives therein, and many other breaches in matters ecclesiastic, and by tyranny and breach of the very leges regnandi in matters civil. For which reason we declare, that several years since he should have been denuded of being king, ruler, or magistrate, or of having any power to act or to be obeyed as such. As also we, being under the standard of our Lord Jesus Christ, Captain of Salvation, do declare a war with such a tyrant and usurper, and all the men of his practices, as enemies to our Lord Jesus Christ, and His cause and covenants; and against all such as have strengthened him, sided with, or anywise acknowledged him in his tyranny, civil or ecclesiastic; yea, against all such as shall strengthen, side with, or anywise acknowledge any other in like usurpation and tyranny—far more against such as would betray or deliver up our free reformed mother Kirk unto the bondage of Antichrist the Pope of Rome. And, by this, we homologate that testimony given at Rutherglen, the 29th of May, 1679, and all the faithful testimonies of those who have gone before, as also of those who have suffered of late: and we do disclaim that Declaration published at Hamilton, June, 1679, chiefly because it takes in the king's interest, which we are several years since loosed from, because of the aforesaid reasons, and other which may, after this, if the Lord will, be published. As also we disown and by this resent the reception of the Duke of York, that professed Papist, as repugnant to our principles and vows to the Most High God, and as that which is the great, though not alone, just reproach of our Kirk and nation. We also, by this, protest against his succeeding to the Crown, and whatever has been done, or any are essaying to do in this land, given to the Lord, in prejudice to our work of reformation. And to conclude, we hope, after this, none will blame us for, or offend at, our rewarding those that are against us as they have done to us, as the Lord gives opportunity. This is not to exclude any that have declined, if they be willing to give satisfaction according to the degree of their offence.[1]

Lord, I die in the faith that thou wilt not leave Scotland, but that thou wilt make the blood of thy witnesses the seed of thy church, and return again and be glorious in our land.

James Renwick
1662–88

SPEECH FROM THE SCAFFOLD · GRASSMARKET · EDINBURGH
17 FEBRUARY 1688

In 1688 the Covenanter James Renwick was arrested for giving 'treasonable sermons'. He confessed his guilt and refused to recant his words. After being sentenced to death, he was asked if he preferred to have more time. 'It is all one to me,' replied Renwick. 'If it is protracted it is welcome. If it is shortened it is welcome. My Master's time is the best.'

On the day of his execution a large crowd gathered round the scaffold in Edinburgh's Grassmarket. Renwick sang the 103rd Psalm, read the 19th chapter of the Book of Revelations, and prayed aloud. 'By and By,' he said, turning his face upwards to the wintry skies, 'I shall be above those clouds; then I shall enjoy Thee and glorify Thee without intermission for ever.'

Aged only 26, after Renwick was hanged, his head was severed and his hands, bound together in a prayerful pose, suspended over one of the gates to Edinburgh. 'When I speak of him as a man,' wrote a contemporary, 'none more comely in features, none more prudent, none more heroic in spirit, yet none more meek, more humane and condescending. He learned the truth and counted the cost, and so sealed it with his blood.'

James Renwick was born in Moniaive, Dumfriesshire, in 1662. He studied religion at Edinburgh University and in 1681 saw several Covenanters martyred, prompting him to join the United Society, a subversive religious group. With their help, he studied abroad and was ordained a minister in the Netherlands. Renwick returned to Scotland in 1683, and spent the next five years giving sermons, and fermenting anti-English sentiment, all over Scotland.

Dear friends, I die a Presbyterian Protestant; I own the Word of God as the rule of faith and manners; I own the Confession of Faith, Larger and Shorter Catechisms, Sum of Saving Knowledge, Directory for Public and Family Worship,

Covenants, National and Solemn League, Acts of General Assemblies, and all the faithful contending that have been for the Covenanted Reformation. I leave my testimony approving the preaching of the Gospel in the fields, and defending the same by arms. To adjoin my testimony to all these truths that have been scaled by bloodshed, either on scaffold, field or seas, for the cause of Christ. I leave

Farewell, be diligent in duty, make your peace with God through Christ; there is a great trial coming.

my testimony against Popery, Prelacy, Erastianism, against all profanity, and everything contrary to sound doctrine and the power of godliness; particularly against all usurpations and encroachments made upon Christ's right, the Prince of the kings of the earth, who alone must bear the glory of ruling in his own kingdom, the church; and in particular against the absolute power affected by this usurper, that belongs to no mortal, but is the incommunicable prerogative of Jehovah, and against his Toleration flowing from this absolute power.'

At this point, Renwick was ordered to stop. 'I have near done,' he protested, before adding:

> Ye that are the people of God, do not weary to maintain the testimony of the day in your stations and places; and, whatever ye do, make sure of an interest in Christ; for there is a storm coming – that shall try your foundation. Scotland must be rid of Scotland before the delivery come: and you that are strangers to God, break off your sins by repentance, else I will be a sad witness against you in the day of the Lord.

Again, Renwick was made to stop. He climbed the ladder where he prayed, saying:

> Lord, I die in the faith that thou wilt not leave Scotland, but that thou wilt make the blood of thy witnesses the seed of thy church, and return again and be glorious in our land. And now, Lord, I am ready. The bride, the Lamb's wife, hath made herself ready.

A napkin was then tied over Renwick's face, and he said to a friend:

> Farewell, be diligent in duty, make your peace with God through Christ; there is a great trial coming. As to the remnant I leave, I have committed them to God. Tell them from me, not to weary nor be discouraged in maintaining the testimony, and the Lord will provide you teachers and ministers, and when he comes he will make these despised truths glorious in the earth.

Renwick was then turned over 'with these words in his mouth':

> Lord, into thy hands I commend my spirit, for thou hast re-deemed me. Lord God of truth.'

From my infancy to this moment, I have devoted myself to the cause of the people.

Thomas Muir
1765–99

SPEECH AT TRIAL FOR SEDITION · HIGH COURT OF JUSTICIARY · EDINBURGH
30 AUGUST 1793

Like many radicals, Thomas Muir was from a wealthy family based just north of Glasgow. A lawyer, in the late 18th century he felt himself drawn to various reform movements that had developed all over Scotland. After the revolution in France these gathered momentum, and in 1792 Muir, along with William Skirving, helped set up Scottish Reform Clubs open to Scots of every class.

Thomas Muir was born in Glasgow in 1765, the son of a hop merchant. Educated at Glasgow's Grammar School and University, he worked as a lawyer while becoming involved in radical political reform movements. In 1793 Muir was tried for sedition, found guilty and sentenced to 14 years transportation. Rescued by a US ship, he was then captured by the Spanish and eventually ended up in France, where he died in 1799.

He wrote and spoke widely, but in 1793, after giving a particularly radical speech to the Scottish Reform Movement General Convention (on behalf of the United Irishmen) he was arrested and charged with sedition. This is the speech Muir made at his trial in Edinburgh, considered such a fine piece of oratory that it was published as a text to be used in English exams in some parts of the United States until 1860.

Muir sat down to a unanimous burst of applause, but he was still found guilty of having 'created disaffection by means of seditious speeches' by Lord Braxfield and a hand-picked jury of anti-reformists. Sentenced to be banished to Botany Bay for 14 years, Muir was rescued by the USS *Otter*, sent by George Washington to take him to the safety of the new American Republic. But when the *Otter* was wrecked near Panama, Muir was arrested by the Spanish; later released, he settled in France, dying there in 1799. A fine memorial at Edinburgh's Calton Cemetery commemorates Muir and other 'Scottish Martyrs'.

This is now perhaps the last time that I shall address my country. I have explored the tenor of my past life. Nothing shall tear me from the record of my departed days. The enemies of reform have scrutinised, in a manner hitherto unexampled in Scotland, every action I may have performed, every word I may have uttered. Of crimes, most foul and horrible, have I been accused: of attempting to rear the standards of civil war; to plunge this land in blood, and to cover it with desolation. At every step, as the evidence of the crown advanced, my innocence has brightened. So far from inflaming the minds of men to sedition and outrage, all the witnesses have concurred, that my only anxiety was, to impress upon them the necessity of peace, of good order, and of good morals.

What then has been my crime? Not the lending to a relation a copy of Mr Paine's works; not the giving away to another a few numbers of an innocent and constitutional publication; but for having dared to be, according to the measure of my feeble abilities, a strenuous and active advocate for an equal representation of the people, in the house of the people; for having dared to attempt to accomplish a measure, by legal means, which was to diminish the weight of their taxes, and to put an end to the effusion of their blood.

From my infancy to this moment, I have devoted myself to the cause of the people. It is a good cause. It will ultimately prevail. It will finally triumph. Say then openly, in your verdict, if you do condemn me, which I presume you will

*Of crimes, most foul and horrible,
have I been accused:
of attempting to rear the standards of civil war;
to plunge this land in blood,
and to cover it with desolation.*

not, that it is for my attachment to this cause alone, and not for those vain and wretched pretexts stated in the indictment, intended only to colour and disguise the real motives of my accusation. The time will come, when men must stand or fall by their actions; when all human pageantry shall cease; when the hearts of all shall be laid open to view.

If you regard your most important interests; if you wish that your consciences should whisper to you words of consolation, rather than speak to you in the terrible language of remorse, weigh well the verdict you are about to pronounce.

As for me, I am careless and indifferent to my fate. I can look danger, and I can look death in the face; for I am shielded by the consciousness of my own rectitude. I may be condemned to languish in the recesses of a dungeon. I may be doomed to ascend the scaffold. Nothing can deprive me of the recollection of the past; nothing can destroy my inward peace of mind, arising from the remembrance of having discharged my duty.[1]

O sister,
rule your realm in peace;
I give up every claim to these domains

Mary Queen of Scots
1542–87

FRIEDRICH SCHILLER'S ACCOUNT OF MARY BEGGING TO BE FREED

1800

Mary Stuart was a play by the German writer Friedrich Schiller (translated by Joseph Mellish in 1847 and revised by Henry G Bohn) that depicted the final days of Mary, Queen of Scots. Premiered in Weimar on 14 June 1800, the play also formed the basis for Donizetti's 1834 opera *Maria Stuarda*. The drama focuses on Mary who, imprisoned in England, is hopeful of a reprieve from her cousin Queen Elizabeth I, who prevaricates over signing her relative's death sentence.

Mary, Queen of Scots or Mary Stuart was only six years old when she succeeded her father, King James V, as Queen. After spending most of her childhood in France, where she was briefly queen consort, Mary returned to Scotland in 1561. Forced to abdicate in 1567, she fled to England to seek the protection of her cousin, Queen Elizabeth I, but after spending more than 18 years in custody, Mary was executed on suspicion of plotting to assassinate Elizabeth.

After Mary finds out that Mortimer (created by Schiller), the nephew of her custodian, is on her side, she entrusts her life to him. Mortimer is supposed to give Robert Dudley, the Earl of Leicester, a letter from Mary, in which she pleads for help. After numerous requests, Mary finally gains the opportunity to meet Queen Elizabeth (something that, in reality, never happened).

This meeting ends in an acrimonious argument, caused by Mary's unwillingness to submit entirely to Elizabeth's wishes. Much of the argument is a monologue by Mary in which she begs to be freed and, as Elizabeth refuses, slowly loses her temper, building up to a fiery crescendo.

"Oh! how shall I begin? Oh, how shall I
So artfully arrange my cautious words
That they may touch, yet not offend your heart?
Strengthen my words, O Heaven! and take from them
Whate'er might wound. Alas! I cannot speak

In my own cause without impeaching you,
And that most heavily, I wish not so;
You have not as you ought behaved to me:
I am a queen, like you: yet you have held me
Confined in prison. As a suppliant
I came to you, yet you in me insulted
The pious use of hospitality;
Slighting in me the holy law of nations,
Immured me in a dungeon — tore from me
My friends and servants; to unseemly want
I was exposed, and hurried to the bar
Of a disgraceful, insolent tribunal.
No more of this; — in everlasting silence
Be buried all the cruelties I suffered!
See — I will throw the blame of all on fate,
'Twere not your fault, no more than it was mine.

Strengthen my words,
O Heaven! and take from them
Whate'er might wound.

An evil spirit rose from the abyss,
To kindle in our hearts the flame of hate,
By which our tender youth had been divided.
It grew with us, and bad, designing men
Fanned with their ready breath the fatal fire:
Frantics, enthusiasts, with sword and dagger
Armed the uncalled-for hand! This is the curse
Of kings, that they, divided, tear the world
In pieces with their hatred, and let loose
The raging furies of all hellish strife!
No foreign tongue is now between us, sister,
Now stand we face to face; now, sister, speak:
Name but my crime, I'll fully satisfy you, —
Alas! had you vouchsafed to hear me then,
When I so earnest sought to meet your eye,
It never would have come to this, nor would,
Here in this mournful place, have happened now
This so distressful, this so mournful meeting...

O sister, rule your realm in peace;
I give up every claim to these domains —

Alas! the pinions of my soul are lamed;
Greatness entices me no more: your point
Is gained; I am but Mary's shadow now —
My noble spirit is at last broke down
By long captivity: — you've done your worst
On me; you have destroyed me in my bloom!
Now, end your work, my sister; — speak at length
The word, which to pronounce has brought you hither;
For I will ne'er believe that you are come,
To mock unfeelingly your hapless victim.
Pronounce this word; — say, "Mary, you are free:
You have already felt my power, —learn now
To honour too my generosity."
Say this, and I will take my life, will take
My freedom, as a present from your hands.
One word makes all undone; — I wait for it; —
Oh, let it not be needlessly delayed.

An evil spirit rose from the abyss,
To kindle in our hearts the flame of hate,
By which our tender youth had been divided.

Woe to you if you end not with this word!
For should you not, like some divinity,
Dispensing noble blessings, quit me now,
Then, sister, not for all this island's wealth,
For all the realms encircled by the deep,
Would I exchange my present lot for yours...
My sins were human, and the faults of youth:
Superior force misled me. I have never
Denied or sought to hide it: I despised
All false appearance, as became a queen.
The worst of me is known, and I can say,
That I am better than the fame I bear.
Woe to you! When, in time to come, the world
Shall draw the robe of honour from your deeds,
With which thy arch-hypocrisy has veiled
The raging flames of lawless, secret lust.
Virtue was not your portion from your mother;
Well know we what it was which brought the head
Of Anna Boleyn to the fatal block...

Moderation! I've supported
What human nature can support: farewell,
Lamb-hearted resignation, passive patience,
Fly to thy native heaven; burst at length

My sins were human, and the faults of youth.

Thy bonds, come forward from thy dreary cave,
In all thy fury, long suppressed rancor!
And thou, who to the angered basilisk
Impart'st the murderous glance, oh, arm my tongue
With poisoned darts!...

(raising her voice).
A bastard soils,
Profanes the English throne! The generous Britons
Are cheated by a juggler, whose whole figure
Is false and painted, heart as well as face!
If right prevailed, you now would in the dust
Before me lie, for I'm your rightful monarch![1]

We may very effectually destroy our own integrity of judicial system.

Sir Walter Scott
1771–1832

SPEECH AT THE FACULTY OF ADVOCATES, EDINBURGH, 28 FEBRUARY 1807

By the early 19th century Walter Scott was already famous as a poet, although he had yet to produce the historical novels that would carry his literary fame around the world. He was also a lawyer, and one of his most enduring speeches was a spirited defence of Scotland's legal traditions delivered to the Faculty of Advocates in February and March 1807.

This considered a Bill 'for better regulating the Courts of Justice in Scotland and the Administration of Justice therein' and Scott's son-in-law (and biographer) John Gibson Lockhart recalled him being 'earnest and serious in his belief that the new rulers of the country were disposed to abolish many of its most valuable institutions'. Several of those present told Lockhart the speech had 'a flow and energy of eloquence for which those who knew him best had been quite unprepared'.

Sir Walter Scott was born in Edinburgh in 1771, the son of a lawyer. Educated at Edinburgh's High School and University, he was called to the Bar in 1792. An avid reader, he combined a literary career with his legal work, initially producing poetry before turning to the historical novel in 1815. Scott was made a baronet in 1820.

Afterwards, Scott walked across the Mound in Edinburgh, accompanied by some of his legal friends who complimented him on his rhetorical powers. Irritated by their irreverence, Scott said: 'No, no – 'tis no laughing matter; little by little, whatever your wishes may be, you will destroy and undermine, until nothing of what makes Scotland shall remain.' With that, one of those present witnessed tears gushing down Scott's cheeks. 'Seldom, if ever, in his more advanced age,' wrote Lockhart, 'did any feelings obtain such mastery.'

He disliked the proposed bill, as being founded and defended on what he should venture to call Anglomania – a rage of imitating English forms and practices, similar to what prevailed in France about the time of the Revolution, respecting their manners and dress. This might be called "playing at being

Englishment;" a sort of *make believe*, as the children say, which by no means took the imitators out of the *Servum Pecus*, the brute herd, to which they are consigned by the poet. He cautioned the Faculty to beware of this. We may very effectually destroy our own integrity of judicial system; but we can no more make it the English law, than a Frenchman could make his feelings those of an Englishman, by wearing boots, a drab great coat, and a round hat instead of a cocked one...

On the subject of the trial by jury, no man could be more devoutly attached to it than he was; others might blazon it on their plate, and on their carriages, – he trusted it was engraved on his heart: But he saw no magic in a name; it was not the sound, but the spirit and efficacy, of a law with which he was enamoured. He

We may very effectually destroy our own integrity of judicial system; but we can no more make it the English law, than a Frenchman could make his feelings those of an Englishman, by wearing boots, a drab great coat, and a round hat instead of a cocked one...

saw its constitutional and indispensible utility in questions between the king and the subject, or between the criminal law and the accused; where, if the prosecutor did not fully and plainly make out his case, the party was entitled to his acquittal. But in a question of civil right, the trial by jury did not appear to him to possess any such paramount advantage. There was no latitude for the jury to exercise their faculties; they were not at liberty to bring in what might be called by a vulgar phrase, a rough and round verdict...

The English were always remarkable for caution in their own judicial regulations... and he feared there was something in this proposal like the well-known aphorism of medical men, which, however, they keep carefully to themselves – *fiat experimentum in corpore vili*. – These learned gentlemen of the south wished we should be their *tasters*; and, very prudently, were desirous of knowing, how this distilled essence of trial by jury suited a Scottish constitution, before they tried it on their own. He deprecated such experiments; nor did he give credit to the professions of those who press a practice in others, very, very different from what they themselves have adopted, or ever proposed to adopt, in similar circumstances...

As great events turn on such trifling causes, he was often tempted to suspect that the English owed the unanimity of their juries to what, according to their great moralist Johnson, made the principal object of their thoughts during the day, their respect for their *dinner*. Did the supporters of the bill suppose this motive equally strong in Scotland; or had they forgot, in the abundance of place and power, the degree of abstinence which a Scotsman is capable of practicing?

A Scotchman by no means fell under Dr Johnson's rule: he prefers many things to his dinner – his religion, especially on speculative points: his interest; but perhaps above all, his inherent love of argument and disputation...

He appealed to the Solicitor-General if it was well, or seemly, that he, whose grandfather had been one of the commissioners for the Union, should be first to lift his hand to the removal of the ancient landmarks which his fathers had placed. He hoped, that even if his honourable friend considered the Union as an old and useless toy, he would respect it as one of his grandfather's fashioning.

That the children of Holland took pleasure in making
What the children of England took pleasure in breaking.

He hoped it would never be said of a family whom he loved and respected, that, in respect to this same ancient plaything, the nursery rhyme might be applied in contrasting the disposition of only three generations:

That the children of Holland took pleasure in making
What the children of England took pleasure in breaking.

He knew the honourable gentleman must have considered deeply the measure he brought forward. Still it was the law of Scotland; that law which had trained his abilities, and led him on to distinction. It was the law of his country which was at stake. Was there occasion for precipitation, when few of the Faculty had the bill a week in their possession. Could he not, in her death-agony, watch with her one little hour? He recommended farther investigation, patience, delay and consultation with the Judges, and with the country. He added, that though somewhat abstracted from professional pursuits, he could not forbear delivering his sentiments on this important crisis, with the freedom of a Scottishman, and concluded, *liberavi animam meam.*

You may condemn me to immolation on the scaffold, but you cannot degrade me.

James Wilson
1760–1820

SPEECH IN THE HIGH COURT, GLASGOW

20 JULY 1820

On 1 April 1820 a notice was posted in Glasgow and its surrounding areas urging people to rise against the British government. Signed by the Organising Committee for a Provisional Government, this alarmed London and troops were stationed in Glasgow. In an attempt to smoke out Scotland's radical leaders, government spies also encouraged the insurrection by telling them that England too was in the throes of a revolution.

James Wilson, who was leading a band of radicals marching from Strathaven to Glasgow, fell for the trap. Carrying a banner that declared 'Scotland Free or a Desert', eventually they realised there was no such uprising and returned, disappointed and dejected, to Strathaven.

Upon his return home Wilson was arrested on a charge of high treason. This is his short but impassioned speech from his trial in Glasgow, although it had little effect. Determined to make an example of Wilson in order to deter future radical activity, on 24 July 1820 he was found guilty of treason by a special English Court of Oyer and Terminer, a royal commission with the power to hear and determine criminal cases. Sentenced to death by Lord President Hope, on 30 August Wilson was both hanged and beheaded.

James Wilson was born in Avondale in 1760 and initially worked as a weaver. After reading Thomas Paine's Rights of Man he became active in campaigning for political reform, particularly in his local branch of the 'Friends of the People' group. In 1820, Wilson was arrested and charged with high treason, for which he was hanged and beheaded. In 1846 a monument to Wilson was erected in Strathaven.

You may condemn me to immolation on the scaffold, but you cannot degrade me. If I have appeared as a pioneer in the van of freedom's battles – if I have attempted to free my country from political degradation – my conscience tells me that I have only done my duty. Your brief authority will soon cease, but the vindictive proceedings this day shall be recorded in history.

Your brief authority will soon cease, but the vindictive proceedings this day shall be recorded in history.

... do you carry out the work which I have begun. I leave it with you.

David Livingstone
1813–73

SPEECH AT SENATE HOUSE, CAMBRIDGE UNIVERSITY

4 DECEMBER 1857

The famous Victorian explorer and missionary David Livingstone spent the latter part of 1857 on a speaking tour. To one listener he appeared 'plainly and rather carelessly dressed, of middle height, bony frame and Gaelic countenance'. 'When he speaks to you,' continued the description, 'you think him at first to be a Frenchman; but as he tells you a Scotch anecdote in the Glaswegian dialect, you make up your mind that he must be, as his face indicates, a countryman from the north.'[1]

David Livingstone was born 19 March 1813 to a working-class family in Blantyre, Scotland, the second of seven children. He worked in a mill from the age of ten but, largely self-taught, managed to study medicine at Anderson's University in Glasgow. Later he was ordained a missionary and sailed to South Africa, spending much of the rest of his life exploring – and writing about – Africa, where he died in 1873.

Livingstone also spoke in Dublin, Glasgow, Blantyre, Edinburgh, Leeds, Liverpool, Birmingham, and Oxford – where, as in Glasgow, he received an honorary degree. On 4 December 1857 William Whewell and the geologist Adam Sedgwick introduced him at Cambridge University's Senate House to a rapturous reception.

After his main speech Livingstone suddenly looked up at his audience and shouted: 'I beg to direct your attention to Africa. I know that within a few years I shall be cut off in that country, which is now open; do not let it be shut again! I go back to Africa to try to make an open path for commerce and Christianity; do you carry out the work which I have begun. I leave it with you.' The applause was prolonged and the impact palpable; the Oxford and Cambridge Mission, later renamed the Universities Mission to Central Africa, was formed soon after.

My desire is to open a path to this district, that civilisation, commerce, and Christianity might find their way there. I consider that we made a great mistake, when we carried commerce into India, in being ashamed of our Christianity; as a matter of common sense and good policy, it is always best to appear in one's true character. In travelling through Africa, I might have imitated certain Portuguese, and have passed for a chief; but I never attempted anything of the sort, although endeavouring always to keep to the lessons of cleanliness rigidly instilled by my mother long ago; the consequence was that the natives respected me for that quality, though remaining dirty themselves...

A prospect is now before us of opening Africa for commerce and the Gospel. Providence has been preparing the way, for even before I proceeded to the Central basin it had been conquered and rendered safe by a chief named Sebituane, and

Pioneers in every thing should be the ablest and best-qualified men, not those of small ability and education.

the language of the Bechuanas made the fashionable tongue, and that was one of the languages into which Mr Moffat had translated the Scriptures. Sebituane also discovered Lake Ngami some time previous to my explorations in that part. In going back to that country my object is to open up traffic along the banks of the Zambezi, and also to preach the Gospel. The natives of Central Africa are very desirous of trading, but their only traffic is at present in slaves, of which the poorer people have an unmitigated horror: it is therefore most desirable to encourage the former principle, and thus open a way for the consumption of free productions, and the introduction of Christianity and commerce. By encouraging the native propensity for trade, the advantages that might be derived in a commercial point of view are incalculable; nor should we lose sight of the inestimable blessings it is in our power to bestow upon the unenlightened African, by giving him the light of Christianity. Those two pioneers of civilisation – Christianity and commerce – should ever be inseparable; and Englishmen should be warned by the fruits of neglecting that principle as exemplified in the result of the management of Indian affairs. By trading with Africa, also, we should at length be independent of slave labour, and thus discountenance practices so obnoxious to every Englishman.

Though the natives are not absolutely anxious to receive the Gospel, they are open to Christian influences. Among the Bechuanas the Gospel was well received. These people think it a crime to shed a tear, but I have seen some of them weep at the recollection of their sins when God had opened their hearts to Christianity and repentance. It is true that missionaries have difficulties to encounter; but what great enterprise was ever accomplished without difficulty? It is deplorable to think that one of the noblest of our missionary societies, the Church Missionary Society, is compelled to send to Germany for missionaries, whilst other societies are amply supplied. Let this stain be wiped off. The sort of men who are wanted for missionaries are such as I see before me; men of education, standing, enterprise, zeal, and piety. It is a mistake to suppose that any one, as long as he is pious, will do for this office. Pioneers in every thing should be the ablest and best-qualified men, not those of small ability and education. This remark especially applies to the first teachers of Christian truth in regions which may never have before been blest with the name and Gospel of Jesus Christ. In the early ages the monasteries were the schools of Europe, and the monks were not

Is that a sacrifice which brings its own blest reward in healthful activity, the consciousness of doing good, peace of mind, and a bright hope of a glorious destiny hereafter?

ashamed to hold the plough. The missionaries now take the place of those noble men, and we should not hesitate to give up the small luxuries of life in order to carry knowledge and truth to them that are in darkness. I hope that many of those whom I now address will embrace that honourable career. Education has been given us from above for the purpose of bringing to the benighted the knowledge of a Saviour. If you knew the satisfaction of performing such a duty, as well as the gratitude to God which the missionary must always feel, in being chosen for so noble, so sacred a calling, you would have no hesitation in embracing it.

For my own part, I have never ceased to rejoice that God has appointed me to such an office. People talk of the sacrifice I have made in spending so much of my life in Africa. Can that be called a sacrifice which is simply paid back as a small part of a great debt owing to our God, which we can never repay? Is that a sacrifice which brings its own blest reward in healthful activity, the consciousness of doing good, peace of mind, and a bright hope of a glorious destiny hereafter? Away with the word in such a view, and with such a thought! It is emphatically no sacrifice. Say rather it is a privilege. Anxiety, sickness, suffering, or danger, now and then, with a foregoing of the common conveniences and charities of this life, may make us pause, and cause the spirit to waver, and the soul to sink, but let this only be for a moment. All these are nothing when compared with the glory which shall hereafter be revealed in, and for, us. I never made a sacrifice. Of this we ought not to talk, when we remember the great sacrifice which HE made who left His Father's throne on high to give Himself for us.[2]

*We live in a great city –
our merchants are princes.*

Alexander 'Greek' Thomson
1817–75

SPEECH TO GLASGOW ARCHITECTURAL SOCIETY · BATH STREET · GLASGOW
22 FEBRUARY 1859

In 1857 Alexander Thomson joined his younger brother George in an architectural partnership that produced a range of Gothic and Romanesque villas in the new suburbs of Glasgow. By the mid-1850s he had also developed the refined and abstracted Grecian style with which he became closely associated. Thomson was also a theorist, developing the concept of 'sustainable housing'.

Alexander 'Greek' Thomson was born in Stirlingshire in 1817. Home-schooled, he also worked from an early age and was eventually apprenticed to a Glasgow architect. In 1848, Thomson set up his own practice and nine years later he entered practice with his brother. Responsible for a range of designs in the city, it was only decades after his death he came to be appreciated as an architectural visionary.

The Presbyterian Thomson grew to hate arches, associating them with the Roman Catholic architecture of Victorian Gothicism, and over time he became the most ambitious architect Glasgow ever produced, drawing on Egyptian and Greek elements in his plans for the city. Although his grander schemes were left unrealised, he nevertheless left his mark on the Second City of Empire.

This speech, a veritable call to arms, was delivered in the Thomson-designed Scottish Exhibition Rooms on Bath Street, and as Robert Crawford has written, had 'something of a manifesto quality' to it. He evangelises about the possibilities of architecture and design, imploring his audience to think not only big but also beautiful.

We live in a great city – our merchants are princes... The last 30 years have seen immense sums expended on engineering works, which must necessarily exist for generations to come. But, with very few exceptions, little artistic skill has been bestowed on them... With our Derrick cranes and our steam-engines we could lift and set stones on our walls of three or four tons weight... [architects now possessed] aids and facilities in the practice of their art which, in no former age, was ever dreamt of. They are built about with books, containing examples of every known style. If an architect wants an idea, he does not require to fly away into the region of imagination to fetch it – it is ready at hand on the adjoining shelf, and needs only to be reached down. Treatises upon everything connected with building are multiplied and piled up to an extent that defies perusal. Our builders, besides having access to all these mountains

If an architect wants an idea, he does not require to fly away into the region of imagination to fetch it – it is ready at hand on the adjoining shelf, and needs only to be reached down.

of knowledge, have mechanical aids unknown in the days of our fathers. For building materials, besides iron and brick, our neighbourhood abounds in stone, which for quality, variety, and abundance, is unequalled in the kingdom, and what have we made of it all?[1]

... when the union takes place, and we become the great country which British North America is certain to be.

Sir John A Macdonald
1815–91

ON CONFEDERATION · CANADIAN PARLIAMENT · TORONTO
FEBRUARY 1865

By 1864 the forces that would lead to the greater Canadian Confederation were already well under way. The American Civil War raged across the United States and the political philosophy of American federalism was becoming well established. It also posed a threat to British North America, for many in the US felt it was the 'Manifest Destiny' of that country to take over all of North America.

Sir John A Macdonald was born in Glasgow in 1815, but when he was a boy his family emigrated to Kingston, Upper Canada (later eastern Ontario). He initially worked as a lawyer, entered the colonial parliament in 1844 and by 1857 had become premier. Upon confederation in 1867 Macdonald was knighted and became the first Prime Minister of Canada. He dominated Canadian politics for the next two decades, dying in 1891.

That same year John A Macdonald, the Scottish-born Canadian politician formed a coalition government and thereafter sailed to Prince Edward Island to convince maritime leaders assembled to Charlottetown that a grander Canadian Union ought to be forged. They reassembled in Quebec City and hammered out the Quebec resolutions that formed the basis of the British North America Act.

Although Macdonald was a late convert to federalism he did become its main supporter. In 1865 he and several other fathers of confederation set sail for England where they met the Queen, enjoyed themselves and lobbied to get the required acts passed in Westminster. In February, however, he had addressed the Canadian Parliament on the subject of confederation.

"I have had the honor of being charged, on behalf of the government, to submit a scheme for the confederation of all the British North American Provinces — a scheme which has been received, I am glad to say, with general if not universal approbation in Canada. This subject is not a new one. For years it has more or less attracted the attention of every statesman and politician in these provinces, and has been looked upon by many far-seeing politicians as being eventually the means of deciding and settling very many of the vexed questions which have retarded the prosperity of the Colonies as a whole, and particularly the prosperity of Canada...

I say to this House, if you do not believe that the union of the Colonies is for the advantage of the country, that the joining of these five peoples into one nation under one sovereign is for the benefit of all, then reject the scheme. Even if you do not believe it to be for the present advantage and future prosperity of yourselves and your children. But if, after a calm and full consideration of this scheme, it is believed, as a whole, to be for the advantage of this Province — if the House and country believe this union to be one which will ensure for us British laws, British connection, and British freedom, and increase and develop the social, political, and material prosperity of the country — then I implore this House and the country to lay aside all prejudices and accept the scheme which we offer. I ask this House to meet the question in the same spirit in which the delegates met it. I ask each member of this House to lay aside his own opinions as to particular details and to accept the scheme as to a whole, if he think it beneficial as a whole...

All the statesmen and public men who have written or spoken on the subject admit the advantages of a union if it were practicable; and now, when it is proved to be practicable, if we do not embrace this opportunity, the present favourable time will pass away, and we may never have it again. Because, just so surely as this scheme is defeated, will be revived the original proposition for a union of the Maritime Provinces irrespective of Canada; they will not remain as they are now, powerless, scattered, helpless communities; they will form themselves into a power which, tho not so strong as if united with Canada, will nevertheless be a powerful and considerable community, and it will be then too late for us to attempt to strengthen ourselves by this scheme, which, in the words of the resolution, "is for the best interests and present and future prosperity of British North America."

No one can look into futurity and say what will be the destiny of this country.

... by a resolution which meets with the universal approval of the people of this country, we have provided that for all time to come, so far as we can legislate for the future, we shall have as the head of the executive power the sovereign of Great Britain. No one can look into futurity and say what will be the destiny of this country. Changes come over nations and peoples in the course of ages. But so far as we can legislate we provide that for all time to come the sovereign of Great Britain shall be the sovereign of British North America. By adhering to the monarchical principle we avoid one defect inherent in the Constitution of the United States...

I think it is well that in framing our Constitution our first act should have been to recognise the sovereignty of her majesty. I believe that while England has no desire to lose her Colonies, but wishes to retain them — while I am satisfied that the public mind of England would deeply regret the loss of these Provinces — yet, if the people of British North America, after full deliberation, had stated that they considered it was for their interest, for the advantage of the future British North America, to sever the tie, such is the generosity of the people of England that, whatever their desire to keep these Colonies, they would not seek to compel us to remain unwilling subjects of the British Crown...

We place no restriction on her majesty's prerogative in the selection of her representative. As it is now, so it will be if this Constitution is adopted. The sovereign has unrestricted freedom of choice. Whether in making her selection, she may send us one of her own family, a royal prince, as a viceroy to rule over us, or one of the great statesmen of England to represent her, we know not. We leave that to her majesty in all confidence. But we may be permitted to hope that when the union takes place, and we become the great country which British North America is certain to be, it will be an object worthy the ambition of the statesmen of England to be charged with presiding over our destinies.[1]

Do not be ambitious;
do not too much need success;
be loyal and modest.

Thomas Carlyle (1795–1881)

RECTORIAL ADDRESS · UNIVERSITY OF EDINBURGH
2 APRIL 1866

At the beginning of 1865, Thomas Carlyle finally finished his sprawling biography of Frederick the Great and promptly fell into a depression mingled with relief. In November, however, he learned that William Ewart Gladstone was to retire as Lord Rector of Edinburgh University after two terms. A new Rector was to be elected by the student body and two names were proposed: Carlyle and Disraeli.

To his surprise Carlyle was elected to the office by a margin of more than two-to-one. He pitched his inaugural address to 'Young Scotland', offering advice to the students on how to make the most of university and beyond. Carlyle concluded with his favourite poem by Goethe and tumultuous applause burst from the enthusiastic students: everyone was on his feet, arms waving, caps flying. In a telegraph to Mrs Carlyle, Tyndall described the address as 'a perfect triumph'.

Thomas Carlyle was born in 1795 in Ecclefechan, Dumfriesshire, the eldest son of a stonemason. Educated at Annan Academy and Edinburgh University, he later became a teacher, married and, in the mid-1820s, turned increasingly to writing. Carlyle moved to London in 1834, beginning work on a history of the French Revolution, the first of numerous volumes of history, biography and commentary. He died in 1881.

A few days later, still in Scotland, Carlyle received tragic news of Jane, his wife. At about 3 p.m. on Saturday 21 April she had gone for her regular afternoon carriage ride in Hyde Park; after several circuits of the park the driver, alarmed by Mrs Carlyle's lack of response to his request for further instructions, asked a lady to look into the carriage. Jane 'was leaning back in one corner of the carriage, rugs spread over her knees; her eyes were closed, and her upper lip slightly, slightly opened'. She was dead.

I dare say you know, very many of you, that it is now some 700 years since universities were first set up in this world of ours. Abelard and other thinkers had arisen with doctrines in them which people wished to hear of, and students flocked toward them from all parts of the world. There was no getting the thing recorded in books as you now may. You had to hear the man speaking to you vocally, or else you could not learn at all what it was that he wanted to say. And so they gathered together, these speaking ones—the various people who had anything to teach—and formed themselves gradually, under the patronage of kings and other potentates who were anxious about the culture of their populations, and nobly studious of their best benefit, and became a body corporate, with high privileges, high dignities, and really high aims, under the title of a university.

It remains, however, practically a most important truth, what I alluded to above, that the main use of universities in the present age is that, after you have done with all your classes, the next thing is a collection of books, a great library of good books, which you proceed to study and to read. What the universities can mainly do for you—what I have found the university did for me, is, that it taught me to read, in various languages, in various sciences; so that I could go into the books which treated of these things, and gradually penetrate into any department I wanted to make myself master of, as I found it suit me.

On the whole, avoid what is called ambition; that is not a fine principle to go upon — and it has in it all degrees of vulgarity, if that is a consideration.

Well, gentlemen, whatever you may think of these historical points, the clearest and most imperative duty lies on every one of you to be assiduous in your reading. Learn to be good readers — which is perhaps a more difficult thing than you imagine. Learn to be discriminative in your reading; to read faithfully, and with your best attention, all kinds of things which you have a real interest in — a real not an imaginary — and which you find to be really fit for what you are engaged in. Of course, at the present time, in a great deal of the reading incumbent on you, you must be guided by the books recommended by your professors for assistance toward the effect of their predilections. And then, when you leave the university, and go into studies of your own, you will find it very important that you have chosen a field, some province specially suited to you, in which you can study and work. The most unhappy of all men is the man who can not tell what he is going to do, who has got no work cut out for him in the world, and does not go into it. For work is the grand cure of all the maladies and miseries that ever beset mankind—honest work, which you intend getting done...

... in regard to all your studies and readings here, and to whatever you may learn, you are to remember that the object is not particular knowledges,—not that of getting higher and higher in technical perfections, and all that sort of thing.

There is a higher aim lying at the rear of all that, especially among those who are intended for literary or speaking pursuits, or the sacred profession. You are ever to bear in mind that there lies behind that the acquisition of what may be called wisdom — namely, sound appreciation and just decision as to all the objects that come round you, and the habit of behaving with justice, candour, clear insight, and loyal adherence to fact. Great is wisdom; infinite is the value of wisdom. It can not be exaggerated; it is the highest achievement of man: "Blessed is he that getteth understanding." And that, I believe, on occasion, may be missed very easily; never more easily than now, I sometimes think. If that is a failure, all is failure! However, I will not touch further upon that matter...

For that is the thing a man is born to in all epochs. He is born to expend every particle of strength that God Almighty has given him, in doing the work he finds he is fit for; to stand up to it to the last breath of life and do his best. We are called upon to do that; and the reward we all get — which we are perfectly sure of, if we have merited it — is that we have got the work done, or at least that we have tried to do the work. For that is a great blessing in itself; and I should say there is not very much more reward than that going in this world. If the man gets meat and clothes, what matter it whether he buy those necessaries with seven thousand a year, or with seven million, could that be, or with seventy pounds a year? He can get meat and clothes for that; and he will find intrinsically, if he is a wise man, wonderfully little real difference.

On the whole, avoid what is called ambition; that is not a fine principle to go upon — and it has in it all degrees of vulgarity, if that is a consideration. "Seekest thou great things, seek them not"; I warmly second that advice of the wisest of men. Do not be ambitious; do not too much need success; be loyal and modest. Cut down the proud towering thoughts that get into you, or see that they be pure as well as high. There is a nobler ambition than the gaining of all California would be, or the getting of all the suffrages that are on the planet just now.

On the whole, I would bid you stand up to your work, whatever it may be, and not be afraid of it; not in sorrows or contradictions to yield, but to push on toward the goal. And do not suppose that people are hostile to you or have you at ill will, in the world. In general, you will rarely find anybody designedly doing you ill. You may feel often as if the whole world were obstructing you, setting itself against you; but you will find that to mean only that the world is travelling in a different way from you, and, rushing on in its own path, heedlessly treads on you. That is mostly all: to you no specific ill will; only each has an extremely good will to himself, which he has a right to have, and is rushing on toward his object. Keep out of literature, I should say also, as a general rule — tho that is by the by. If you find many people who are hard and indifferent to you, in a world which you consider to be inhospitable and cruel — as often indeed happens to a tenderhearted, striving young creature — you will also find there are noble hearts who will look kindly on you; and their help will be precious to you beyond price. You will get good and evil as you go on, and have the success that has been appointed you.[1]

*Nothing will come of it
but trouble and shame.
And now it has come with a vengeance!*

Sheriff Alexander Nicolson
1827–93

'ADDRESS TO THE PEOPLE' · KIRKCUDBRIGHT

24 APRIL 1882

Alasdair Mac Neacail, better known as Sheriff Nicolson, was one of the leading Gaelic-speaking Scotsmen of his generation. Born on Skye, he originally planned to become a Free Church minister before working as a journalist and finally turning to the law. Nicolson was called to the Scottish Bar in 1860 and became sheriff-substitute of Kirkcudbright in 1872.

Sheriff Alexander Nicolson was born at Husabost on Skye in 1827. Educated in Skye and at Edinburgh University, he became sheriff-substitute of Kirkcudbright in 1872. A member of the 1883 Napier Commission on crofters in 1885, Nicolson became sheriff-substitute in Greenock, retiring in 1889. Among his publications were a revised edition of the Gaelic Bible, writing on mountaineering and a short volume of verse. He died in Edinburgh in 1893.

By the early 1880s there was widespread unrest on Nicolson's native island. There were land raids in the outer isles, rent strikes and attacks on policemen that culminated in the sending of a gunboat with a regiment of marines to Portree in order to impose order. It was in early 1882, when the crofters' agitation against high rents was at its height, that Sheriff Nicolson delivered this address several times on the island.

Nicolson's background as the son of a minor Skye landowner who had gained prominence on the mainland as a lawyer and writer meant his remarks carried considerable weight. The following year he was appointed a member of the Napier Commission, which a nervous government had established to investigate and act upon the crofters' grievances, lest the situation parallel that of Ireland. Although Nicolson was generally viewed as sympathetic, in this speech he is determined to ensure crofters do not indulge in non-payment of rents.

Do Thuath an Eilean Sgiathanaich, gu h-àraid an Gleanndail 's am Braigh Phortrigh.

A mhuinntir mo chridhe!

Dè seo na naidheachdan eagalach a tha a' tighinn h-ugainn oirbh! 'S beag a shaoil mi riamh gun tigeadh an là a chluinninn a leithid a' tighinn à Eilean mo rùin, à Gleanndail gu h-àraid, dùthaich m'oige, 's à Braigh Phortrigh, dùthaich mo shinnsre, dha 'm bu dual a bhi nan daoine sìochail!

'S mi tha cianail an diugh. 'S beag mo shùnnd 's mo cheòl gàire mu'n Eilean 's tric a tha mi a' luaidh! Bha sinn muladach 'n uair a chuala sinn mun chall mhòr a thainig oirbh toiseach a' gheamhraidh, ach 's miosa leinn a' naigheachd a tha seo. 'S ioma duine, tha mise cinnteach, ann an cearnaibh fad às, a bhios dhe'n fhaireachadh cheudna.

Bha mi bho chionn ghoirid an Dùn Eideann, a' toirt eachdraidh bheag, le mòran toilinntinn, mu na Gàidheil chaomh; agus thuirt mi, ged is mòr a dh'fhuiling iad, 's a tha cuid dhiubh fhathast a' fulang, nach ionnan iad 's na h-Eireannaich thruagh. Mun tuirt am fear roimhe, 'Cha b'ionnan O' Brian 's na Gàidheil'. Tha'n Gàidheal, arsa mise, fearail, tapaidh, ach tha e ciallach, cneasda, stòlda, onorach, modhail. Cha toir e droch cainnt airson droch dhìol; cha tog e làmh an aghaidh uachdarain no ùghdarrais; cha diùlt e màl a phàigheadh, ge duilich gum bi e; chan eil e ag iarraidh an fhearainn dha fhèin; chan eil e ag iarraidh ach ceartas, agus a bheò far an d'rugadh e.

The Highlander is manly, spirited, but he is sensible, devout, quiet, honest, courteous.

Ach a nis, – mo chreach! Tha Sgiathanaich ag atharrais air na h-Eireannaich, gan deanamh fhèin nan cuis-bhùird 's nan cuis-eagail.

Mo chàirdean gràdhach, na smaoinichibh gur h-ann mar sin a gheibhear ceartas no buaidh. Chan ann! Chan ann! Cha tig as ach trioblaid agus nàire. Tha mo chridhe goirt a' smaoineachadh air. Chuala mi le uamhas gu robh cuid as an Eilean gam ainmeachadh fhèin am measg na feadhnach a tha a' brosnachadh nan Sgiathanach gu aimlisg, ag ràdh gur h-ann aca fhèin a tha còir air an fhearann. Builgean air teanga nam briag! Cha tuirt mi facal dheth – chan eil mi cho aineolach 's cho baoth 's gun canainn a leithid!

Mar thuirt Pòl beannaichte, 'O Ghalatianacha amaideach, Cò chuir druidheachd oirbh?' Tha mi a' guidhe oirbh, na dichuimhnaichibh an teagasg ciallach ud, *Lean gu dluth ri cliù do shinnsre*. Be'n cliù-san riamh a bhi earbsach, rianail, uasal, umhal do'n lagh. Ma tha fìor adbhair gearain agaibh, chan eagal nach fhaigh sibh ceartas; ach chan ann le ainneart agus ùpraid agus làmhachas-làidir a gheibh sibh e gu bràth. Esan a bhriseas an lagh, brisidh e a' cheann fhèin. An ainm na h-uile nì a tha math agus ionmhalta, na toiribh masladh air ar n-ainm, agus adbhar bròin do ur fìor chàirdean, eadar Ghàidheil 'us Ghoill.

Fa dheòidh, a bhràithre, ge b'e nì a tha urramach, ge b'e nìthe a tha ceart, ge b'e nìthe a tha fìor-ghlan, ge b'e nìthe a tha ion-ghràidhe, ge b'e nìthe a tha ion-mholta; ma tha deadh-bheus air bith ann, ma tha moladh air bith ann, smuainichibh air na nìthibh sin!

Bho ar caraid dìleas agus ur fear-dùthcha.'

People of my Heart, – What dreadful news is this that has come to us about you! Little did I think I should ever here of the like coming from the island I love, particularly from Glendale, the country of my youth, and the Braes of Portree, the country of my ancestors, whose nature it was to be peaceable people. I am very sorrowful today. Small is my delight in thinking of the island that I have so often praised. We were sorrowful to hear of your great losses at the beginning of winter; but this news is far more grievous. Many a man, I am sure, in places far away will feel the same. I was lately in Edinburgh giving a short account, with much satisfaction, of the Highlanders, and I said, "though they have suffered much, and some of them suffer still, they are very different from the miserable Irish. As the old saying has it, 'O' Brien was very different from the Gael.' The Highlander is manly, spirited, but he is sensible, devout, quiet, honest, courteous. He will not give bad language in return for bad usage. He will not refuse to pay the rent, thought it be difficult for him. He does not seek the land for himself; he seeks only justice, and to be allowed to live in the place where he was born." But now, alas, Skyemen are imitating the Irish, and making themselves objects of derision and of dread. My dear friends, don't think it is so you will get justice. Nothing will come of it but trouble and shame. And now it has come with a vengeance! My heart is sore to think of it. I heard with disgust that I was mentioned myself in Skye as one of those who were stirring up the people to mischief, and telling them that the land belonged to themselves. I said nothing of the kind. I am not so ignorant or so mad as to use such language. As St Paul said, "Oh, foolish Galatians, who hath bewitched you!" I beseech you do not forget that excellent old saying. *Follow close the fame of your fathers.* Their fame ever was to be trustworthy, orderly, honourable, obedient to the law. If you have any real causes of complaint, there is no fear but you will get justice; but it is not by violence, and uproar, and high-handedness that you will ever get it. "He that breaks the law breaks his own head." In the name of everything that is good and praiseworthy, bring no shame on our name, and sorrow to all your true friends, whether Highland or Lowland. "Finally, brethren, whatsoever things are true, whatsoever things are honest, whatsoever things are just, whatsoever things are pure, whatsoever things are of good report; if there be any virtue, and if there be any praise, think on these things."[1]

Think,
I beseech you, think well,
think wisely, think, not for the moment,
but for the years that are to come,
before you reject this Bill.

William Ewart Gladstone 1809–98

SPEECH ON HOME RULE FOR IRELAND · HOUSE OF COMMONS
7 JUNE 1886

In late 1885 the Grand Old Man of Liberal politics, William Ewart Gladstone, made it known (his nephew flew the famous 'Hawarden Kite') he had resolved in favour of Home Rule, or rather devolution, for Ireland. This precipitated the fall of Lord Salisbury's Conservative government, for the Irish Nationalist MPs, led by Charles Stuart Parnell, held the balance of power in Parliament and switched their support to the Liberals.

William Ewart Gladstone was born in 1809 to Scottish parents, although he was raised in Liverpool. Initially a Tory, he first entered Parliament in 1832 and in a career lasting more than six decades served as Chancellor four times, as well as Prime Minister in four different administrations. He resigned as premier in 1894 and died four years later.

But this was not the end of the Irish Question, for Gladstone's decision split the Liberal Party down the middle, so when he kicked off a Second Reading debate on his Home Rule Bill on 7 June 1886, it was not guaranteed to pass. Today it looks like a modest constitutional innovation, the establishment of a devolved Irish legislature sitting in Dublin, much like that established in Edinburgh in 1999, but at the time it was considered revolutionary and, by opponents, a slippery slope down which the mighty British Empire would slide.

Gladstone would later talk of 'Home Rule all round', devolved Parliaments for the four component nations of the UK, and indeed he was at the time the Member for Midlothian, a campaign won in no small part on the basis of his oratory. But fine words were not enough and MPs threw out his Irish Bill by 341 votes to 311, ending his third administration after just a few months. The Irish Question, meanwhile, remained unanswered for another 36 – often very violent – years.

This is the earliest moment in our Parliamentary history when we have the voice of Ireland authentically expressed in our hearing. Majorities of Home Rulers there may have been upon other occasions; a practical majority of Irish Members never has been brought together for such a purpose. Now, first, we can understand her; now, first, we are able to deal with her; we are able to learn authentically what she wants and wishes, what she offers and will do; and as we ourselves enter into the strongest moral and honourable obligations by the steps which we take in this House, so we have before us practically an Ireland under the representative system able to give us equally authentic information, able morally to convey to us an assurance the breach and rupture of which would cover Ireland with disgrace...

What is the case of Ireland at this moment? Have honourable Gentlemen considered that they are coming into conflict with a nation? Can anything stop a nation's demand, except its being proved to be immoderate and unsafe? But here are multitudes, and, I believe, millions upon millions, out-of-doors, who feel this demand to be neither immoderate nor unsafe. In our opinion, there is but one question before us about this demand. It is as to the time and circumstance of granting it. There is no question in our minds that it will be granted...

The difference between giving with freedom and dignity on the one side, with acknowledgment and gratitude on the other, and giving under compulsion — giving with disgrace, giving with resentment dogging you at every step of your path — this difference is, in our eyes, fundamental, and this is the main reason not only why we have acted, but why we have acted now. This, if I understand it, is one of the golden moments of our history — one of those opportunities which may come and may go, but which rarely return, or, if they return, return at long intervals, and under circumstances which no man can forecast...

What is the case of Ireland at this moment? Have honourable Gentlemen considered that they are coming into conflict with a nation?

There has been no great day of hope for Ireland, no day when you might hope completely and definitely to end the controversy till now — more than 90 years. The long periodic time has at last run out, and the star has again mounted into the heavens. What Ireland was doing for herself in 1795 we at length have done. The Roman Catholics have been emancipated — emancipated after a woeful disregard of solemn promises through 29 years, emancipated slowly, sullenly, not from goodwill, but from abject terror, with all the fruits and consequences which will always follow that method of legislation. The second problem has been also solved, and the representation of Ireland has been thoroughly reformed...

We have given Ireland a voice: we must all listen for a moment to what she says. We must all listen — both sides, both Parties, I mean as they are, divided on this question — divided, I am afraid, by an almost immeasurable gap. We do not undervalue or despise the forces opposed to us. I have described them as the forces of class and its dependents; and that as a general description — as a slight and rude outline of a description — is, I believe, perfectly true. I do not deny that many are against us whom we should have expected to be for us. I do not deny that some whom we see against us have caused us by their conscientious action the bitterest disappointment. You have power, you have wealth, you have rank, you have station, you have organisation. What have we? We think that we have the people's heart; we believe and we know we have the promise of the harvest of the future. As to the people's heart, you may dispute it, and dispute it with perfect sincerity. Let that matter make its own proof. As to the harvest of the future, I doubt if you have so much confidence, and I believe that there is in the breast of many a man who means to vote against us to-night a profound misgiving, approaching even to a deep conviction, that the end will be as we foresee, and not as you do — that the ebbing tide is with you and the flowing tide is with us. Ireland stands at your bar expectant, hopeful, almost suppliant. Her words are the words of truth and soberness. She asks a blessed oblivion of the past and in that oblivion our interest is deeper than even hers...

We have given Ireland a voice:
we must all listen for a moment to what she says.

Go into the length and breadth of the world, ransack the literature of all countries, find, if you can, a single voice, a single book, find, I would almost say, as much as a single newspaper article, unless the product of the day, in which the conduct of England towards Ireland is anywhere treated except with profound and bitter condemnation. Are these the traditions by which we are exhorted to stand? No; they are a sad exception to the glory of our country. They are a broad and black blot upon the pages of its history; and what we want to do is to stand by the traditions of which we are the heirs in all matters except our relations with Ireland, and to make our relations with Ireland to conform to the other traditions of our country. So we treat our traditions — so we hail the demand of Ireland for what I call a blessed oblivion of the past. She asks also a boon for the future; and that boon for the future, unless we are much mistaken, will be a boon to us in respect of honour, no less than a boon to her in respect of happiness, prosperity, and peace. Such, Sir, is her prayer. Think, I beseech you, think well, think wisely, think, not for the moment, but for the years that are to come, before you reject this Bill.[1]

The Government that does not legislate for the unemployed does not deserve the confidence of this House.

Keir Hardie
1856–1915

MAIDEN SPEECH, HOUSE OF COMMONS
7 FEBRUARY 1893

When Keir Hardie, the first 'Labour' politician elected to the UK Parliament, made his maiden speech in February 1893, there was an outcry. For instead of wearing the then obligatory frock coat and top hat, Hardie wore a tweed suit and deerstalker. 'He spoke at first slowly, quietly, almost hesitatingly,' wrote his biographer Emrys Hughes, 'carefully marshalling his figures of the numbers of the unemployed in London, Liverpool, Glasgow, Birmingham and the other big cities.'

(James) Keir Hardie (formerly James Kerr) was born in Lanarkshire in 1856, the illegitimate son of a farm servant. From the age of 11 he worked down the mines as a 'trapper', later progressing to trade unionism and, from 1887, socialism. Hardie moved to London in 1891 and was elected the 'independent Labour' MP for West Ham South the following year. He died from pneumonia in 1915.

'Members on both sides whispered to each other,' continued Hughes. 'He was making a good speech. He had never been to school but he spoke faultless English.' Hardie spoke for about 40 minutes and although his amendment to the Loyal Address was defeated by 276 votes to 109, he 'had impressed the House with his earnestness, ability and courage'.[1]

Even the Grand Old Man, William Ewart Gladstone, paid Hardie the complement of listening to his speech. The press, which claimed Hardie had caused offence by wearing a 'cloth cap' in the Chamber (in fact, it had been a Glasgow MP), dubbed him the 'Member for the Unemployed'. Further afield, it earned Hardie the undisputed leadership of the Independent Labour Party, which he and others formed that year.

I believe all the horrors of sweating, of low wages, of long hours, and of deaths from starvation, are directly traceable to the large numbers of people who are totally unemployed or only casually employed. The worker in the workshop is fettered by the thought that outside his workshop gates there are thousands eager and willing to step into his shoes should he be dismissed in consequence of any attempt to improve his position...

I know that the difficulty is to find a remedy for what everyone admits to be an evil of no little magnitude. Quite a number of remedies have been proposed and discussed. Amongst others, emigration long held the field; but it has been found that emigration is not a cure for the evil, that emigration sends out of the country the best part of our working-classes—the thrifty, prudent, sober and intelligent workers, the very men whom we desire to keep at home; and that we get in exchange for them the Jew, the poor degraded workers of the Continent, who come here to fill the vacuum left by our own people who leave our shores. But even emigration will not long avail as a remedy. America with all its broad acres is closing the door as rapidly as it may against the immigrant from all lands, and what is true of that land is true of many others...

One of the most harrowing features connected with the problem of the unemployed is not the poverty or the hardship they have to endure, but the fearful moral degradation that follows in the train of the enforced idleness; and there is no more pitiable spectacle in this world than the man willing to work, who, day after day, vainly begs a brother of the earth, To give him leave to toil. I am anxious that the Government should have the fullest opportunity of getting to work with their legislative proposals, and I hope that one of them will include something at least being done for the unemployed, because I would again point out that this is not merely making provision for men out of work during periods

I want to ask the Government what have the unemployed to thank Her Majesty for in the Speech which has been submitted to the House?

of bad trade. In every season of the year, and in every condition of trade, men are unemployed. The pressure under which industry is carried on to-day necessitates that the young and the strong and the able should have preference in obtaining employment; and if the young, the strong, and the able are to have the preference, then the middle-aged and the aged are of necessity thrown out upon the streets.

We are now discussing an Address of Thanks to Her Majesty for Her Speech. I want to ask the Government what have the unemployed to thank Her Majesty for in the Speech which has been submitted to the House? Their ease is overlooked and ignored; they are left out as if they did not exist. Their misery and their sufferings could not be greater, but there is no mention of them in the Queen's

Speech. I take it that this House is the mouthpiece of the nation as a whole, and that it should speak for the nation—for the unemployed equally as for the well-to-do classes. But this House will not be speaking in the name of the nation, but only in the name of a section of the nation, if something is not done, and done speedily, for those people whose sufferings are so great, and for whom I plead...

I am sure that if the election addresses and election promises of gentlemen on both sides of the House were examined, it would be found that during election contests they had plenty of professions of sympathy for the unemployed. I ask of them today that they should translate these professions into practice. It is said that this Amendment amounts to a Vote of Want of Confidence in the Government, and that, therefore, hon Members opposite will not vote for it. The Government that does not legislate for the unemployed does not deserve the confidence of this House; and Members representing London constituencies will take care not to go to their constituencies with these arguments on their lips. If the Queen's Speech contained any reference to this question of anything like a satisfactory nature, I would not have raised it on the present occasion; but having raised it, I will, as I have said, take the sense of the House upon it. It may be pointed out to me that the Queen's Speech does contain promises of many great and useful measures. That may be so; but if the Queen's Speech did not contain an allusion to the question of Home Rule, we should have an Amendment proposed protesting against that omission. The unemployed number 4,000,000, which is nearly equal to the population of Ireland, and am I to be told that a question affecting 4,000,000 of people — affecting, not only their patriotism, or their comfort, but affecting their very lives — is of less consequence than the question of Home Rule for Ireland? And if the hon Gentlemen who represent the cause of Nationalism in Ireland would have felt justified in risking the life of the Government on the question of Home Rule, I claim to be more than justified in taking a similar risk in the interests of the unemployed. I beg, Mr Speaker, to move my Amendment.[2]

Such in my opinion is the true gospel concerning wealth, obedience to which is destined someday to solve the problems of the rich and the poor.

Andrew Carnegie
1835–1919

A READING OF HIS ESSAY 'THE GOSPEL OF WEALTH' 1908 (BUT WRITTEN IN 1889)

In his essay 'Wealth' (also known as 'The Gospel of Wealth') published in the *North American Review* in 1889, the Scots-born industrialist Andrew Carnegie argued that capitalists had a duty to play a broader cultural and social role and thus improve the world around them. He argued the best way to deal with the phenomenon of wealth inequality was for the self-made rich to redistribute surplus income in a responsible and thoughtful manner.

Andrew Carnegie was born in Dunfermline in 1835 and emigrated to the United States with his parents in 1848. He started work as a telegrapher and by the 1860s had investments in railroads, bridges and oil. Later he led the massive expansion of the US steel industry in the late 19th century, building Pittsburgh's Carnegie Steel Company, which he sold to J. P. Morgan in 1901 for $480 million (roughly $13.2 billion), creating the US Steel Corporation. He was the highest-profile philanthropist of his day.

Carnegie's approach differed from the traditional bequest, where such wealth was simply handed down to family heirs, and other forms where large sums of money were handed over to the state for public use. To him, responsibility for how it was spent should be the personal concern of the philanthropist, in which case it would produce the greatest net benefit to society. Carnegie also argued that the wealthy themselves resist using their wealth in extravagant, irresponsible or self-indulgent ways in order to set an example.

Carnegie practiced what he preached, devoting the last few decades of his life to large-scale philanthropy, funding a vast network of local libraries, education and scientific research. He also built Carnegie Hall in New York City and founded the Carnegie Endowment for International Peace and, closer to home, endowed the Carnegie Trust for the Universities of Scotland. Although 'Wealth' was written as an essay rather than a speech, in 1908, aged 73, Carnegie recorded a portion of it for posterity.

I quote from the Gospel of Wealth published 25 years ago. This then is held to be the duty of the man of wealth. First: to set an example of modest, unostentatious living, shunning display; to provide moderately for the legitimate wants of those dependent upon him, and after doing so, to consider all surplus revenues which come to him simply as trust funds, which he is strictly bound as a matter of duty, to administer in the manner which in his judgment is best calculated to produce the most beneficial results for the community.

The man of wealth must become a trustee and agent for his poorer brethren, bringing to their service his superior wisdom, experience, and ability to administer. Those who would administer wisely must indeed be wise. For one of

The man of wealth must become a trustee and agent for his poorer brethren.

the serious obstacles to the improvement of our race is indiscriminate charity. It were better for mankind that the millions of the rich were thrown into the sea than so spent as to encourage the slothful, the drunken, the unworthy.

In bestowing charity, the main consideration should be to help those who help themselves. It provides part of the means by which those who desire to improve may do so; to give to those who desire to rise the aids by which they may rise; to assist but rarely or never to do all.

He is the only true reformer who is careful and as anxious not to lead the unworthy as he is to lead the worthy, and perhaps even more so, for in alms giving, more injury may be done by promoting vice than by relieving virtue. Thus is the problem of the rich and poor to be solved.

The laws of accumulation should be left free; the laws of distribution free. Individualism will continue. But the millionaire will be but a trustee for the poor; entrusted for a season with a part of the increased wealth of the community, but

Men may die without incurring the pity of their fellows.

administering it for the community far better than it did, or would have done, of itself. The best in minds will thus have reached a stage in the development of the race in which it is clearly seen that there is no mode of disposing of surplus wealth creditable to thoughtful and earnest men into whose hands it flows save by using it year-by-year for the general good. This day already dawns.

Men may die without incurring the pity of their fellows, sharers in great business enterprises from which their capital cannot be, or has not been withdrawn, upon which is left entirely a trust for public uses.

Yet the day is not far distant when the man who dies, leaving behind him millions of available wealth, which was free for him to administer during life, will pass away "unwept, unhonored, and unsung," no matter to what use he leaves the dross which he cannot take with him. Of such as these, the public verdict will then be: the man who dies thus rich, dies disgraced. Such in my opinion is the true gospel concerning wealth, obedience to which is destined someday to solve the problems of the rich and the poor, to hasten the coming brotherhood of man, and at last to make our earth a heaven.[1]

As long as the world rolls round Liberalism will have its part to play.

Winston Churchill
1874–1965

SPEECH ON LIBERALISM AND SOCIALISM · KINNAIRD HALL · DUNDEE
4 MAY 1908

When Sir Henry Campbell-Bannerman died in 1908 and was succeeded as Prime Minister by HH Asquith, Winston Churchill – then a Liberal MP – was promoted to the Cabinet as President of the Board of Trade. But there was a snag. Under the law at that time, a newly-appointed minister was required to seek a fresh mandate at a by-election. Churchill lost, the electors of Manchester North West having decided they wanted a non-minister instead.

Sir Winston Leonard Spencer-Churchill was educated at Harrow and Sandhurst and after a brief Army and newspaper career was elected to Parliament in 1900. He held many posts in Liberal and Conservative governments until the early 1930s, and became Prime Minister in 1940. Churchill returned to the premiership in 1951 but resigned four years later. He died in 1965.

Within minutes of the count, as Churchill later recalled, he had received a telegram inviting him to become the candidate in another by-election in Dundee, where the sitting Member was about to be elevated to the House of Lords. He travelled up to Scotland that night and on 14 May made an eve-of-poll speech to more than 2,000 people.

Not only did the speech reflect Churchill's transition from concentrating on foreign affairs to social problems, but it was also designed to persuade trade unionists to back Liberalism rather than Socialism, representing a real turning point for the former creed. Churchill considered it the most successful election speech he ever made, and he won the seat with a convincing majority.

There are cross-currents in this election. You cannot be unconscious of that. They flow this way and that way, and they disturb the clear issue which we should like to establish between the general bodies of those whose desire it is to move forward on the lines of modern civilisation and those who wish to revert to the old and barbarous prejudices and contentions of the past to their fiscal systems and to their methods of government and administration, and to their

Jingo foreign policies across the seas, from which we hoped we had shaken ourselves clear. [Cheers.]

Socialism seeks to pull down wealth; Liberalism seeks to raise up poverty.

... Liberalism has its own history and its own tradition. Socialism has its own formulas and its own aims. Socialism seeks to pull down wealth; Liberalism seeks to raise up poverty. [Loud cheers.] Socialism would destroy private interests; Liberalism would preserve private interests in the only way in which they can be safely and justly preserved, namely, by reconciling them with public right. [Cheers.] Socialism would kill enterprise; Liberalism would rescue enterprise from the trammels of privilege and preference. [Cheers.] Socialism assails the pre-eminence of the individual; Liberalism seeks, and shall seek more in the future, to build up a minimum standard for the mass. [Cheers.] Socialism exalts the rule; Liberalism exalts the man. Socialism attacks capital; Liberalism attacks monopoly. [Cheers.] These are the great distinctions which I draw, and which, I think, you will think I am right in drawing at this election between our philosophies and our ideals. Don't think that Liberalism is a faith that is played out; that it is a philosophy to which there is no expanding future. As long as the world rolls round Liberalism will have its part to play – a grand, beneficent, and ameliorating part to play – in relation to men and States. [Cheers.]

... But I have no hesitation in saying that I am on the side of those who think that a greater collective element should be introduced into the State and municipalities. I should like to see the State undertaking new functions, particularly stepping forward into those spheres of activity which are governed by an element of monopoly. [Applause.] Your tramways and so on; your great

Liberalism will not be killed.

public works, which are of a monopolistic and privileged character there I see a wide field for State enterprise to embark upon. But when we are told to exalt and admire a philosophy which destroys individualism and seeks to replace it by collectivism, I say that is a monstrous and imbecile conception which can find no real foothold in the brains and hearts – and the hearts are as trustworthy as the brains – in the hearts of sensible people. [Loud cheers.]

... Liberalism will not be killed. [Cheers.] Liberalism is a quickening spirit – it is immortal. [Loud cheers.] It will live on through all the days, be they good days or be they evil days. No, I believe it will even burn stronger and brighter and more helpful in evil days than in good – [cheers] just like your harbour lights which shine out across the waters, and which on a calm night gleam with soft refulgence, but through the storm flash a message of life to those who toil on the rough waters. [Cheers.] But it takes a great party to govern Great Britain – no clique, no faction, no cabal, can govern the 40 millions of people who live in this island. It takes a great concentration of forces to make a governing instrument.

You have now got a Radical and democratic governing instrument, and if this

Down, down, down would fall the high hopes and elevated aspirations of the social reformer.

Administration is broken that instrument will be shattered. It has been re-created painfully and laboriously after 20 years of courage and fidelity. It has come into being – it is there. It is now at work in legislation and in the influence which it can exercise throughout the whole world, making even our opponents talk our language [laughter] – making all parties in the State think of social reform, and concern themselves with social and domestic affairs. I say, beware of how you injure that instrument – that great instrument as Mr Gladstone called it – or weaken it at a moment when I think the masses of this country have great need of it. Why, what would happen if this present Government were to perish? On its tomb would be written – "Beware of social reform. [Laughter.] The working classes – the labour forces will not support a Government engaged in social reform. Every social reform will cost you votes. Beware of social reform. Learn to think Imperially." [Great laughter and tremendous cheering.]

An inconclusive verdict from Dundee, the home of Scottish Radicalism – [hear, hear] an inconclusive or, still more, a disastrous verdict – [loud cries of "No" and "Never"] would carry a message of despair to everyone in all parts of our island and in our sister island who is working for the essential influences and truths of Liberalism and progress. Down, down, down would fall the high hopes and elevated aspirations of the social reformer. The constructive plans now forming in so many nimble brains would melt into air – the light which had begun to gleam over the mountains would fade and die. The old regime would be reinstated, reinstalled; the Balfours and the Chamberlains, the Arnold-Forsters and the Lansdownes, and the Cecils will return. Like the Bourbons they will have learned nothing and will have forgotten nothing. [Loud cheers.] We shall step out of the period of adventurous hope in which we have lived for a brief spell – we shall step back to the period of obstinate and prejudiced negations. [Cheers.] For Ireland ten years of resolute government; for England dear food and cheaper gin – [great laughter] – and for Scotland – the superior wisdom of the House of Lords. [Laughter.] Is that the work you want to do, men of Dundee? [Loud cries of "No, no."] Is that the work to which you will put your precious franchises – your votes which have been won for you by so much exertion and struggle in the past? Is that the work you want to do on Saturday? No, I think not. I have a great confidence that the message you will send will be to encourage different work to that. [Hear, hear, and cheers.][1]

Look at all the Oriental countries. Do not talk about superiority or inferiority.

Arthur James Balfour
1848–1930

SPEECH ON THE CONSOLIDATED FUND (NO 2) BILL · HOUSE OF COMMONS
13 JUNE 1910

In 1910 Arthur James Balfour was in the middle of his career, which had already peaked with a short spell as Prime Minister between 1902–05; he was leader of the Conservative opposition and could look forward to three years as Foreign Secretary towards the end of the Great War. He had also been an early Secretary for Scotland in the late 19th century (Balfour was from East Lothian), but foreign affairs was his biggest passion.

In this, a long speech delivered to the House of Commons in June 1910, Balfour outlined what Professor Edward Said later analysed as the standard western imperialist stance that proferred the dominant supervising role to the UK and the subordinate role to what Balfour called the 'subject race', in this case Egypt. Said, in an infuential 1978 book, described this as 'Orientalism', a concept wherein a strong cultural, racial, or political body wields power over a weaker one.

Of course, in 1910 Balfour's was hardly a controversial view. He addressed MPs amid rising, and often violent, nationalism in Egypt, which was not yet a formal British Protectorate (that followed in 1914). Indirect British rule had begun in 1882 when the British Army defeated the Egyptians at Tel El Kebir, and would last until the 1952 Egyptian revolution when British 'advisers' were expelled.

Arthur James Balfour was a Conservative Party politician and statesman. Born in Scotland and educated as a philosopher, he entered Parliament in 1874 and became, initially, Secretary for Scotland, then Chief Secretary for Ireland 1887–1891. In 1902 he succeeded his uncle Lord Salisbury as Prime Minister, although he resigned following a split over tariff reform just three years later. Balfour was Leader of the Opposition until 1911, but returned to the Cabinet in 1915 and became Foreign Secretary the following year (he issued the famous 'Balfour Declaration' in 1917). He received an earldom in 1922 and died eight years later.

I take up no attitude of superiority. But I ask... everybody else who has even the most superficial knowledge of history, if they will really try to look in the face the facts with which a British statesman has to deal when he is put in a position of supremacy over great races like the inhabitants of Egypt and countries in the East. We know the civilisation of Egypt better than we know the civilisation of any other country. We know it further back; we know it more intimately; we know more about it. It goes far beyond the petty span of the history of our own race, which is lost in the prehistoric period at a time when the Egyptian civilisation had already passed its prime. Look at all the Oriental countries. Do not talk about superiority or inferiority.

Look at the facts of the case. Western nations as soon as they emerge into history show the beginnings of those capacities for self-government... You may look through the whole history of the Orientals in what is called, broadly speaking, the East, and you never find traces of self-government. All their great centuries — and they have been very great — have been passed under despotisms, under absolute government. All their great contributions to civilisation — and they have been great — have been made under that form of government. Conqueror has succeeded conqueror; one domination has followed another; but never in all the revolutions of fate and fortune have you seen one of those nations of its own motion establish what we, from a Western point of view, call self-government. That is the fact. It is not a question of superiority or inferiority. I suppose a true Eastern sage would say that the working government which we have taken upon ourselves in Egypt and elsewhere is not a work worthy of a philosopher — that it is the dirty work, the inferior work, of carrying on the

You may look through the whole history of the Orientals in what is called, broadly speaking, the East, and you never find traces of self-government.

necessary labour. Do let us put this question of superiority and inferiority out of our minds. It is wholly out of place...

We have got, as I think, to deal with nations who, as far as our knowledge goes, have always been governed in the manner we call absolute, and have never had what we are accustomed to call free institutions or self-government. They have never had it; they have never, apparently, desired it... The time may come when they will adopt, not merely our superficial philosophy, but our genuine practice. But after 3,000, 4,000, or 5,000 years of known history, and unlimited centuries of unknown history have been passed by these nations under a different system, it is not thirty years of British rule which is going to alter the character bred into them by this immemorial tradition.

If that be true, is it or is it not a good thing for these great nations—I admit their greatness — that this absolute Government should be exercised by us? I think it is a good thing. I think experience shows that they have got under it a far better government than in the whole history of the world they ever had before, and which not only is a benefit to them, but is undoubtedly a benefit to the whole of the civilised West... We are in Egypt not merely for the sake of the Egyptians, though we are there for their sake; we are there also for the sake of Europe at

Generations pass. New men arise. Old memories vanish.

large... Generations pass. New men arise. Old memories vanish. Under a policy which casts pain and inconvenience on some members of the community ancient wrongs are forgotten, ancient benefits are forgotten likewise...

Every person, with an intimate knowledge of Egypt, to whom I have spoken, whether he be a recent traveller, a man with a long official experience, or whether he be a man whose business has taken him to Egypt year by year for decade after decade — all these people have agreed with one voice I that the position in Egypt is now eminently unsatisfactory. They also agree that it is eminently unsatisfactory because the authority of what they frankly say is the dominant race — and as I think ought to remain the dominant race — has been undermined. Whether that is the fault of the Egyptian administration, whether it is the fault of His Majesty's Government, or whether it is due to a somewhat unfortunate concatenation of circumstances over which neither the Government at home nor the Government in Egypt have had adequate control, I do not know, and I do not say. What I do know, what I will say, is that the situation, if I read it rightly, calls for prompt and decisive action![1]

I can imagine no length of resistance to which Ulster can go in which I should not be prepared to support them.

Andrew Bonar Law
1858–1923

SPEECH AT BLENHEIM PALACE RALLY

APRIL 1912

Ireland dominated UK politics in the late 19th and early 20th centuries. After many aborted efforts, in 1912 the Liberal government of HH Asquith forged ahead with the second Home Rule Bill, which would have granted the whole of Ireland – north and south – a devolved legislature based in Dublin. To Unionists with ties to Scotland and Ulster such as Andrew Bonar Law, this was unacceptable.

Andrew Bonar Law was born in New Brunswick, Canada, to the Rev James Law, an Ulsterman of Scottish descent. The only Prime Minister to have been born outside the British Isles, he was also the shortest serving of the 20th century, inhabiting 10 Downing Street for just 211 days. A businessman before entering Parliament, Bonar Law made his political reputation opposing Home Rule for Ireland, and in particular for Ulster.

On 9 April 1912 Bonar Law visited Belfast along with around 70 MPs and watched as 100,000 Irish unionists marched past in military formation. 'You are a besieged city,' said Bonar Law melodramatically, before quoting Pitt: 'You have saved yourselves by your exertions, and you will save the empire by your example.'

Two days later Asquith put the Home Rule Bill before the House of Commons. The Unionists responded by organising a huge rally at Blenheim Palace. Bonar Law condemned Asquith's government 'as a Revolutionary Committee which has seized upon despotic power by fraud', and essentially endorsed armed resistance to the plans. As Lord Blake, Bonar Law's biographer, later pointed out, the Unionist leader had broken the conventions upon which Parliamentary democracy is based. Such a tone had not been heard in England since the Long Parliament.

In our opposition to them we shall not be guided by the considerations or bound by the restraints which would influence us in an ordinary constitutional struggle. We shall take the means, whatever means seem to us most effective, to deprive them of the despotic power which they have usurped and compel them to appeal to the people whom they have deceived. They may, perhaps they will, carry their Home Rule Bill through the House of Commons, but what then? I said the other day in the House of Commons and I repeat here that there are things stronger than Parliamentary majorities...

Before I occupied the position which I now fill in the Party, I said that in my belief if an attempt were made to deprive these men of their birthright as part

We shall take the means, whatever means seem to us most effective.

of a corrupt Parliamentary bargain, they would be justified in resisting such an attempt by all means in their power, including force. I said it then, and I repeat now with a full sense of the responsibility which attaches to my position, that in my opinion, if such an attempt is made, I can imagine no length of resistance to which Ulster can go in which I should not be prepared to support them, and in which, in my belief, they would not be supported by the overwhelming majority of the British people.[1]

If you are itching for a rifle, itching to fight, have a country of your own; better to fight for our own country than for the robber empire.

James Connolly
1868–1916

SPEECH AT COMMEMORATIVE MEETING · DUBLIN

30 AUGUST 1914

Although born in Scotland, James Connolly was for most of his life associated with Ireland and its Home Rule movement. In 1912 he was a founder of the Independent Labour Party of Ireland, and when, in 1913, the Dublin Employers' Federation staged a lock-out to prevent workers joining the trade union, Connolly returned to Dublin to rally the workers, although poverty defeated them in February 1914.

James Connolly was born in 1868 at the Cowgate in Edinburgh, the youngest of three sons of Irish immigrants. Brought up in a slum, Connolly left St Patrick's School aged ten and became a printer's devil, bakery hand and tiling factory worker. In 1882, he lied about his age in order to join the Army, and served in Ireland. Connolly deserted in 1889 and joined the Scottish Socialist Federation the following year, beginning his political career.

This speech commemorated the deaths of James Nolan, John Byrne and Alice Brady, who were all killed during that lock-out. Appalled by the outbreak of the Great War in 1914, Connolly had launched a massive anti-recruitment drive, although its failure, combined with the terrible suffering of the Dublin poor, drove him to join forces with the revolutionary nationalist Irish Republican Brotherhood.

Later, his influence was clear in the egalitarian wording of the proclamation declaring an Irish republic published on Easter Monday in 1916. Connolly directed operations at the General Post Office bravely, for the last two days with a shattered ankle. After the surrender on 29 April he was court-martialled on 9 May and shot (while seated, he was unable to stand) at Kilmainham Jail, Dublin, at dawn on 12 May 1916.

He was glad to see so large a gathering to commemorate their comrades, because they were murdered for the sake of great principles. It had not been a mere casual murder, but a cold-blooded and premeditated one, deliberately planned with the idea in mind that as they went to their graves, so went the hopes for which they fought. That when they were murdered all the hopes of the Irish workers would be slain with them; when they were foully done to death all our aspirations for a cleaner, better city and grander nation would be murdered, too.

Where do we stand today? The Irish Transport and General Workers' Union and the hopes of the Irish working class, and that class itself stands erect and resolute, fearing no man, and the British Government is down on its knees praying for the Russians to come and save them. Our fight of last year was not for added wages and reduction of hours; it was for an opportunity of building up in our midst men and women, a chance to develop nobility and grandeur of character for men and women, a time to realise the nobility of life, to study the history of Ireland, to study our rights as well as our duties; time to develop men and women for the coming crisis, so that they might take advantage of it when it came.

He was glad to see so large a gathering to commemorate their comrades.

Abject servility there is in Ireland; whatever of the spirit of a slave that in you lies, lies with those who served to cripple the grandest movement ever started. If labour controlled your destinies, conjure the picture of what might have happened when after Gray and Asquith had plunged England into war, there arose a clamour for [John] Redmond. And Redmond, without consulting you, the people of Ireland, pledged us to war with as kindly, gracious a nation as God ever put the breath of life into – what happened then?

Redmond when they shouted for him might have sat still and let them shout, then before another sun rose got a measure greater than Grattan dreamed of Redmond, as spokesman of the majority of the Irish people might have risen and said: "I and my colleagues will go to Ireland and consult the Irish Nation." Then would Ireland be a nation in reality. "We have waited and now Germany has come, and we will start our own Parliament. Stop us if you can." Help would have come from all sides. Why, the R[oyal] I[rish] C[onstabulary] would have acted as a guard of honour!

Abject servility there is in Ireland.

These men have sold you. Sold you? No, by God, given you away. Whether my speech is pro-German or pro-Irish, I don't know. As an Irish worker I owe a duty to our class; counting no allegiance to the Empire; I'd be glad to see it back in the bottomless pit. The Irish workers hold themselves ready to bargain with whoever can make a bargain. England has been fighting Germany. If it were not for the Russians, French and Japanese, the British would not have made a mouthful for the Germans. The Germans are in Boulogne, where Napoleon projected an invasion of Britain. To Ireland is only a twelve hours' run.

These men have sold you. Sold you? No, by God, given you away.

If you are itching for a rifle, itching to fight, have a country of your own; better to fight for our own country than for the robber empire. If ever you shoulder a rifle, let it be for Ireland. Conscription or no conscription, they will never get me or mine. You have been told you are not strong, that you have no rifles. Revolutions do not start with rifles; start first and get your rifles after. Our curse is our belief in our weakness. We are not weak, we are strong. Make up your mind to strike before your opportunity goes.

Their only righteous purpose is to promote the welfare of their fellow-citizens and the well-being of mankind.

Dedicatory meeting

DEDICATORY MEETING · ST ANDREW'S HALLS AND GLASGOW CITY HALL
NOVEMBER 1922

As the organised left replaced the Liberals as the party of the Scottish working classes, more and more Labour politicians were elected to Parliament. This was most manifest at the general election of 1922, when several of the Red Clydesiders – most of them Independent Labour Party members – were elected to the House of Commons. They included James Maxton, John Wheatley, Manny Shinwell, David Kirkwood, Neil Maclean and George Buchanan.

When the results became known, large meetings were held in St Andrew's Halls and the Glasgow City Hall. In both, the 'atmosphere was tense with enthusiasm and barely concealed emotion'. Herbert Highton presided at the former and Edward Rosslyn Mitchell at the latter. The Labour Members for Glasgow divided themselves between the meetings, and each made short speeches, but at both the 'keynote' of the proceedings lay in the following dedicatory statement.

'Red Clydeside' was a term used to describe an amalgamation of charismatic politicians, organised movements and political forces that lasted from the 1910s to the early 1930s. Centred on Glasgow and nearby urban areas like Clydebank, Greenock and Paisley, the movement – although subject to a lot of historical mythology – played an important part in the British labour movement.

The Labour Party members of Parliament for the City of Glasgow, inspired by zeal for the welfare of humanity and the prosperity of all peoples, and strengthened by the trust reposed in them by their fellow-citizens, have resolved to dedicate themselves to the reconciliation and unity of the nations of the world and the development and happiness of the people of these islands.

They record their infinite gratitude to the pioneer minds of past generations who, by their services and sacrifices, have opened up the path for the freedom of the people.

They send to all peoples a message of goodwill, reconciliation and friendship.

To the sister nations of the British Commonwealth they send fraternal greetings, and offer all encouragement in the difficult task of self-realisation and self-government.

To the men who bore the burden of war they offer their grateful thanks, and promise that those who have suffered shall be generously treated, and that the widows and orphans of those who fell shall be cherished by the nation.

They send to all peoples a message of goodwill.

They promise that they will urge without ceasing the need for providing houses for the people, suitable to enshrine the spirit of Home, that men and women may live in healthy surroundings and that little children may bloom and flourish. They will bear in their hearts the sorrows of the aged, the widowed mother and the poor, that their lives shall not be without comfort.

They will endeavour to purge industry of the curse of unhealthy workshops, to restore wages to the level of adequate maintenance and to eradicate the corrupting effects of monopoly and avarice.

For those who are without work, they will press for the provision of useful employment or reasonable maintenance.

They will have regard to the weak and those stricken by disease, that medical science and skill shall not be wanting to restore them to health and to eradicate preventable disease from our land.

They will bear in their hearts the sorrows of the aged, the widowed mother and the poor, that their lives shall not be without comfort.

For those who have fallen in the struggle of life, and are in prison, they will labour that their lot may be lightened and that they may be strengthened to face the temptations of the world on their release.

To this end they will endeavour so to adjust the finances of their nation that the burden of public debt may be relieved and the responsibility for the maintenance of national administration be borne by those who, by the possession of the land of the nation, or the wealth created by the citizens of the nation, are best able to bear.

In all things they will abjure vanity and self-aggrandisement, recognising that they are the honoured servants of the people, and that their only righteous purpose is to promote the welfare of their fellow-citizens and the well-being of mankind.

Why should we give up the creation of eight centuries in favour of the work of a few hurried and hustled gentlemen in the year 1927?

John Buchan 1875–1940

MAIDEN SPEECH IN THE HOUSE OF COMMONS · LONDON
6 JULY 1927

John Buchan, in 1927 best known as the author of thrillers such as *The 39 Steps*, became an MP after winning a by-election in the Combined Scottish Universities constituency (elected by graduates of Scotland's four ancient universities). In the House of Commons he immediately aligned himself with a small band of articulate and progressive Tory MPs known as the YMCA.

Buchan's maiden speech took place during a key debate on the future of the House of Lords, which Prime Minister Stanley Baldwin had promised to strengthen in response to pressure from the Conservative right wing. Several members of the YMCA led backbench Tory opposition to any reform, while Buchan's speech pointed out the scheme's contradictions, questioned its usefulness and urged his party to trust the people. In the event, more than 100 Conservative MPs opposed the measure, which was then dropped.

John Buchan, 1st Baron Tweedsmuir was a Scottish novelist, historian and Unionist politician. After a brief career as a lawyer, he mixed writing with his political and diplomatic career, serving as private secretary to various colonial administrators in Southern Africa. Buchan was appointed governor-general of Canada in 1935 and occupied that post until his death in 1940, upon which he received a state funeral.

Baldwin congratulated Buchan personally, no doubt relieved to have been saved from a tricky political situation. 'Another Ministerial organ has referred to this revolt as a "Y.M.C.A.,"' observed Oswald Mosley during the debate, 'which, I understand, is a reverent tribute to the evangelical character of that group of young Conservatives.' Buchan was certainly evangelical but, interestingly, always felt he was not taken seriously as a politician due to his day job – writing thrillers.

I do not deny that, judged by a narrow academic logic, there are many anomalies in the House of Lords. But... the strength of the House of Lords is that it represents at present almost every interest, almost every avocation, almost every branch of knowledge, and, since its recent copious dilutions, almost every social grade. It is a most curious microcosm of the life of this country, and, therefore, it seems to me, to have admirable qualities for the work of revising and criticising. If the providence which watches over us has given us this kind of Second Chamber, why tamper with it? Why should we give up the creation of eight centuries in favour of the work of a few hurried and hustled gentlemen in the year 1927? I doubt very much if thereby you would increase its efficiency. I can imagine a House of Lords reformed on the most austere intellectual basis which would be far less efficient. It is notorious that there may be a dangerous collective un-wisdom, and a dense corporate stupidity in bodies, every member of which is a distinguished man.

If the providence which watches over us has given us this kind of Second Chamber, why tamper with it?

We are told that the present system is unfair to the Labour party, that the Labour party on their return to power will be embarrassed by finding in the House of Lords so few men who adhere to their political creed. I confess that the Labour party does not seem to me to be very grateful to the Government for its tender consideration for its welfare... It seems to me that the embarrassment would continue and be inevitable in any Second Chamber, however constituted. Surely it would be better to put the onus on the Labour party of meeting this difficulty when they return to power. I have no doubt that they have in their ranks a number of patriots who would be willing to be sacrificial lambs on the altar of public duty... I can imagine that the day may yet come when the last supporters of a discredited, antiquated, and almost forgotten creed called Socialism will be a small group of Noble Lords deriving their titles from various spots in the Clyde valley.

I see no practical advantage in the changes proposed under this head, and I see very real practical disadvantages. I strongly object to the principle which is behind it. It is an attempt to rationalise, to make more logical, to make less anomalous one of our institutions. But we have never worried about that question. The one question which our practical-minded people have always asked has been: Does it work? Hon. Members may remember the famous words of Edmund Burke:

I have no doubt that they have in their ranks a number of patriots.

"The old building stands well enough, though part Gothic, part Grecian, part Chinese, till an attempt be made to square it into uniformity. Then, indeed, it may come down upon our heads altogether in much uniformity of ruin." If we once give in to the minor intellectual and attempt to rationalise our politics entirely, we may end in very deep waters...

The British Empire from first to last has been illogical and anomalous, and if at any time we had attempted to make it a logical structure, we should have smashed it to pieces. The political genius of our countrymen lies in the fact that they can tolerate anomalies, that they can respect anomalies which are deep-rooted and close to the life of the country, and that they can make them work. The British Constitution seems to me like a pin-cushion, stuck full of the thin ends of wedges, which the common sense of our people has refrained from driving further in.

My second difficulty is far more fundamental and far more important. The Lord Chancellor's scheme proposes to take the powers and composition of a reformed House of Lords altogether out of the Parliament Act. It proposes at

Just as there are certain things which no civilised country can do and yet retain its claim to civilisation, so there are certain things which Britain cannot do and remain Britain.

the same time to abolish the power of the Crown to create Peers at the request of the Government of the day. That must happen. If you limit the number of Peers it is bound to happen. The result is that the House of Lords, on this scheme, will become a permanent and unchallengable corporation. I think that is a most dangerous doctrine... What does it involve? It means that we take an important part of our Constitution and give it the rigidity of a written document, a thing which is not only repugnant to Conservatism but wholly alien to the tradition of our public life. What is the argument used in support of this startling change? It is the fear of some future revolutionary intention of some future Government... I am as credulous and as imaginative as most men, but my imagination and my credulity cannot rise to these apocalyptic heights. But suppose there was any such danger of revolution, how could any paper barrier prevent it? There will be no revolution, no constitutional revolution, in Britain until the great bulk of the British people resolutely desire it, and if that desire is ever present what Statute can bar the way?

... Just as there are certain things which no civilised country can do and yet retain its claim to civilisation, so there are certain things which Britain cannot do and remain Britain. That is the law fundamental; that is the true barrier against foolish and perilous change, the inherited political aptitude of our people, what our greatest political thinker described as the "ancient, inbred integrity, honesty, good nature and good humour of the people of Britain." I should be sorry indeed if in any fleeting moment of pedantry or of panic we were false to what is the first principle not only of the Conservative party but of the British Constitution.[1]

I can only describe it as a mixture of cant, corruption and incompetence

Jennie Lee
1904–88

MAIDEN SPEECH DURING FINANCE BILL DEBATE · HOUSE OF COMMONS
25 APRIL 1929

When Jennie Lee entered Parliament in a 1929 by-election, she was the youngest Member of Parliament, being only in her mid-20s. After graduating from university and working as a teacher in Cowdenbeath, she was adopted as the Independent Labour Party (ILP) candidate for the North Lanarkshire constituency. Even before making her maiden speech Lee found herself in conflict with the Labour leadership.

Jennie Lee was born in 1904 in Lochgelly, Fife, the daughter of a miner. Her childhood was steeped in socialist politics, and she later studied at Edinburgh University. After losing her seat in 1931, she remained active politically, not least through her marriage to Nye Bevan, and in 1945 re-entered the House of Commons as the MP for Cannock in Staffordshire. In the 1960s Lee held various ministerial posts and played a key role in founding the Open University. She lost her seat in 1970 and joined the House of Lords as Baroness Lee of Asheridge. Lee died in 1988 aged 84.

She insisted on being sponsored by Robert Smillie and her old friend James Maxton rather than by her party's choice of Members to formally introduce her to the House of Commons. Her maiden speech, meanwhile, spared little time on pleasantries. 'I must confess that this dying House is not exactly a place of inspiration,' she informed MPs, 'and I look upon myself more as a chip of the next Parliament, which has made a rather precipitate arrival, than as one really belonging to the present House.'

Lee's contribution went on to attack the Budget proposals of Winston Churchill, comments he apparently congratulated her on following the speech. Thereafter she forged a Parliamentary reputation as a left-winger, aligning herself with Maxton and other ILP Members. She lost her seat in 1931 and married, in 1934, the left-wing Welsh Labour MP Aneurin Bevan, a 26-year marriage that ensured Lee became Labour royalty.

In listening to the Debates in this House, I have throughout been wondering how those things affect the great mass of working men and women in the country. Is there anything in the statement which has been made which may lead us to believe that a glimmer of hope is held out to such people that more employment, better conditions of labour, or higher wages in the future than they have had in the past, will be the result of this Budget? The greatest indictment of this Budget is that it holds out to the great mass of the people of this country absolutely no hope that the years ahead will be any better or brighter for them than the years which have passed. I regret that, because, surely, there could be no greater opportunity than a Budget statement for the Government of this country, if they so desired, to do something to readjust the inequalities of income in this country.

I have throughout been wondering how those things affect the great mass of working men and women in the country.

I do not think that anyone so far has disputed the figures that have been given already from these benches, showing that, out of a national income of approximately £4,000,000,000, only some £1,600,000 is paid as wages to the workers of this country. That represents only two-fifths of the total income, and, surely, a Chancellor of the Exchequer who was genuinely concerned to improve the life of the people of this country would have had a very substantial margin, in the remaining three-fifths, in which to readjust the burdens of taxation...

We say to hon. Members opposite that there is only one explanation of this Budget, and that explanation is that, in the eyes of the Chancellor of the Exchequer, the people of this country are made up in this way — the great majority of them are fools, and the remaining minority knaves. That is the only possible explanation of such a Budget as has been put before us, and I can only describe it, and with it the whole policy for which the party at present in office has been responsible, as a mixture — let me choose my words deliberately — I can only describe it as a mixture of cant, corruption and incompetence...

In expressing my criticism of this Measure, which seeks to perpetuate the inequality of things as they are, which lacks even an ordinary sense of self-preservation, as it makes little or no provision for developing the resources of this country, and is allowing Great Britain to lag far behind in the race, while America,

I can only describe it as a mixture of cant, corruption and incompetence...

Germany, France and all the other countries steal ahead, I feel that these matters will never be treated seriously in this House until the Government of this country is changed. Although comfortable Gentlemen opposite may smile, and may be little concerned about these problems, they matter very intensely to Members on this side of the House, they matter very intensely to the great majority of our people outside, and I hope and believe that the Chancellor of the Exchequer, in putting before this House the Budget statement that he has, has made it absolutely certain that, when the Election comes, all honest, honourable citizens of this country will rise in revolt and hound from office this Government which has so misused its opportunities and its power.[1]

They died for a world that is past, these men, but they did not die for this that we seem to inherit.

Robert Colquhoun

SERMON · KINRADDIE

1932

The writer Lewis Grassic Gibbon is best known for his 1932 novel *Sunset Song*, widely regarded as one of the most important Scottish novels of the 20th century. Part of the trilogy *A Scots Quair*, it concerns a young woman called Chris Guthrie growing up in a farming family on the fictional estate of Kinraddie in the north-east of Scotland.

Guthrie's life is hard and her family's dysfunctionality takes up much of the novel: suicide, infanticide, domestic abuse and ill health. Eventually she finds happiness with a young farmer called Ewan Tavendale, with whom she has a son, also called Ewan. Then the First World War intervenes, taking Ewan senior from Guthrie and the experience brutalises him. Eventually he is shot as a deserter.

Guthrie begins a relationship with the new minister of Kinraddie, Robert Colquhoun, and *Sunset Song* ends with her watching as he dedicates the War Memorial at the Standing Stones above her home, the sun setting to the strains of 'Flowers of the Forest' on the bagpipes. This is Colquhoun's sermon, 'his short hair blowing in the wind that had come', (as Grassic Gibbon wrote) 'his voice not decent and a kirk-like bumble, but ringing out over the loch'.

Lewis Grassic Gibbon was born James Leslie Mitchell in Auchterless in 1901. He worked as a journalist for the Aberdeen Journal and Scottish Farmer aged 16, while in 1919 he joined the Royal Army Service Corps and served in Iran, India and Egypt before enlisting in the RAF. Mitchell began writing full time in 1929 but died prematurely young in 1935 of peritonitis brought on by a perforated ulcer.

"In the sunset of an age and an epoch we may write that for epitaph of the men who were of it. They went quiet and brave from the lands they loved, though seldom of that love might they speak, it was not in them to tell in words of the earth that moved and lived and abided, their life and enduring love. And who knows at the last what memories of it were with them, the springs and the winters of this land and all the sounds and scents of it that had once been theirs, deep, and a passion of their blood and spirit, those four who died in France? With them we may say there died a thing older than themselves, these were the Last of the Peasants, the last of the Old Scots folk. A new generation comes up that will know them not, except as a memory in a song, they pass with the things that seemed

They went quite and brave from the lands they loved.

good to them, with loves and desires that grow dim and alien in the days to be. It was the old Scotland that perished then, and we may believe that never again will the old speech and the old songs, the old curses and the old benedictions, rise but with alien effort to our lips. The last of the peasants, those four that you knew, took that with them to the darkness and the quietness of the places where they sleep. And the land changes, their parks and their steadings are a desolation where the sheep are pastured, we are told that great machines come as soon to till the land, and the great herds come to feed on it, the crofter is gone, the man with the house and the steading of his own and the land closer to his heart than the

It was the old Scotland that perished then.

flesh of his body. Nothing, it has been said, is true but change, nothing abides, and here in Kinraddie where we watch the building of those little prides and those little fortunes on the ruins of the little farms we must give heed that these also do not abide, that a new spirit shall come to the land with the greater herd and the great machines. For greed of place and possession and great estate those four had little heed, the kindness of friends and the warmth of toil and the peace of rest – they asked no more from God or man, and no less would they endure. So, lest we shame them, let us believe that the new oppressions and foolish greeds

They died for a world that is past.

are no more than mists that pass. They died for a world that is past, these men, but they did not die for this that we seem to inherit. Beyond it and us there shines a greater hope and a newer world, undreamt when these four died. But need we doubt which side the battle they would range themselves did they live to-day, need we doubt the answer they cry to us even now, the four of them, from the places of the sunset?

Do not try to stop us on the road along which we are travelling.

Willie Gallacher
1881–1965

MAIDEN SPEECH · HOUSE OF COMMONS

4 DECEMBER 1935

The Communist politician Willie Gallacher first stood for Parliament in Dundee at the 1922 and 1923 general elections, and again in West Fife (1929 and 1931) and also Shipley in 1930. In 1925 he had been one of 12 members of the Communist Party convicted under the Incitement to Mutiny Act 1797, and one of the five defendants sentenced to 12 months' imprisonment.

In 1935, he was eventually elected the MP for West Fife, and served 15 years in the House of Commons, one of only three Communist MPs elected in the UK without the endorsement of the Labour Party. Most of his impassioned maiden speech dealt with the situation in Abyssinia; he supported independence, as he did 'for all colonial peoples', while he also broke with convention in not praising his predecessor's speech.

A lifelong teetotaller, Gallacher was above all uncompromising. 'I hope I may never see the day when I win applause from the opposite side of the House', he declared, while railing against the evils of war, which 'does not come from the heart of human beings; it comes as a consequence of the greed for territory and trading profits. 'Take away the incentive of the element of profit', he added, 'and you take away the incentive for war.'

William 'Willie' Gallacher was born in Paisley in 1881 to mixed Irish-Scottish parentage. He began work aged only ten and did a number of manual jobs while becoming politically active via the Independent Labour Party and Social Democratic Foundation. An active trade unionist, by the 1920s Gallacher was a leading Communist and served as an MP from 1935–50.

What of defence? Have you defended the miners' families in Wales, Lancashire, on the north-east coast and in Scotland? Have you defended these places — go and look at them — which give the appearance of a country that has been devastated by the enemy? Have you defended the miners? There were over 1,000 men killed in the pits last year and nearly 200,000 injured. Have you defended them? Come with me to the mining villages, and, day after day, you can see the terrible tragedy of the pit, and the tragedy of the miners' homes. Have you defended the unemployed? We have heard about the means test. Yesterday the hon Member for Bridgeton (Mr Maxton) drew attention to the gyrations of hon Gentlemen opposite in connection with the means test during the Election. There

Come with me to the mining villages, and, day after day, you can see the terrible tragedy of the pit

was not one Member on the other side prepared to stand up for the means test as it was being operated in any industrial constituency in the country. Why? Because of the terrible effects the means test was having upon men, women and children in the country. Not one of them would defend it or stand for it. When pressure is brought to bear upon the matter, we hear some flippant talk about going to change it. You are going to change it, but are you going to compensate in any way for the evil you have done during the past four years?

I have heard of hundreds of cases, but one of the most outstanding in my mind at the moment is that of one of the heroes who came back from the war paralysed. He has lain in bed since the end of the War and has never moved. Do you remember the promise we made as to the treatment that these heroes were to receive? Do you remember how the duke and the worker were to walk along the road hand-in-hand, with roses on every side and happiness lying close at hand? Here is a paralysed man lying in bed. His boy grows to manhood — he is 21 years of age — and gets a job. The means test is operated in that home. He is persuaded to leave home and live with relatives so that the family income shall not be interfered with. He leaves his bedridden father and weeping mother and goes to his new home. He cannot eat; he cannot sleep. Despair settles upon him, and in a week comes the end — suicide. He is driven to death by the means test, as thousands of others have been done to death. Were you anxious for them? Are you

You are going to change it, but are you going to compensate in any way for the evil you have done.

going to change it because you have seen the ghastly work which you have done? I have seen it, and I cannot forget it. You have not defended the unemployed and the mothers and the children... Where does the trouble come from? It comes from low wages and low unemployment relief. The mothers and children have to suffer. You may pay tribute to, or worship, the Madonna and Child, but day after day you are doing the Madonna and Child to death.

On this side of the House we represent and speak for the workers of this country, the men who toil and sweat. [HON. MEMBERS: "So do we."] Oh, you do speak for the workers, do you? [HON. MEMBERS: "Yes."] All right. We shall see. The leader of the miners says that theirs is the hardest, most dangerous and poorest paid job in the country. Is there anybody who will deny it? The miners make a demand. They ballot for it, and the ballot is a record, and we who speak for and on behalf of the miners demand an increase of 2s a day for the miners. That is how we speak for the miners. Now it is your turn. Speak now. Two shillings a day for the miners. Speak, you who claim to represent the miners.

Do not try to stop us on the road along which we are travelling.

We say not a penny for armaments. It is a crime against the people of this country to spend another penny on armaments...

I would make an earnest appeal to hon Members of the House who have not yet become case-hardened in iniquity. The National Government are travelling the road of 1914, which will surely lead to another and more terrible war, and to the destruction of civilisation. Are hon Members going to follow them down that road? The party which is represented on these benches, from which, at the present moment, I am an outcast, has set itself a task of an entirely different character, that of travelling along the road of peace and progress and of spending all that can be spent in making life higher and better for all. We invite those of you who are prepared to put service to a great cause before blind leadership of miserable pygmies who are giving a pitiful exhibition by masquerading as giants, to put first service not to a National Government such as is presented before us, but to a Labour Government drawing towards itself all the very best and most active and progressive elements from all parties and constituting itself, as a consequence, a real people's Government concerned with the complete reconstruction of this country, with genuine co-operation with the other peace nations for preserving world peace, a Government that follows the road of peace and progress. I make an appeal even while I give a warning. Do not try to stop us on the road along which we are travelling. Do not try to block the road by the meshes of legal entanglements or by Fascist gangs. Do not try it, lest an evil day come upon you and you have to pay a price far beyond any present reckoning.[1]

Whither thou goest, I will go; and where thou lodgest, I will lodge; thy people shall be my people, and thy God my God.

Harry Hopkins
1890–1946

SPEECH AT DINNER FOR WINSTON CHURCHILL · STATION HOTEL · GLASGOW
14 JANUARY 1941

Following Winston Churchill's oratorical triumph in Glasgow City Chambers during a visit to the city on 14 January 1941, another memorable speech followed that evening, when the Prime Minister and Harry Hopkins, President Roosevelt's personal emissary, were given dinner by the Regional Commissioner for Scotland, Tom Johnston (shortly to become one of the greatest Secretaries of State for Scotland) at the Station Hotel.

Harry Lloyd Hopkins (1890–1946) was one of Franklin Delano Roosevelt's closest advisers and one of the architects of the New Deal, particularly the Works Progress Administration, which he directed and turned into the largest employer in the country. During the Second World War Hopkins was Roosevelt's chief diplomatic advisor and troubleshooter. He was instrumental in the $50 billion Lend Lease programme that supplied aid to war-torn Europe.

Churchill was clearly in a good mood, impressed by the warmth of his reception in Glasgow and its civil defence preparations. 'I was struck by the evident keenness and efficiency of the various Civil Defence services,' he wrote to Glasgow's Lord Provost a few days later, 'and came away fortified by the assurance that, if the full force of the enemy's attack should be turned upon Glasgow, as upon so many cities in the South, her citizens will endure and surmount it.'

This sentiment must have rubbed off on Hopkins too, although Churchill's doctor, Lord Moran, recorded the US emissary as 'an unkempt figure' in his diary. But Hopkins' short, moving speech altered this initial impression. 'I was surprised to find the PM in tears,' noted Moran. 'He knew what it meant… Even to us, the words seemed like a rope thrown to a drowning man.'

I suppose you wish to know what I am going to say to President Roosevelt on my return. Well, I'm going to quote you one verse from that Book of Books in the truth of which Mr Johnston's mother and my own Scottish mother were brought up: "Whither thou goest, I will go; and where thou lodgest, I will lodge; thy people shall be my people, and thy God my God." [Then he added very quietly]: 'Even to the end.'

Whither thou goest, I will go;
and where thou lodgest, I will lodge;
thy people shall be my people,
and thy God my God.

If men use society merely as a means to their own ends, then society is justified in putting them outside society.

Sir David Maxwell Fyfe
1900–67

CLOSING SPEECH AT THE NUREMBERG TRIAL · GERMANY
28–29 AUGUST 1946

As the Second World War drew to a close the Allies began to discuss how the German high command should be dealt with following their defeat. Winston Churchill had initially pushed for a 'summary' method of justice but the US delegation, led by Justice Robert Jackson, lobbied heavily for a trial. As a result of Labour's 1945 landside victory Sir David Maxwell Fyfe, the UK Attorney General and chief British prosecutor, was replaced by Sir Hartley Shawcross, although Fyfe was appointed as his deputy and *de facto* chief prosecutor at Nuremberg.

Sir David Maxwell Fyfe was born in Edinburgh in 1900 and later established himself as a barrister in Liverpool. Elected as a Conservative MP for the city, he served as Solicitor and Attorney General in Winston Churchill's wartime administration. After the Nuremberg Trial he played a key role in the production of the European Convention on Human Rights. When the Conservatives returned to office in 1951, Fyfe was appointed Home Secretary and latterly Lord Chancellor.

During the trial Fyfe won praise for his skillful cross-examination of a number of the lead defendants, most famously Hermann Göring. His unrelenting capacity for administration and detailed nitty-gritty not only assured the trial's success but also its international credibility. While Justice Jackson provided the moral blueprint for the proceedings Fyfe was undoubtedly its principal engineer.

The trial lasted 216 days in total and following a general closing speech by Shawcross, Fyfe wound up on the specifics of the indictment for which the British delegation was responsible. The risk of the condemned men becoming martyrs weighed heavily on his mind, but nevertheless the outcome provided the basis for the subsequent development of international criminal law, including the establishment of the International Criminal Court in the Hague in 2002.

The law is a living thing. It is not rigid and unalterable. Its purpose is to serve mankind, and it must grow and change to meet the changing needs of society. The needs of Europe today have no parallel in history. Never before has the society of Europe faced the problem or the danger of having in their midst millions of ruthless, fanatical men, trained and educated in murder and racial hatred-and in war. It is a situation which, were there or were there not precedents from the past, would justify, and indeed compel, unusual legal provision. In fact, as the Tribunal will remember from the speech of Mr Justice Jackson, there

The needs of Europe today have no parallel in history.

are ample precedents for the proceedings which we are asking you to institute. If you are satisfied that these organisations as a whole are criminal, that the great majority of the members of these organisations knowingly and voluntarily supported the criminal policies and participated in the criminal activities of the leaders of the Nazi Party, then it is your duty under the Charter to declare them criminal. You may well think that your duty under the Charter is only commensurate with your duty to Germany, to Europe, and to the world...

The principle on which their condemnation is asked for is clear. It is a practical application of the sound theory of punishment which we learnt in our youth-from, among others, that great German thinker, Kant. If men use society merely as a means to their own ends, then society is justified in putting them outside society. The immensity of the problem does not excuse its non-solution. The failure to perform this legal duty may well spell terror and racial persecution throughout a continent and, for the third time in our adult lives, world war...

You have now seen and heard many witnesses who, some on their own admission, were themselves deeply involved in hideous crime. Have you been able to discern a sense of guilt or shame or repentance? Always it is someone who gave the orders that is to blame; never he who puts these orders into execution. Always it is some other agency of the State who was responsible; to support that State and co-operate with those other agencies is without criticism. If this is

If men use society merely as a means to their own ends, then society is justified in putting them outside society.

the mind of these people today, there can be no more pressing need nor greater justification for branding the guilty as criminal... The evidence of all of them is the same. They are asked if they knew of the persecution and annihilation of the Jews, of the dread work of the Gestapo, of the atrocities within the concentration camps, of the ill-treatment of slave labor, of the intention and preparation to wage aggressive war, of the murder of brave soldiers, sailors, and airmen. And they reply with "the everlasting No."

... These men, of all men, knew their leader to be a callous murderer, yet for years they had met in conference after conference to sit at his feet and listen to his words. They fed his lust for power and enslavement with the best of their professional skill, while the defenceless peoples of the East, the men, women and children of Poland, of the Soviet Union, and of the Baltic states, were being deliberately slaughtered and deported into slavery to allow for German "Lebensraum," these men talked of the necessities of war. When their own cities were bombed and Germans killed, they called it murder. Only in July 1944, when

These men, of all men,
knew their leader to be a callous murderer.

Hitler's star was dimmed, did three Field Marshals and five Colonel Generals recognize that he was murdering also their own country and took action. When that star was rising in victory they had hailed it and ignored the blood-red colour of the clouds from which it rose...

My Lord, I am deeply conscious that one of the greatest difficulties, and not the least of the dangers, of this Trial is that those of us who have been engaged day in and day out for nine months have reached the saturation point of horror... It is not merely the quantity of horrors-although these organisations have been the instruments of death for 22,000,000 people – it is the quality of cruelty which produced the gas chambers of Auschwitz or the routine shooting of Jewish children throughout a continent claiming to be civilised. There is not one of these organisations which is not directly connected with the sorry trade of murder in a brutal form. Who can doubt that the Reich Cabinet knew of the euthanasia used to conserve the physical resources of Germany for war? It is beyond question that the High Command and General Staff passed on these orders of which you have heard so much and which are all reduced in the end to plain murder; the Leadership Corps shared in killing Jews and ruining the bodies of slave labourers. I have simply to mention the SS and the crimes come unbidden into the mind without any words of mine. Conniving, assisting, and finding a reason for these crimes were the SD and the Gestapo...

Some things are surely universal:
tolerance, decency, kindliness.

If Europe is to be cleansed of Nazi evil it is indispensable that you and the world should know these organisations for what they are... It has been our sombre task to assist you to this knowledge; having done so, we sometimes wonder if the stench of death will ever wholly pass from our nostrils. But we are determined to do our utmost to see that it will pass from Germany, and that the spirit which produced it will be exorcised. It may be presumptuous for lawyers, who do not claim to be more than the cement of society, to speculate or even dream of what we wish to see in its place. But I give you the faith of a lawyer. Some things are surely universal: tolerance, decency, kindliness. It is because we believe that there must be a clearance before such qualities will flourish in peace that we ask you to condemn this organisation of evil... When such qualities have been given the chance to flourish in the ground that you have cleared, a great step will have been taken. It will be a step towards the universal recognition that... [these]... are not the prerogative of any one nation. They are the inalienable heritage of mankind.[1]

The Scottish predicament today calls for the same ruthless and objective appraisal which a general demands from his staff before action.

Hamish Henderson
1919–2002

'SCOTLAND'S ALAMEIN' SPEECH TO THE SCOTTISH CONVENTION'S NATIONAL ASSEMBLY

c.1949

The Scottish Covenant was a petition to the UK government to create a 'Home Rule' Scottish Parliament in Edinburgh. First proposed in 1930, the National Covenant movement reached its peak during the late 1940s and early 1950s after John MacCormick initiated a draft in October 1949 during the third National Assembly of the Scottish Convention, a pressure group that eventually became the Scottish Covenant Association.

James (Hamish) Scott Henderson was born in Blairgowrie in 1919. Educated at Blairgowrie High School and London's Dulwich College, during the Second World War he served as an intelligence officer in Europe and North Africa. From the early 1950s Henderson devoted himself to collecting Scottish folk music and material, and also composed his own material. In 1983 he refused an OBE in protest at nuclear weapons. He died in 2002.

Hamish Henderson, at that time an enthusiastic supporter of the movement, often spoke at National Assembly meetings and the speech below is a composite from his contributions to various meetings at around this time. As his biographer Timothy Neat explained: 'He was not interested in demonstrating his opposition to government policy, he wanted results. He wanted a Scottish Parliament but his recent experience of the war (and that of his readers') meant he kept military metaphors to the fore.'

But despite the enthusiasm of figures such as Henderson, the National Assembly and Covenant achieved little success; the petition was signed by around two million Scots (although there was much talk of forged signatures and joke entries) between 1947 and 1950, but its demands were flatly rejected by the then Prime Minister Clement Attlee, and indeed by the entire political establishment. Only in the 1970s would the devolution debate resurface.

During the recent war the Highland Division became a kind of symbol of Scotland... Scots in the field can still function with energy, initiative and courage. One felt in fact, seeing the preparations for Alamein and Sicily, that something like the perfervid spirit of our ancestors was entering the lists against Rommel. It is all the more bitter, therefore, to contrast this picture of Scotland at war with the spectre of our countrymen in peace time, for it scunners you to see how tame, mean-spirited and ineffectual the craturs look. They doff their spirit, their bonnet and hackle. When warfare's over, they grip the rudder with foisonless fingers.

They had better wake up to the fact that Scotland's national situation today is fully as perilous as the Eighth Army's when it faced the defensive battle of El Alamein. During those critical months of 1942, the issue of the war was at stake. It was necessary to check the Axis army, then throw it back – nothing else would do. For Scotland, here and now, the same situation presents itself. If this nation does not forthwith rally and hurl back once and for all the forces which for two centuries have been encompassing its obliteration, it will henceforward be fighting nothing but a forlorn rear-guard action. It will have had it.

Scots in the field can still function with energy, initiative and courage.

The National Assembly... is the first sign on a national scale that Scotland is throwing off the dreadful apathy of the interwar years, is beginning to gather its strength for decisive conflict. But without a resolute follow-up it will be a mockery. The Scottish predicament today calls for the same ruthless and objective appraisal which a general demands from his staff before action. Any attempt to fob us off with pious platitudes (especially religious) must be met with uncompromising hostility. The Scots had better realise that spiritual up-lift is no substitute for earthly élan...

The fight to maintain and develop a distinctive Scottish way of life must be invigorated and sustained by political action. Without the latter, the former is – in the last analysis – only an elaborate shadow-play, which in time must become inept and meaningless. Cultural and political movements are, in occupied states, invariably complementary. Nothing could be more pathetic, for example, than the idea that we can defend our ancient Gaelic civilisation merely by organising bigger and better Mods, or railing at the Highland people for no longer speaking their language. We shall defend it only by energetic political action which will make life liveable in the glens and along the shores of the sealochs. And the indispensible preliminary to *that* is the existence of a Parliament in Scotland... if these facts and figures are not made the grounds for action, without delay, we shall find that the day and the hour have slipped from us... But if the convening of this National Assembly means that our country is stirring at last, if it means that, in the coming months and years, Scotland is going to leave far behind her this slough of national degradation in which she is at present lying, then the battle will be won, and I see a vision of Alba in the years before us that would take the sting out of predestined damnation![1]

...probably this is the first occasion in 900 years that the voice of a woman has been heard in the deliberations of this House.

Baroness Elliot of Harwood 1903–94

MAIDEN SPEECH IN THE HOUSE OF LORDS

4 NOVEMBER 1958

Harold Macmillan's government presented its proposals for 'life peers' to the House of Lords in October 1957. In doing so, the Earl of Home, Leader of the House, also indicated the intention to make women eligible to belong to the House as life peeresses, adding in an aside (very much of its time) that 'taking women into a parliamentary embrace seemed to be only a modest extension of the normal functions of a peer'.[1]

Katharine Elliot, Baroness Elliot of Harwood was born in 1903, the daughter of the Scottish industrialist and politician Sir Charles Tennant, Bt. Presented at court to King George V, she declared herself 'more interested in politics than parties' and studied at the London School of Economics. In 1934 Katharine married the MP Walter Elliot and became active herself in Conservative politics and public life more generally. She served in the House of Lords for 35 years, dying in January 1994.

One of the first to be appointed was Katharine Elliot, the popular and respected (in her own right) widow of the former Scottish Conservative MP and minister Walter Elliot. Following his death in 1958, Kay (as she was known) stood in the resulting Glasgow Kelvingrove by-election but lost narrowly. But given the Life Peerages Act had just become law it was possible for Elliot to join the Upper House instead, as Baroness Elliot of Harwood.

Her speech, the first by a woman or 'peeress' – as she remarked – in several centuries, was historic in itself, but the content, Commonwealth affairs, drew on her experience as a delegate to the United Nations. Elliot's career in the Upper House saw other firsts: later she became the first peeress to propose the Loyal Address and the first to pass a private bill through the House of Lords. Following her maiden speech, the Earl of Home praised the 'courage' Lady Elliot had 'shown throughout her life: courage tempered by an acute mind and practical common sense'.

My Lords, it was with great trepidation that I put down my name on the list of speakers for the debate this afternoon. It is only a week since the new Life Peers were introduced into this House and it might seem presumptuous on my part to speak so early in this august Assembly. But I have always found in life that if there is something difficult to do it does not get any easier when you do not do it but put it off. I am very conscious of the importance of the first speech to be made by one of the Life Peers...

This is a maiden speech, my Lords, and I would crave your indulgence. I would ask you to follow the suggestion of Matthew Prior, a Member of the other place in 1701: "Be to her virtues very kind," "Be to her faults a little blind." In case your Lordships should be nervous at all, I have been studying the Standing Orders of the House of Lords, of which I am sure everybody here is very cognisant, and No. 29, passed in 1626, and No. 30, passed in 1641, are well in my mind at the moment. Indeed, I am very conscious that, except for Her Majesty's gracious Opening of Parliament, probably this is the first occasion in 900 years that the voice of a woman has been heard in the deliberations of this House...

I have always found in life that if there is something difficult to do it does not get any easier when you do not do it but put it off.

In the gracious Speech we read: "My Government will neglect no opportunity to promote the advance of the Colonial territories and the increasing association of their peoples with the management of their own affairs." This is a principle which wins for us great support in the councils of the world. I was present in the General Assembly when Ghana took her seat as an independent country, and the Federation of Malaya, and even the most caustic critics of the colonial system stayed to praise on that occasion. All the world is searching for a way to govern in freedom. We have all seen authoritarian methods, both of the Right and of the Left. Never have I been more conscious of the differences that stand between the free world and the Communist world than in New York, sitting there, as we do, in alphabetical order, with the USSR on one side and the USA on the other, and around the Assembly the representatives of the Commonwealth—free, independent, voting as they wish, steeped in the traditions of democratic government, while the Soviet satellites all vote as they are instructed by the USSR and no one dares raise a voice in dissent.

In this world search for the art of government I believe that the Commonwealth countries can play a great part. They stretch all round the world. The Far East for us is the Near North for Australia; and everywhere, all over the world, there are centres which are linked to the Commonwealth. The leaders of our Commonwealth countries have, in many cases, been educated in our universities. They value their independence and they develop their own traditions, but they are wedded to the free world and not to the Communist world. Wherever Mr Speaker takes the Chair, whether he be African, Indian, Malay, Ceylonese, Canadian, Australian or New Zealander, he presides over a free Parliament where

In this world search for the art of government I believe that the Commonwealth countries can play a great part.

the rights of the Opposition to object are as rigorously safeguarded as the rights of the Government to govern. What is more, in many of these assemblies the words of the great Elizabethan prayer, which we listen to every day in Parliament, here, are heard in the language of the country before the Parliament begins its deliberations...

In the great division which separates the free world and the Communist world the nations of the Commonwealth are on the side of the free world. There are many nations, both old and new—and one sees them and meets them in New York—in the category of "uncommitted" as between this great issue which faces the 20th century world. I am convinced that we must try, through the

I hope, however, that we who are women may be regarded as having come here not because we are women but rather because women are now admitted

Commonwealth countries, through our experience, and through our "know-how", to lead those countries into the free world, and not allow them to slip into the Communist world. We can do much to lead the world in the future as we have done in the past.

My Lords, I thank you for the kind and courteous manner in which you have received what I fear is a rather inadequate contribution to this important debate. I suppose that in some way, poor though it be, it has made history as the first speech made by a woman from the Benches of your Lordships' House. I hope, however, that we who are women may be regarded as having come here not because we are women but rather because women are now admitted, and because, like others of your Lordships of first creation, Her Majesty has been graciously pleased to confer Life Peerages upon us in the same way as upon the distinguished gentlemen who are in this House to-day. I beg to support the Motion.[2]

We must think in terms of communities and not just of individuals.

Judith Hart 1924–91

MAIDEN SPEECH · HOUSE OF COMMONS

3 NOVEMBER 1959

Although Judith Hart was born in Burnley, Lancashire, she quickly became an adopted Scot after moving north with her husband in the mid-1950s. She first came to prominence during the 1955 general election when she took on the Unionist Lady Tweedsmuir in Aberdeen South. Hart's good looks ensured this hard-fought 'battle of the housewives' (although Tweedsmuir was hardly that) a high media profile.

During this period Hart made broadcasts on BBC's *Woman's Hour*, wrote articles on Scottish affairs for *The Tribune* (she was an early devolutionist), and lectured in sociology, but when she was offered the more promising constituency of Lanark she decided to quit academia for Parliament. Her husband Tony even withdrew as the prospective Labour candidate for Glasgow Hillhead in order to campaign for his wife.

Judith Hart was born in Lancashire in 1924 and educated at Clitheroe Royal Grammar School and the London School of Economics (LSE). Hart taught briefly before deciding on a political career. She entered Parliament in 1959 and held various ministerial positions in Harold Wilson's government. Hart joined the House of Lords in 1988 and died three years later.

Hart won the seat comfortably and made an immediate impact with her maiden speech, which followed an upbeat contribution from the Chancellor. Admitting she found it 'particularly difficult to observe the usual courtesies of being uncontroversial' given his remarks, Hart spoke knowledgably about her constituency and its economic problems, many of her remarks anticipating political battles that came to a head in the 1980s.

In my constituency, we have two very different kinds of community. In the constituency of Lanark, there are mining villages and a new town. The underlying problem of both these types of community is exactly the same. The mining villages are very much afraid of what may happen as a result of the next pit closures soon to be announced. We have suffered very grievously from one pit closure in the last year and, since our villages are on a declining coalfield, we are afraid of what may happen in the future. I beg hon Members opposite to consider, in relation to the future of the mining industry, not only the salvation of the individual miner, which to some extent can be achieved by moving the miner away from his former home to a new and developing coalfield elsewhere... but also what will happen if the whole social fabric of community life is grievously disturbed. We must think in terms of communities and not just of individuals...

We should like to see the kind of industry of which Scotland is in such great need—industry based on science and on modern technological developments. I have no need to say this to hon Members, for the claims were so frequently made in the last Parliament and are constantly being made by people outside Parliament, but it is well known that Scotland needs the lighter, modern industries, such as chemicals and plastics, in order to balance its dependence on heavy industries. We want that kind of lighter industry in the Lanark area...

Elsewhere in my constituency we have a very different kind of community—a new town. The Prime Minister said in the House last week that perhaps we ought to stop calling the new towns "new" and to regard them in the same way as we regard other towns. I hope that this in no way indicated that he believes that the period of hard thinking about the future of the new towns has passed, because,

We must think in terms of communities and not just of individuals...

if the new town of East Kilbride, in my constituency, is typical of the other new towns of Britain, I am certain that we are entering a period in which a great deal of hard thinking must be done if we are to avoid a crisis threatening their whole future development.

The theme is just the same: it is one of providing employment where it is needed. Here, however, we are not considering people displaced from a declining industry but thousands of boys and girls growing up and leaving school. I do not want to elaborate this point, although it is one in which I am very interested, but there has been much discussion of the lack of balance in the populations of our new towns. I believe that a great mistake is being made in the attitude taken towards the lack of balance. It has been generally argued, frequently by chairmen of Development Corporations and others interested in the subject, that the lack of balance concerns social classes and occupational groupings, and great efforts have been made by some of the new town development corporations to bring in more and more white-collar workers, middle-class people, with some effects which we have recently seen very clearly.

The balance of population which is important is not that of occupation or social class. There is nothing intrinsically virtuous in a new town which has a high proportion of middle-class people in it. The lack of balance which is important, particularly for the future, is a lack of balance in the age structure. This lack of balance in East Kilbride means that within the next ten to fifteen years between one-third and one-half of our population will be leaving school and needing jobs. This will provoke a recurring cycle of crises as these young people grow up, marry and have children.

The problems of the new towns are just beginning, but if they are to be solved, and if the new towns are to achieve their aim of being places where people go to live and to work, a tremendous move forward must now be made by the

There is nothing intrinsically virtuous in a new town which has a high proportion of middle-class people in it.

Government in planning to bring new industry into them at this time, when it is needed. I hope that they will do so. I hope that they will consider more adequately than they have in the past the need for much greater research about the future not only of the new towns but of all new communities and new housing schemes as we develop them. We need far more research to determine precisely what the problems are and how they can best be tackled. I hope that the Government will consider setting up a research unit in one of their Departments and that they will give money to the universities to sponsor research on these subjects...

Early in his speech the Chancellor of the Exchequer said that we on this side of the House had tended to get our priorities wrong. We are quite certain that our priorities, in so far as they concern people first and foremost, have never been wrong. They are certainly not wrong today. We hope that we can persuade hon Members opposite to share our point of view that dynamic social action must be taken in the next year if our people are to be saved from economic disaster.[1]

”

To have a measure of determination over their own life and their own living, so that they may no longer be merely sleeping partners.

John Bannerman
1901–1969

MAIDEN SPEECH · HOUSE OF LORDS
6 DECEMBER 1967

Although never elected to the House of Commons, by the 1960s John Bannerman was well-known as an energetic Liberal politician but perhaps more so as a famous Scottish rugby player. He championed Highland culture and politics, promoting the Highlands and Islands Development Board, which was established in 1965. He also broadcast Gaelic programmes on BBC Scotland.

John MacDonald Bannerman, Baron Bannerman of Kildonan, was a Scottish farmer, rugby union internationalist and Liberal politician. Educated at the Glasgow High School, Glasgow University and Balliol College, Oxford, he was a celebrated rugby player during the golden period of Scottish rugby in the mid-1920s. Bannerman worked as a factor to the Duke of Montrose while trying several times to become an MP, usually for the Inverness constituency. He died in 1969.

Bannerman's long political service was recognised in December 1967 when he was created a life peer. Unusually, he delivered his maiden speech just two hours after being introduced to the Upper House. 'It was a fighting speech,' wrote the editor of his posthumous memoirs, 'delivered with a fire and passion strange in that House.' Indeed, Bannerman's maiden speech created such a stir that he was immediately interviewed for a weekend Westminster television programme, 'during which he launched into Gaelic for good measure.'

As a Highland Scot, I welcomed the formation of the Highlands and Islands Development Board, but I am bitterly disappointed at the obvious limitation on its enterprise up to date... If the Scottish Highlander is not to die off in a nature reserve the Highlands Board must renew the whole economic fabric of the Highlands. This it can do by making the owner of land—and I put this advisedly to your Lordships' House—in the Highlands a trustee of the nation for the production of folk and food. I do not suggest nationalisation or expropriation, but I feel that if the owner of land cannot do what he ought to do for the land he owns, then a fair rental should be paid to him to allow others to do the job. There are in the Highlands one million acres, undeveloped and bracken-covered, which, after survey and reclamation, could be allocated to the production of folk and food and timber...

I am surprised that in all of your Lordships' discussions concerning conditions in Scotland to-day the question of land was never raised. I do not want the question of agriculture to be raised particularly, but the question of land is basic to the survival of our area of the Highlands, and of Scotland, and it must enter into any debate which concerns itself with the condition of Scotland. So I

If the Scottish Highlander is not to die off in a nature reserve the Highlands Board must renew the whole economic fabric of the Highlands.

feel that the improvident neglect of our limited land resources in Scotland is a constant rebuke to Government.

One would imagine that the need to replace 100,000 acres of land taken from farming, and used for building and housing, since the last war would at least spur the Government to do something to look for new acres in Scotland. But these erstwhile fertile areas have become, through careless apathy, more waterlogged and useless as the years pass... I feel that the Highlands Board should first sponsor and encourage, by grant and loan, widespread land settlement throughout the Highlands, introducing also light industries...

The Board must follow two comprehensive practical policies; and that right away. These should be widespread land settlement and the establishment of good communications, with sharply tapering freight rates, between the Highlands area and the main markets of Britain, and to the North East of Scotland, where Aberdeen and the fishing industry would benefit tremendously. These measures would be enough to bring spontaneous growth without any more incentive. Then might the Akan heart at Invergordon pump live blood throughout the Highlands, instead of sucking the remaining blood from depopulated areas to maintain a selfish urban existence. But I am afraid that this will remain another of our

So I feel that the improvident neglect of our limited land resources in Scotland is a constant rebuke to Government.

Scottish pipe-dreams so long as we have to accept the decisions of others: for I understand that we are to receive new transport legislation from Whitehall which, in the Highlands anyhow, can act only as another blockade against enterprise.

I thank your Lordships for the courtesy and the kindness you have shown me. I have many faults, and one of these may be my enthusiastic regard for Scotland. But there can be nothing surer in this life than the truth which we Liberals proclaim; and that is that the growth in stature of man depends on the extent to which he can control his own destiny. This is equally true of nations;

I have many faults, and one of these may be my enthusiastic regard for Scotland.

and Scotland is a nation. That is why Liberals advocate federalism to replace the present form of centralised power government in Britain, so that all parts of Britain may be helped. There is a Border poet called Will H. Ogilvie, and he says in one of his poems: "There is a fresh wind blowing" "Over moorland and dale." Aye, there is a fresh wind in the byways and in the highways, in the main streets of our villages and towns today. There is in it the warm purpose of the Scottish people to have a measure of determination over their own life and their own living, so that they may no longer be merely sleeping partners. That is not a selfish ambition. This is an ambition which we are determined is better for the United Kingdom set-up.

Finally, I would say this: that even Old England herself, in these proposals of federalism, would find peace and quiet and time to put her own house in order. So, my Lords, I hope you will agree that, for a Scotsman, I have made quite a non-controversial maiden speech.

The greatest Scots have always deplored the union with England.

Hugh MacDiarmid
1892–1978

'A POLITICAL SPEECH' TO THE 1320 CLUB SYMPOSIUM
GLASGOW UNIVERSITY
6 APRIL 1968

Like many Scottish writers of the early 20th century, the poet Hugh MacDiarmid was fiercely political, and a strong believer in socialism. He felt deeply that Scottish life and culture was ill served by its constitutional status as part of Great Britain and, in 1928, was a founding member of the National Party of Scotland, which later merged with the Scottish Party to form the Scottish National Party (SNP) in 1934.

Hugh MacDiarmid was born Christopher Murray Grieve in Langholm in 1892. Abandoning plans to teach, MacDiarmid started his career as a journalist before joining the Royal Army Medical Corps at the beginning of the First World War. Returning to journalism after the war, he began writing poetry as well as becoming politically active. MacDiarmid lived near Biggar for much of his life and died in 1978.

In later years his political stance shifted even further left and, in 1964, he stood as Communist Party candidate against the then Prime Minister, Sir Alec Douglas-Home, in the safe Unionist seat of Kinross and Western Perthshire (he polled 127 votes). This speech, delivered at Glasgow University a few years later, gives a flavour of MacDiarmid's uncompromising style.

The context is important, for he was speaking just months after Winnie Ewing achieved an astonishing victory in the Hamilton by-election, while the SNP would, in that year's local government elections, go from strength to strength. MacDiarmid clearly believed independence (or 'devolution') was the inevitable consequence, and also makes his dislike of the English clear. Famously, of course, he listed 'Anglophobia' among his hobbies in *Who's Who*.

Scotland is emerging again, culturally at any rate, into the modern world as a separate entity with something of its own to say, some contribution to make to the common pool of culture that no other people can make... It is the cultural questions, the language and literary questions, that have been the decisive factor in the national regeneration movements of many European countries, and it will not be otherwise with Scotland. No nation was ever restored to its proper dignity owing to a demand for merely practical measures, better wages, better conditions of employment, better transport, and all the rest of it. These are vitally important, but they are subsidiary and first things must be put first. It is because too many people in the [Scottish] National Party have no concern with the things

We have a great deal of violence in Scotland today.

of fundamental importance, with the great spiritual issues underlying the mere statistics of trade and industry, with the ends to which all other things should merely be means, that I don't feel the destiny of Scotland lies with it. At present they are anxious above all not to go too far, they deprecate Anglophobia, many do no envisage armed action. Well, no one in his senses wants warfare, but if we are determined to be absolutely independent, it may be, and almost certainly will be forced upon us. I do not believe the English have learned anything from the Irish affair and I believe that they will be more determined to hang on to Scotland than ever, by fair means or preferably foul, since their world rule has diminished so greatly. In any case, even if it doesn't come to that, we'll have violence anyway in Scotland. Scotland never fought while it was independent any aggressive war, but since the Union, it has been dragged at the heels of England into scores of

What is the difference between the Scots and the English, how important is it?

wars, none of which were of any value to Scotland itself. We have a great deal of violence in Scotland today; I could only wish that it were possible that it could be chanelled in better directions.

What is the difference between the Scots and the English, how important is it? ...there are not two nations under the firmament that are more contrary and different from each other than Englishmen and Scotsmen, howbeit they be within one island, and neighbours, and of one language. For Englishmen are subtle and Scotsmen are facile, Englishmen are ambitious in prosperity and Scotsman are humane in prosperity, Englishmen are humble when they are subdued by force and violence, and Scotsmen are furious when they are violently subdued. Englishmen are cruel when they get victory, and Scotsmen are merciful when they get victory. And to conclude, it is impossible that Scotsmen and Englishmen can remain in concord under one government because their natures and conditions are as different as is the nature of sheep and wolves...

I want complete independence, I don't believe in the difficulties that are alleged to exist in the way. I want a Scottish working-class republic, based on our ancient traditions, because the difference in democracy in Scotland and England is fundamental and dates back to our Gaelic basis, to the old clan system; we never had the segregations, snobberies, class distinctions that the feudal system gave the English...

The Scots people are not inferior in intelligence, in ability, to any people in the world, and if they address themselves to their own affairs, they will speedily

We're going for devolution right to the end.

find solutions if solutions can be found. The eyes of the fool are on the ends of the earth, and for far too long, the eyes of Scots have been directed away from their own affairs, but they're no use to Scotland, and they certainly can't make any contribution to international culture if they don't first of all put their own house in order, tackle the things that are nearest to the hand, and tackle them with all their might... I don't think it is necessary now to argue this question of devolution for Scotland. We are going to have it, and we're going to have it very soon, and we can safely reconcile all our religious and other divergences on the basis of one of the profoundest statements in the Bible: "Be ye not unequally yoked together." We'll choose our own equals, our own peers. At large, we've been internationalists to a far greater extent than the English ever were, we've never had any imperialist longings, our moral position is infinitely stronger than the position of England in any connection has been for centuries past, and it's on that basis that I suggest to you that we don't allow ourselves to be fobbed off with any talk about the problems and difficulties that varying degrees of devolution would present us with. We don't requite to bother about that. We're going for devolution right to the end, that's to say for complete independence and we rest our case on the virtue of our own personality and the strength of our own determination.

The nationalism I see expressed in Scotland at present is not real nationalism.

Willie Ross
1911–88

SPEECH TO SCOTTISH TRADES UNION CONGRESS · BEACH BALLROOM ABERDEEN

18 APRIL 1968

Although largely forgotten in the New Labour era, Willie Ross dominated the Scottish Labour movement for almost two decades. As Harold Wilson's man in Scotland, Ross, it was often said, treated it as his personal fiefdom during two stints as Secretary of State for Scotland (1964–70 and 1974–76). He was also a fine orator in the Ayrshire tub-thumbing tradition.

Willie Ross was born in 1911, the son of a train driver in Ayr. He was educated at Ayr Academy and Glasgow University, and after spells as a teacher and wartime service, he entered Parliament in 1946 following a by-election in Kilmarnock. Appointed Scottish Secretary in 1964, Ross held the position – with a four-year break – until 1976. In 1979 he was created Lord Ross of Marnock and died of cancer in 1988.

This typically uncompromising speech to the annual Scottish Trades Union Congress gives a flavour of his caustic wit and the subtlety of his argument, deployed here against the rising tide of Nationalism that appeared to be sweeping Scotland following Winnie Ewing's victory in the 1967 Hamilton by-election.

Stern-faced and authoritarian, Ross also included allusions to the grim economic context that had derailed Wilson's government and its vision of a nation forged in the 'white heat' of modern technology. But his main target was the SNP, whom he hated with a primordial passion.

Despite recent press forecasts to the contrary, he was still Secretary of State for Scotland,[1] and intended in his address to try to give delegates – and he thought some of them were in need of the information – an indication of what was really happening in Scotland and an account of what the Government were doing in the face of tremendous national economic difficulties...

He didn't know where the eyes of Clive Jenkins and others had been during the past three years, but he would refute any claim that the Government had reduced the standard of living of the working people of Britain over this period. This was one thing they had not done.

He could recall those days when shipyard after shipyard on the Clyde was being closed down.

In the face of international difficulties they had certainly been compelled to take some unpopular decisions, but they had realised there were no alternatives to these other than the Tory ones of mass unemployment and the cutting down of the social wage...

He could recall those days when shipyard after shipyard on the Clyde was being closed down; when, at the request of Congress, he had fought in vain to get the Tory Government to do something about unemployment and unemployment benefit. Things were just allowed to drift, in that period, and if the Tories were ever to return the same thing would happen again...

Instead of apologising for the Government it was time delegates should be telling the people of Scotland what the Government were doing in such places as Dundee, Greenock, Kilmarnock and Kirkcaldy... All of these things... had just not happened by chance. They had come about because the Government had made them take place, and therefore he maintained delegates should not allow the Scottish TUC to become the *Scottish Trades Union Congrouse*. They should be a little bit more constructive and not take refuge in the quicksands of nationalism.

Nobody knew better than the ordinary worker in Scotland, the organised worker, that separation was nonsense and would mean economic suicide, and examination demonstrated the truth of this. How could a separate Scottish Government sit in Edinburgh and put the squeeze on firms in the south-east and in the Midlands to force and drive them to Scotland? They just couldn't do it, but the Labour Government were doing it, and he hoped that all representatives of those unions who had come to Congress from London and heard the demands being made at Aberdeen on behalf of Scotland would return to London and assist them. It was just not enough for them to attend Congress and make speeches...

He was the kind of Scot that was not afraid to stand up for the kind of things that Robert Burns represented.

The work which his colleagues and he were doing was the work which Congress wanted done for the benefit of the people of Scotland as a whole. The Government were doing this work because they believed that with new security and new prosperity there would be some release of the human spirit; some appreciation that they were not nationalists but internationalists, insofar as they were demonstrating that the benefits of their policies would surely show the world that under democracy and freedom the economic and social problems of Scotland could be solved.

Some might wonder why he as a perfervid Scot was not also a perfervid Nationalist. The reason was that the nationalism which he saw expressed in Scotland at present was not real nationalism: it was petty and parochial, and,

Personal advantages had to be laid aside for the greater good of all

he was sorry to say it, had signs of a kind of latent hatred. It had a sort of chip-on-the-shoulder hatred that could create very considerable trouble if it were not recognised as such and opposed. He was the kind of Scot that was not afraid to stand up for the kind of things that Robert Burns represented. He would ask, as the Bard did, that Scots should not "like snarling curs in wrangling be divided."

He exhorted Scots to grasp hold of their vision again, because only if they held fast by that could they make the right kind of progress. He was proud to be a member of the Labour Government, and although some of their decisions might be unpopular he was confident that they were the right ones. Personal advantages had to be laid aside for the greater good of all, because only if this were done could the nation be placed on a sound economic basis and abiding economic and social progress won.[2]

I'll have unity with the Church of Rome when that church returns to its original purity…

Pastor Jack Glass
1936–2004

SPEECH DURING A DEBATE ON THE REFORMATION
UNIVERSITY OF ST ANDREWS
1971

Pastor Jack Glass was a Scottish protestant preacher and political activist. Seen by some as Scotland's answer to the similarly fiery Rev Ian Paisley, he was never far from controversy with his anti-Catholic speeches and generally uncompromising views. The Zion Baptist Church, which he founded in 1965, was at once Calvinist, Baptist and Separatist.

In 1971, when he took part in this debate at St Andrews University, Glass had been editing the *Scottish Protestant View*, an evangelical Protestant newspaper, since 1969, while serving as chairman of the Twentieth Century Reformation Movement, which he considered the 'political arm' of his church. He had also recently contested the Glasgow Bridgeton seat at the 1970 general election, attracting a respectable 1,180 votes.

John Thomas Atkinson Glass, often known as Pastor Jack Glass or simply as Jack Glass, was born in Glasgow in 1936, the son of a brushmaker. He was 'born again' aged 11 at a Salvation Army Sunday School and ordained to the ministry in 1968. Glass went on to minister at Zion Baptist Church, which he had founded in 1965, and was a prominent figure in Scottish religious life until his death in 2004.

The motion debated at St Andrews was 'this house regrets the Protestant Reformation'. It was no surprise where Glass stood. 'I want to say right away that I consider the Protestant Reformation a glorious revival,' he declared, 'for the Protestant Reformation delivered this land from the bondage of the Church of Rome which I do not consider to be a Christian church at all, for I would say with John Knox that the Church of Rome is the synagogue of Satan.' He continued in a similar vein.

I thank God for the Reformation because the Reformation delivered this land from the ignorance of Popery. Do you know that up until the time of the Reformation there were Roman Catholic Priests who believed that Martin Luther wrote the New Testament; then of course, among the Bishops, there was hardly one who could preach a sermon. Read "The Satire of the Three Estates" by Sir David Lyndsey, and you'll find the RC Church lampooned there by Lyndsay because of its immorality and ignorance...

Let the New Testament loose and you will bring confusion again into the Church of Rome because what the Reformation did for us was this — it put an open Bible into the hands of the man in the street, who could read it in his own language, and see for himself the errors of the Roman Catholic Church. That was one of the blessings of the Reformation. John Knox, the great Reformer, said if any man could show him out of God's Holy Book where he was wrong, he would endeavour to put himself or the complainer right. Martin Luther said, "My conscience is captive to the word of God."

Now I recall some people saying that it is good for all Christians to get together today in this Ecumenical Movement. Of course this is to seek unity at the expense of truth as Ecumenism has no time for truth. If you read John 17, that famous chapter quoted by the Ecumenical Movement, you'll find there the words of the Lord Jesus Christ. He said, "Sanctify them through Thy truth, Thy word is truth." The Bible teaches unity based on truth. Read the Acts of the Apostles. "They continued stedfast in the apostles' doctrine and fellowship." It was doctrine first and fellowship second.

My conscience is captive to the word of God.

So let's get our facts right, theologically. I'll have unity with the Church of Rome when that church returns to its original purity as when Paul wrote his Epistle to the Romans. Only then will I have unity with the Church of Rome... the Reformation delivered us from the Idolatry of Popery. Is it not Idolatry for Roman Catholics to prostrate themselves in worship before the wafer God of their church and to believe that the very piece of bread is turned into the actual bones and nerves and Divinity of our Lord Jesus Christ? That's the teaching of the Church of Rome. They also teach, of course, that the wine is changed by the priest into the actual blood of Christ. This is still Rome's teaching today as it was at the Council of Trent centuries before. Truly the Reformation delivered us from the Idolatry of Popery...

The Reformation also delivered us from the Immorality of Popery. If you look at the Register of the Great Seal of Scotland 1513–1546 you will find the records of the legitimisation of eleven of the bastard sons and three daughters of Cardinal Beaton, Cardinal Gray's predecessor. That's the so-called Christian Cardinal; a Cardinal that produced 11 bastard sons. Thank God the Reformation delivered us from the Immorality of Popery.

The Intolerance of Popery is another thing that the Reformation delivered us from. A friend said to me that when I went to St Andrews I was to make certain that I would return again because when Patrick Hamilton made his stand for truth there he never came back again. There is the Intolerance of Popery and even in this very area you'll find the spots marked where Patrick Hamilton, George Wishart, and Walter Myln were burned. Now Walter Myln was about 82 years of age and they couldn't find one magistrate in St Andrews to pronounce sentence

I'll have unity with the Church of Rome when that church returns to its original purity

until they found some sychophant of the Church of Rome to do so. Thank God for Myln's last words. He said you may burn me but out of my ashes shall rise a hundred more to preach the glorious teachings of the Reformation and God answered his prayer. The Reformation delivered us from the Intolerance of Popery.

Do you know that we owe religious liberty in this land and the right of private judgement to the Reformation? Where is your religious liberty in Spain tonight? But thank God, because of the Reformation we can meet this way tonight. We can discuss these things and a Roman Catholic can preach what he wants and I can preach what I want. The Reformation also brought forth this great truth of the Priesthood of all believers. You don't have to go to some mass-mongering priest to get forgiveness of sins, for the priest who forgives sins has got nailprints in his hands. I can go direct into the presence of God and since Calvary every Romanist priest has been on the Unemployment Exchange. If anybody wants to come to Christ tonight they can go straight to God through Christ and not through a priest who is a sinner himself.

These are my reasons for supporting the motion that I do not regret the Reformation and I'd just like to say this. You may say that I'm living four centuries too late but the truth of God is unchanged and unchanging and thank God there is one man here tonight, although he is in the minority, to speak God's truth in a day of ecumenical apostacy. The Apostle Paul said, "Though we or an angel from heaven preach any other gospel, let him be accursed." You must define, tonight, what is the gospel and Paul's gospel was the gospel of God's free grace while the gospel, of the Church of Rome is the gospel of man's salvation through works. I prefer Paul of the New Testament to Pope Paul of the Church of Rome.[1]

I have been a coward ever since I could run. Cowardice runs in my family

John Cleese
1939–

RECTORIAL ADDRESS · ST ANDREWS UNIVERSITY

21 APRIL 1971

Rectorial addresses, particularly at St Andrews University, have tended to expound lofty themes. Rudyard Kipling praised 'Independence' and J.M. Barrie (author of Peter Pan, see volume one of this book) spoke of 'Courage'. Both those addresses were published, and indeed Barrie's sold in significant numbers. So when the British actor and comedian John Cleese was elected Rector in 1970, he realised he had a tough act to follow.

John Marwood Cleese was born in Weston-super-Mare in 1939. He was educated at Clifton College in Bristol and at Cambridge University he joined the Footlights, the amateur theatrical club. A career in comedy and television followed, culminating in Monty Python's Flying Circus, which ran from 1969 until 1974 on the BBC. The cult series also spawned three films, while Cleese enjoyed solo fame with Fawlty Towers, about a dysfunctional hotel in Torquay. He still appears in a variety of film and television parts around the world.

'For the first time in St Andrews' long and distinguished history you have elected a Silly Rector,' acknowledged Cleese in his speech. 'Where stood John Stuart Mill, Balfour, Marconi, Kipling, Earl Haig, Smuts and Sir James Barrie, now stands a 31-year-old TV funny-man... an electronic buffoon who peddles jokes to the subversively inclined in order to scrape together his humble fortune.'

Thus Cleese chose not to be serious, but to lampoon his illustrious predecessors by choosing 'Cowardice' as his Rectorial theme. But despite his irreverence that day, his three-year term as Rector was actually viewed as an important period in which the university modernised its practices. For example, Cleese appointed an elected student to deputise for him when he was unable to be in Scotland.

All I have discovered is that I have to talk to you on some subject of importance... and so, in my search of likely topics I read other Rectorial Addresses, and found that moral qualities have been very popular in the past. But then to my dismay I realised that all the good ones had been done. Courage has gone. Sir James Barrie nicked that. And independence and magnanimity and freedom...I've been left with things like good taste and chastity. And frankly, I feel whatever I speak on I should have some genuine feeling for. And the only quality that I am aware of possessing more than my fellow man is that of physical cowardice. I don't wish to boast, but I am widely regarded as one of Europe's Six Leading Cowards. I have been a coward ever since I could run. Cowardice runs in my family. The Duke of Wellington encountered my great great grandfather running full pelt from the field at Waterloo. He was merely anticipating Ambrose Bierce's definition of a coward as "one who in a perilous emergency, thinks with his legs". But the Duke didn't know this. "Why", he thundered, "are you running away?" "I am running", replied my great-great, "because I am physically unable to fly".

Consequently I feel it is something I am qualified to talk about. I know about cowardice. I put my own down to my sincere dislike of physical pain. It is my ever present hope, as I rise from my bed every morning, that this day my head will not get gashed, and that no large men will try to force a tea chest down my throat. Some nights I lie awake in bed, paralysed by the thought that one day I may be tortured for information, vital to the interests of this country, which I do not possess.

And the only quality that I am aware of possessing more than my fellow man is that of physical cowardice.

And because I have these quite normal fears, I am reviled as a coward. At school my housemaster hated me because I was not prepared to risk getting kneed in the head, simply to prevent the Brown's House third from scoring another try against the North Town third XV. It seemed to me that the adding of another three points to their already enormous total was nothing compared with the possibility of my sudden demise. And for this rational approach my life was made a living hell.

And why? For one reason only, that cowardice is badly thought of. Now I would put it another way. I would say it is badly underrated. Dr Johnson asserted that "Mutual Cowardice keeps us in peace". I believe it could, that this fundamentally realistic behaviour could be a great force for social cohesion. And I suggest that the reason why there is so much more internecine behaviour within the human species than within any other species of animals is because cowardice has got itself a bad name.

Man is a social animal. So let us look at the behaviour of other social animals. Take the wolf – he lives in a pack. Like man he is a hunter. Now, whenever a conflict breaks out between two members of a pack, either wolf can bring it to an immediate halt by making a ritual act of submission, by offering the side of his neck, his most vulnerable part, to his opponent. This immediately stops his opponent's aggressive behaviour. What a sensible system! No feeling of shame for the submittor. Just peace.

A Canadian zoologist who had been studying wolves' behaviour tried this out in a human context. He was stopped by a traffic policeman for speeding. As the zoologist saw the policeman approaching his car he noticed that the policeman, for some reason, seemed particularly angry. So he adopted sensible wolf behaviour. First he got out of his car, because to remain seated while someone is talking to you is standing suggests superior status which is

Man is a social animal.

clearly not submissive. He then took off his spectacles, because spectacles have connotations of wide staring eyes, which in terms of animal behaviour is also aggressive. And then he stood hanging his head and offering the side of his neck to the cop. The policeman's anger immediately subsided, and the zoologist was let off. The ritual submission, the cowardly behaviour, had worked.

An interesting experiment. Nothing more perhaps. But these gestures of appeasement, these acts of ritual submission, are found in all social animals. Wherever there is trouble, gulls turn away their beaks, puppies roll on their backs, jackdaws offer the napes of their necks, dogs present their throats and baboons proffer their buttocks. And what happens? The stroppy gulls and dogs and jackdaws and baboons lay off. Peace reigns. But you and I have been conditioned to despise such sensible behaviour as the seagull's. And the carnage and destruction within the human species continues unabated.

Liberalism is an attitude.

Russell Johnston
1932–2008

SPEECH TO SCOTTISH LIBERAL CONFERENCE · PERTH
19 JUNE 1976

Russell Johnston, latterly Lord Russell-Johnston, was the Grand Old Man of Scottish Liberal politics, a fixture on its political scene since his election to Parliament in 1964. When the Liberal Party seemed on the brink of extinction, even in Scotland, Johnston retained his campaigning zeal. Typically for a Liberal, he was also deeply interested in political ideology, something his Scottish Liberal conference speeches often explored.

Russell Johnston was born on Skye in 1932 and educated at the University of Edinburgh. Following National Service he was a teacher before being elected the Liberal MP for Inverness in 1964. Successively chairman (1970–74) and leader of the Scottish Liberal Party (1974–88), he was also president of the Scottish Liberal Democrats (1988–94) and deputy leader of the UK party (1988–92). Active in the Council of Europe, Johnston was given a peerage in 1997 and died in 2008.

Johnston slaved over these set-piece orations, and delegates usually found them inspirational. Although not the best of orators in a technical sense, the content was always remarkably lucid, as was the case in 1976 when he examined the 'fundamentals' of the Liberal creed, explaining what made it distinct from Socialism and Conservatism.

The context was important. As Johnston rose to speak the UK Liberal Party was in the midst of a leadership contest to replace Jeremy Thorpe, a charismatic figure who had finally resigned after months of tabloid allegations and legal proceedings relating to his personal life. The party was traumatised, thus this speech can be read as an attempt to rise above the tittle-tattle of daily politics and look at something more fundamental.

Liberalism in Scotland is clearly on the advance...While it is true that Liberalism is a philosophy of reason, Liberals throughout history have not, nor can we now, rely on reason alone. If we are to make our contribution to the finding of solutions to the divisions of interest and blood and prejudice which sunder humanity, there must be more. There must be emotional devotion. There must be passion. There must be idealism. There must be the will to climb the Matterhorn of human cupidity, up its impossible face and the belief that this can be done.

Let me take a moment to look again at the fundamentals of Liberalism. No definition of Liberalism can ever be wholly acceptable to another Liberal. Liberals are individuals and individuals disagree as inevitably as the sun rises each day – only much more frequently!

It is the way of solving problems and the attitudes we believe that make their resolution possible, rather than the specific means which bind us together... Because Liberalism is an attitude. While recognising interests it refuses to base its approach upon them (as do the Labour and Conservative Parties). It is a never-to-be-completed effort, to build a community, not of communally imposed standards (Socialism) or endlessly built-in conflicts between the haves and have-nots (Conservatism) – I accept that this is a very broad generalisation, but one has to make such generalisations – but a lively, individualistic community of free persons, pushing for achievement, but conscious of the responsibility their talents lay upon them and ever anxious to reconcile.

There must be emotional devotion. There must be passion. There must be idealism.

Reconciliation on the basis of radical reform. This, for me, is what Liberalism is about... The wish for the maximum freedom of persons to have their say which leads one to talk of proportional representation, of federalism (giving positive release to communal energies), of industrial democracy (closing the medieval gap between management and worker by creating common commitment through co-ownership and profit-sharing to progress), to the right of each of us to live the kind of lives we want to live so long as they do not impose things on others, whatever our race or colour or sex.

This is the heart of Liberalism. Because it is about the individual, it makes the assumption that if we concentrate on him/her, justice for the group of which he/she is a part will follow logically, while the converse is untrue. In this it is fundamentally set apart from political philosophies like Communism, Socialism and Nationalism, which start from this converse, seek to better the group and believe that this will lead, in time, to the improvement of the individual's lot. Conservatism is not a philosophy but a resistance to change, valuable in clarifying arguments about the way we are to go, but valueless in providing signposts. As I have said before, Conservatism is a consensus of prejudices moderated by remorse.

Liberalism then is an attitude, which may, pragmatically, support different administration of social legislative solutions but always in relation to the doctrinal concept (and we should not be afraid of recognising that it is a doctrine) that the roles society fashions for itself should be based on precepts which are (in the translation of the Latin for 'Liberal'), 'free and generous'.

We are therefore not talking simply about power: we are talking about changing a whole set of human relationships, perhaps indeed the whole basis upon which human relationships are presently founded.

It is not enough to be the government: one must change the governed... Liberalism, whatever its definition – and I have given you mine – cannot be about the replacement of one injustice by another. It only has meaning, emotional and philosophical validity if, having given every man and woman and child the equal value as human personalities to which they are entitled, it directs its energies to finding ways whereby their unequal situations are resolved fairly and compassionately and they are led to will it.

You may say this is evangelical. You may say this has no contact or relation to the realities of now and specific things we face – the shame and the misery of deprivation and poverty; the agony of unemployment, itself in our pretty civilised land, incomparably to be preferred to the utter despair of millions rotting in disease and despair in Asia and Africa... like little birds in a nest whose mother is killed, waiting hour after hour opening their mouths trustingly for the food that never comes...

Of course Liberals must be indefatigable in the pursuit of systems which reduce conflict, of laws which protect the weak, of methods which marry initiative and caring, of schemes which promote co-operation as they satisfy nationalism.

But the moment, fellow Liberals, that we forget our way along the great compassionate road to reconciliation and slip down the sidetracks of pragmatism, of short-term solutions, of bartering support for bolstered privilege, we sell our soul and become just like the rest.

If we do that, though we win, we lose...For Liberalism is a concept which knows no boundaries and whose responsibilities have no limitation. The working out of these ideas, like the dedication to the principles upon which they are based, has long depended on a few, but over the years, their numbers have steadily grown...

An alternative way of life towards which more and more people are reaching. People who have heard what we have to say, recognise its validity and are moving to join, for there is no other way, carrying the same conviction whereby the free and generous society all in their hearts seek may be created.[1]

For nearly ten years I have campaigned [for] an Assembly for Scotland within the United Kingdom. I do not intend to change my position now.

Alick Buchanan-Smith
1932–1991

SPEECH ON THE SCOTLAND AND WALES BILL · HOUSE OF COMMONS
14 DECEMBER 1976

Since his appointment as Margaret Thatcher's Shadow Scottish Secretary in 1975, Alick Buchanan-Smith had been a standard bearer for the Conservative Party's pro-devolution wing. Mrs Thatcher, however, merely tolerated Edward Heath's commitment to establish a devolved Scottish Assembly. And when the Labour government of James Callaghan published its Scotland and Wales Bill in November 1976, these divisions were exposed publicly.

Alick Laidlaw Buchanan-Smith was a Scottish Conservative politician, the second son of Lord Balerno. Educated at Edinburgh Academy, Glenalmond College, Pembroke College, Cambridge, and the University of Edinburgh, he entered Parliament as the MP for North Angus and Mearns (1964–83), and later Kincardine and Deeside until his death. He was an under-secretary at the Scottish Office (1970–74), Minister of State for Agriculture (1979–83) and Minister of State for Energy (1983–87).

All hell broke loose after a marathon Shadow Cabinet meeting the following month, at which the decision was taken to oppose the Scotland and Wales Bill's Second Reading, while maintaining a commitment to some form of devolution. 'I had no illusion that this could be done without some resignations,' recalled Thatcher in her memoirs. 'I wanted to minimise them, but not at the expense of failing to lance the devolution boil.' Some Scottish Tories argued that Buchanan-Smith should be given special dispensation to abstain in the vote, but Mrs Thatcher refused. Five days later Buchanan-Smith and his deputy Malcolm Rifkind resigned from the Conservative front bench.

'Whatever the niceties of parliamentary procedure,' Buchanan-Smith explained to reporters, 'in reality to vote against the second reading of the Bill would be a vote against the principle of devolution.' When the Second Reading was debated on 13/14 December, his speech confirmed his intention to defy a three-line whip. Although Buchanan-Smith would be appointed a minister by Mrs Thatcher in 1979, his chance of Cabinet office was gone forever.

Although we are playing for high stakes in these deliberations, the subject in hand is important not only for Parliament but for the great national parties in this country. We must demonstrate in what we do and say in the House that we are sensitive and that we can show our sensitivity towards individual parts of the United Kingdom that make up the whole. If we take that course, we shall truly show that we believe in the integrity and unity of the whole nation...

I emphasise to my hon Friends that simply to criticise the Government's proposals without spelling out any alternative will not do. Of course there will be conflicts which require explanations. There are conflicts in our proposals, just as there are conflicts under the present system. In fact, the present conflicts have given fire to the desire for devolution in Scotland.

Having listened to the criticisms of the Leader of the Opposition [Margaret Thatcher] yesterday I was tempted to say, just as the hon Member for Berwick and East Lothian (Mr Mackintosh) said, that, if these criticisms are so valid, perhaps the Government proposals do not go far enough. If we are not prepared

There are conflicts in our proposals, just as there are conflicts under the present system.

to consider some framework of devolution, as the Government are trying to do in this Bill, then perhaps we should not dismiss out of hand the idea of some federal solution which might cope effectively and adequately with the conflict to which my right hon Friend referred yesterday. That is not necessarily the right thing to do, but if we are exposing some of the risks, we must face up to the consequences, consider them constructively, and then either accept or reject them.

Be that as it may, the worst course of all is to do nothing. Opinion in Scotland cannot be ignored. This is not something which will just go away. If we in the House appear to frustrate the genuine aspirations of the Scottish people, this is the very thing which turns moderates into extremists. Scotland is not a country of extremists—Socialist, nationalist, or anything else. It is up to us in this debate to ensure that we do not turn moderates into extremists...

There is a broad desire in Scotland for the proposals for an Assembly to be debated in detail. In the course of the past week I have had more representations made to me, and have received more letters, than at any time in my whole period in this House. Not all the letters and representations have been in favour of devolution. In fact, many are openly against any form of Scottish Assembly. But there is one thing which all the letters and representations have in common. They cannot understand why we should vote against this Bill on Second Reading and thus seek to curtail any other detailed discussion on this, the first devolution proposal which has come forward to the House of Commons...

There are alternatives. This is a constitutional matter and there are deep convictions on it, as my right hon Friend the Member for Chipping Barnet [Reginald Maudling] said. It could have been dealt with by a free vote, although I know that is not welcome in certain quarters. But, if it is necessary for us on this side to register our opposition on this, surely, if we are in favour of the principle of devolution and of a Scottish Assembly, we can do so by tabling amendments spelling out our objections to the inclusion of Wales and the dangers we see in the proposals for Scotland.

The Union to which we all rightly pay allegiance will not be preserved and strengthened by us ignoring the aspirations of one party to that Union.

A vote against the Bill—I say this in particular to my right hon and hon Friends from south of the border—will be misunderstood by many of the people in Scotland if we are to remain true to our commitment to an Assembly for Scotland. The Prime Minister has promised to consider constructive amendments in Committee. If we were unsuccessful in Committee, there would still be Third Reading. But at this stage we should get the debate going.

Finally, I appreciate that there are many hon. Members on both sides of the House who oppose the Bill out of fear for the future integrity of the United Kingdom. I respect that view, and I paid tribute to it earlier. The view is sincerely held, I know, and I yield to no one in my support for the United Kingdom. But I ask my right hon and hon Friends to consider one fact. The Union to which we all rightly pay allegiance will not be preserved and strengthened by us ignoring the aspirations of one party to that Union; the Union will not be preserved and strengthened by denying the opportunity to discuss one possible way of meeting those aspirations; and the Union will not be preserved and strengthened if we ignore the views of the majority of Scottish MPs on a matter so deeply affecting Scotland.

On the other hand, I believe that the Union will be preserved and strengthened if we in this House can recognise and react to the fact that the majority of those in Scotland who want more say in the running of their own affairs want it to be within the framework of the United Kingdom... For nearly ten years I have campaigned within my party and in Scotland for what is embodied in the principle of the Bill—an Assembly for Scotland within the United Kingdom. I do not intend to change my position now.

I cannot forget that I was crowned Queen of the United Kingdom of Great Britain and Northern Ireland.

Queen Elizabeth II
1926–

REPLY TO AN ADDRESS FROM BOTH HOUSES OF PARLIAMENT
WESTMINSTER
4 MAY 1977

In 1977 Queen Elizabeth II celebrated her Silver Jubilee with visits throughout the UK and overseas. At the start of the celebrations, on 4 May 1977, the Queen replied to an address from both Houses of Parliament in which she reflected on her reign. The constitutional context was important: not only was the SNP at its pre-2011 electoral peak with 11 MPs, but devolution was also firmly on the political agenda.

Queen Elizabeth II was born in 1926, the eldest daughter of Prince Albert, the Duke of York (later King George VI). When her uncle, King Edward VIII, abdicated in 1936, it made the ten-year-old Elizabeth first in line to the throne. In 1947 she married Prince Philip of Greece and Denmark and gave birth to the future Prince Charles in 1948. In 1952 George VI died and Queen Elizabeth was crowned the following year.

Unusually, the monarch's remarks – normally expected to be studiously dull – actually referred directly to contemporary events, and not in a neutral way. The Queen recalled her coronation vows and even ventured to suggest the Jubilee might be a good time to 'remind ourselves of the benefits which union has conferred'; which the SNP complained – with good reason – strayed into party political territory.

At this time the SNP was going out of its way to emphasise that the Queen was not under threat from either devolution or its preferred option of independence. The party even debated a written constitution that year, and despite a degree of dissent, endorsed its inclusion of the Queen as head of state in an independent Scotland. It was a debate which, to varying degrees, lingered for the next few decades.

My Lords and Members of the House of Commons, I am deeply grateful for your Loyal Addresses and for the kind and generous words in which the Lord Chancellor and Mr Speaker have expressed them. Thank you also for what you have said about my family and the service they have given over the years. You will understand that for me personally their support has been invaluable.

It is appropriate that I should come to Westminster at the start of the Jubilee celebrations in the United Kingdom. Here, in a meeting of Sovereign and Parliament, the essence of Constitutional Monarchy is reflected. It is a form of Government in which those who represent the main elements of the community can come together to reconcile conflicting interests and to strive for the hopes and aims we all share. It has adapted itself to the changes in our own society and in international relationships, yet it has remained true to its essential role. It has

These 25 years have seen much change for Britain.

provided the fabric of good order in society and has been the guardian of the liberties of individual citizens.

These 25 years have seen much change for Britain. By virtue of tolerance and understanding, the Empire has evolved into a Commonwealth of 36 Independent Nations spanning the five Continents. No longer an Imperial Power, we have been coming to terms with what this means for ourselves and for our relations with the rest of the world.

We have forged new links with other countries and in joining the European Economic Communities we have taken what is perhaps one of the most significant decisions during my reign. At home there are greater opportunities for all sorts and conditions of men and women. Developments in science, technology and in medicine have improved the quality and comfort of life and, of course, there has also been television!

We in Government and Parliament have to accept the challenges which this

At home there are greater opportunities for all sorts and conditions of men and women.

progress imposes on us. And they are considerable. The problems of progress, the complexities of modern administration, the feeling that Metropolitan Government is too remote from the lives of ordinary men and women, these among other things have helped to revive an awareness of historic national identities in these Islands. They provide the background for the continuing and keen discussion of proposals for devolution to Scotland and Wales within the United Kingdom.

I number Kings and Queens of England and of Scotland, and Princes of Wales among my ancestors and so I can readily understand these aspirations. But I cannot forget that I was crowned Queen of the United Kingdom of Great Britain and Northern Ireland. Perhaps this Jubilee is a time to remind ourselves of the benefits which union has conferred, at home and in our international dealings, on the inhabitants of all parts of this United Kingdom.

A Jubilee is also a time to look forward! We should certainly do this with determination and I believe we can also do so with hope. We have so many advantages, the basic stability of our institutions, our traditions of public service and concern for others, our family life and, above all, the freedom which you and your predecessors in Parliament have, through the ages, so fearlessly upheld.

My Lords, Members of the House of Commons. For me the 25th anniversary of my Accession is a moving occasion. It is also, I hope, for all of us a joyous one. May it also be a time in which we can all draw closer together. Thank you again! I begin these celebrations much encouraged by your good wishes and expressions of loyalty.

The waves of international subversion and terrorism are already lapping our shores and may have all sorts of unpredictable consequences...

Duke of Edinburgh
1921–

RADIO CLYDE BROADCAST

OCTOBER 1977

It was not only the Queen who strayed into political commentary during the course of 1977, her Silver Jubilee year. Her husband the Duke of Edinburgh contributed to a series of broadcasts on Radio Clyde, looking forward to the year 2000. Some of his predictions were very prescient, foreseeing an upsurge of interest in climate change and warning of the dangers of international terrorism.

Prince Philip, the Duke of Edinburgh was born Prince of Greece and Denmark in Corfu in 1921, Queen Victoria being his (and the Queen's) great-great-grandmother. In 1947 he married Princess Elizabeth and renounced his Royal title, becoming a naturalised British subject. In 1951 Philip gave up his naval career and instead became patron or president of some 800 organisations.

Other elements, not least an attack on an overbearing state, could have been construed as almost Thatcherite in tenor, and indeed Philip's speech was later included in a volume published by the Institute of Economic Affairs, alongside contributions from Hayek the future Chancellor of the Exchequer Nigel Lawson. The Duke of Edinburgh, as the historian Mark Garnett once wrote, 'was a constitutional crisis waiting to happen'.

Even in 1977 he was known to be fond of speaking his mind. As Prince Philip had written in a volume of his earlier speeches: '...these speeches embody the reflections of an unprejudiced observer on the life and some of the problems of the middle of the twentieth century. True, I have rather exceptional opportunities to observe what is going on but I have no axe to grind and nothing to sell. I have to make speeches as a matter of duty but the line I take is my own.'[1]

It is one thing to predict technological developments; it is rather more difficult to predict general social and political conditions. And there is a considerable difference between what is likely to happen and what we may want to happen. I am going to be concerned only with what I think may happen. What I would like to see happen is an entirely different story...

Quite apart from the techniques of forecasting, there is the attitude of the forecaster to bear in mind. I suppose it may be humanely possible to be utterly objective, but I rather doubt it. If you have grown up with or acquired a certain set of principles, they will inevitably colour your selection of historical factors and the emphasis you give to the conclusions you draw from them. In any event there is such a vast choice of material that the less scrupulous prophets find it easier to start with the conclusion they wish to reach and then simply search around for the appropriate cases to prove it. I cannot avoid selecting historical factors, but I hope I have not fallen into the trap of pre-selecting my conclusions...

Some years ago the issues of starvation, malnutrition and world population

We cannot exist totally isolated from the rest of the world.

gave rise to the Freedom from Hunger Campaign. This was followed by a sudden concern for the conservation of nature and the environment. More recently, interest switched to energy resources and alternative sources of energy. Each has had quite a significant influence on popular attitudes. Who knows what will be next to attract public attention? Perhaps it will be the problems of a changing world climate, or it may be a revival of interest in religion. Whatever it is, it is bound to make predictions based on current attitudes which turn out to be less accurate, if not completely wrong.

Secondly, we cannot exist totally isolated from the rest of the world. There is no way of knowing what ideas and attitudes will sweep into this country from abroad, or what political or practical events will have repercussions here. The waves of international subversion and terrorism are already lapping our shores and may have all sorts of unpredictable consequences...

It looks as if we can expect to see an increasing bureaucratic involvement in virtually every aspect of the lives of individual citizens. If the experience of other countries is anything to go by, this will mean a gradual reduction in the freedom of choice and individual responsibility, particularly in such things as housing, the education of children, healthcare, the ability to acquire or inherit personal property, to hand on commercial enterprises, and the ability to provide for old age through personal savings and, perhaps, most important of all, the freedom of the individual to exploit his skills or talents as suits him best.

Judging from the experience of other countries, individual initiative in commerce and industry will become considerably restricted, although the opportunities for marginally legal and illegal activities will increase as a consequence of the growing volume of legislation which it will not be possible to enforce. The situation will also be aggravated if there is any further decline in moral standards...

The major financial and commercial markets will begin to flourish. Consumer products will tend towards an average standard, with the gradual elimination of items of better quality. The social services, and particularly the Health Service, will suffer as government finds it progressively more difficult to meet the rising costs and as it comes up against the rule that the bigger the organisation the more difficult it is to manage.

The take-home element of wages and salaries will become relatively less important as all the major necessities will be provided "free" – in other words, out of taxation – and also because fringe benefits associated with employment and trade unions will increase. This dependence on fringe benefits for even the basic elements of existence will ensure a very high degree of job discipline. The loss of a job will not be cushioned by the accumulation of savings or property. Employment direction may make unemployment benefits more difficult to obtain. Slavery is no more than a system of directed labour and fringe benefits.

Slavery is no more than a system of directed labour and fringe benefits.

Whereas individuals recognise an affinity with individuals in similar occupations in other countries, the existence of an exclusive nation is the vested interest of national governments. The more powerful governments become, the more they tend to encourage a spirit of exclusive nationalism and a hatred and suspicion of anything foreign or multi-national. Official nationalism will lead to increasing state responsibility for cultural, sporting and economic activities and the gradual suppression of anything which does not suit national economic policies or which does not appear to do justice to the national cultural ideal.

These predictions sound almost fanciful in the British context. Some of the things I have said may seem unthinkable in this country with its tradition of freedom and tolerance. There were people in many other countries who felt the same way, but the unthinkable happened to them. The Russian dissident Alexander Solzhenitsyn said:

"It is not how the Soviet Union will find a way out of totalitarianism, but how the West will be able to avoid the same fate."[2]

If they believe in what they have been told about opinion in Scotland, they have absolutely nothing to fear from my amendment.

George Cunningham
1931–

SPEECH DURING DEBATE ON THE SCOTLAND BILL · HOUSE OF COMMONS
25 JANUARY 1978

The very mention of George Cunningham's name still riles Scottish Nationalists and veteran campaigners for a Scottish Assembly (or Parliament) more than three decades after his infamous 'Cunningham Amendment' effectively killed any chance of devolution for Scotland.

An Anglo-Scot, Cunningham was strongly opposed to the Scotland Bill, which was making its way through Parliament in early 1978. He proposed an amendment, ultimately passed by a majority of MPs, which stipulated that at least 40 per cent of the total Scottish electorate (as opposed to 40 per cent of those voting) would have to vote 'yes' in a referendum planned for 1 March 1979 in order for the Scotland Act to come into force.

As expected, this threshold was not achieved and the Scotland Act was repealed shortly after Margaret Thatcher swept to power at the 1979 general election. In that sense, ironies abound. Cunningham's amendment was instrumental in the downfall of his own Labour government, and thereafter his party was plunged into ideological turmoil that resulted in his own defection to the centrist SDP. Even more ironically, that new party favoured radical decentralisation, or devolution, to which Cunningham was vehemently opposed.

George Cunningham was initially educated in Scotland but settled in England and pursued his political career there. He was elected MP for Islington South West in 1970, renamed Islington South and Finsbury in 1974. In 1981 Cunningham resigned from the Labour Party and defected to the Social Democratic Party in 1982, narrowly losing his seat the following year.

Then there is the question of what kind of minimum test we need to impose. There is, of course, a minimum test implicit in having a referendum at all—namely, that more people should vote "Yes" than should vote "No". The only question is whether we impose a minimum majority.

There are two ways in which to do that. First, we could require a minimum percentage of the electorate to vote, however they voted, and, secondly, we could require a minimum majority of those who vote "Yes" over those who vote "No"... My hon Friend the Member for Mitcham and Morden [Mr Douglas-Mann]

We should all recognise that there is nothing magic or sacred about any figure in this context...

suggests 33⅓ per cent; I suggest 40 per cent. We should all recognise that there is nothing magic or sacred about any figure in this context... I am suggesting a very modest figure—that 40 per cent of the electorate in Scotland should declare positive support for the proposal, or the referendum does not bind us morally to go ahead with devolution.

I do not think that that can be called a wrecking amendment for devolution, first because it is not a figure which was not met in the EEC referendum. The EEC figure for the whole of the United Kingdom was that just under 43 per cent voted "Yes". That is, 43 per cent of the electorate in the United Kingdom as a whole voted "Yes". Therefore, my test, if imposed in the referendum, would have been very comfortably met...

This referendum will not be mandatory. Nothing will be legally binding upon the House of Commons. Whatever comes before the House in the way of an order from the Government will be passed or not passed according to the discretion of the House. Anyone who feels that a referendum is all right if it is not binding should not be worried about my amendment, because these changes would have no effect upon that point...

The only effect of this threshold is that, if the threshold is not met, the House has to reconsider the matter the Government would have to bring in an order which required the House of Commons to reconsider the matter. It does not seek to terminate devolution automatically, and in practice it would not necessarily do so. It simply imposes a level and provides that if that level is not reached the House of Commons will want to look at the matter again. In my view, it would not be fair to hold a referendum without giving any indication to the Scottish people that we propose to take account of the size of the poll and of the size of the majority, both of which are involved in this type of amendment.

The test is a reasonable one for such a fundamental and irrevocable change as is being proposed. The figure is even perhaps a shade too modest. If the SNP

This referendum will not be mandatory. Nothing will be legally binding upon the House of Commons.

and the Government are even remotely right in saying that a significant majority of Scottish people want this change, they have nothing to worry about. Yet we are observing that they are worried. The Scottish Labour Party is to vote against my amendment, and the hon Member for South Ayrshire [Jim Sillars] will no doubt make his own points.

The SNP, which says that Scotland wants this change, is against the amendment, and so are the Government. The only people who should be against it are those who, whether they say so or not, suspect that there is not a majority of people in Scotland positively in favour of the amendment but who are determined to impose it whether that majority exists or not. If they believe in what they have been told about opinion in Scotland, they have absolutely nothing to fear from my amendment.'

There is no doubt that tonight the Scotland Act will be repealed

Malcolm Rifkind
1946–

WINDING UP SPEECH ON REPEAL OF THE SCOTLAND ACT
HOUSE OF COMMONS
20 JUNE 1979

Debates over devolution dominated British politics throughout the 1970s. The Conservative Party, committed to a devolved Scottish Assembly since 1968, suffered particular ructions, not least because several of its MPs – and not just in Scotland – were determined to scupper such plans. Finally, in late 1976, Mrs Thatcher (party leader since early 1975), decided to ditch Ted Heath's pledge.

Sir Malcolm Leslie Rifkind was born in 1946 in Edinburgh, where he attended school and university. After a brief career as a teacher and Advocate, he entered Parliament in February 1974, rising rapidly through the Conservative ranks and spending 18 years as a minister between 1979 and 1997. Having lost his seat, Sir Malcolm re-entered Parliament for Kensington and Chelsea in 2005, unsuccessfully contesting the Conservative Party leadership later that year.

As a keen devolutionist Malcolm Rifkind, who had entered Parliament in February 1974, resigned from his front bench post as Scottish Affairs spokesman in protest at the move. He argued that as the Conservative Party still supported the *principle* of devolution, then it ought to have backed Government plans for a Scottish Assembly or abstained.

Just over two years later, when Scots voted on the plans for a Scottish Assembly in a referendum, Rifkind stuck to his supportive line and voted 'yes'. But when the result failed to reach a required 40 per cent threshold (of the total electorate), he withdrew his support, arguing that Scotland was divided over the proposal. After the May 1979 election that resulted in Mrs Thatcher becoming Prime Minister, Rifkind found himself – as a junior Scottish Office minister – winding up the debate on repealing the 1978 Scotland Act. Speaking without a note and, aged only 33, it made his reputation.

It is now more than 10 years since the devolution debate began in earnest in Scotland. It is a debate that was, in part at least, precipitated by the voice of the Scottish people as expressed through the ballot box. It is perhaps fitting that this phase of the devolution debate should now be ending also largely as a result of the voice of the Scottish people as expressed through the ballot box. Let no one be mistaken. It was the referendum on 1 March that caused the House to have to consider these matters today and to come to the decision that will shortly have to be voted on...

There has been considerable discussion in this debate on the 40 per cent rule that was written into the Act, but I think that there are few hon Members who would doubt that, even if that rule had never been introduced into the Act, given the result of the referendum we would still be here today and still about to come to a very similar decision. Even without the 40 per cent rule, the referendum was advisory. There was never any question but that this House would have to take into account the express views of the Scottish electorate on 1 March in making the final decision. Few people correctly predicted what would happen on that date. Nevertheless, we are facing the result today. First, 32.8 per cent of the Scottish people voted "Yes" and roughly 68 per cent either voted "No" or stayed at home... The majority was a mere 77,000, the size of a largish constituency. That is no basis for embarking on the most fundamental constitutional reform since the Act of Union...

That is no basis for embarking on the most fundamental constitutional reform since the Act of Union...

Where do we go from here? There is no doubt that tonight the Scotland Act will be repealed. The Conservative Party and the Government have said that they are willing and anxious to enter into talks with other political parties to seek agreement on methods of constitutional change... There are various ways in which the government of Scotland can be improved within the structure of the United Kingdom legislation. The success of the all-party talks depends on the response of the other parties, and their willingness to involve themselves in proposals for improving our system of government...

I turn to the point argued by both the Shadow Leader of the House—the right hon. Member for Ebbw Vale (Mr Foot)—and the former Secretary of State for Scotland—the right hon. Member for Glasgow, Craigton (Mr Millan). They have asked why we are repealing the Scotland Act before the talks take place. The reason is simple and obvious. No one member of the Labour Party has today argued that the Scotland Act should be implemented now. No one representative of the Opposition has suggested that the result of the referendum was such as to entitle or require us to implement that Act immediately and establish an Assembly... The reason why the Opposition are voting against this repeal order has nothing to do with conviction, but everything to do with tactics. They know that if they were to vote with the Government, recognising the results of the referendum, they would have a rebellion on their hands from the Scottish Council of the Labour Party, the hon. Member for West Stirlingshire (Mr Canavan) and from certain other supporters of the Scotland Act. But they equally know that if they were to vote against the repeal order on the basis that the Act should be immediately implemented and an Assembly immediately established, they would have a rebellion on their hands, not from 50, but from 150 of their hon. Friends. Therefore, the Opposition are forced into this tactical manoeuvre. They are saying that they are against the repeal order, not because they believe that an Assembly should be established, but because they believe that the order is premature. They hope that in that way they can reconcile their lack of principle with their political objectives. I do not believe that either the House or the country as a whole will be fooled by that manoeuvre...

The reason why the Opposition are voting against this repeal order has nothing to do with conviction but everything to do with tactics...

We believe that it would be against the interests of all concerned if further discussions were to extend throughout the life of this Parliament. [HON. MEMBERS: "Oh."] This subject has been discussed and debated for ten years. We believe that discussions can usefully be carried out and can come to a conclusion in the course of this year, and indeed in the course of the next few months. But that will depend on the response of Opposition parties. If they do not respond constructively, the whole concept of all-party agreement cannot be achieved. When the House votes tonight to repeal the Scotland Act, it will in some respects be doing what the House in its own instinct has wanted to do for some time. But it will be doing more than that. It will also be responding to the decision of the Scottish electorate on 1 March when the people of Scotland refused to endorse the Scotland Act. That is a fact of history which cannot be denied. On that basis we invite the House to vote for the order.[1]

...in this instance the state of our law is no better than that in the Soviet Union.

Robin Cook
1946–2005

SPEECH MOVING AMENDMENT TO CRIMINAL JUSTICE (SCOTLAND) BILL
HOUSE OF COMMONS
22 JULY 1980

It is often forgotten that while homosexual acts between two men were decriminalised in England and Wales by the 1967 Sexual Offences Act, they remained a criminal offence in Northern Ireland and Scotland. Throughout the 1970s various equalities groups – including some based in Edinburgh – campaigned to address this anomaly and bring Scots Law into line with that of the rest of Great Britain.

Robin Cook's was one of those voices raised in support; indeed he often joined forces with the Conservative MP Malcolm Rifkind to argue the case. Nevertheless, the Sexual Offences (Scotland) Act 1976 retained the clause that made homosexual acts a criminal offence, while a 1977 Bill introduced in the House of Lords by Lord Boothby failed to progress.

When Margaret Thatcher's government introduced a routine Criminal Justice Bill in 1980, however, Cook saw an opportunity to have another go and tabled an amendment which attracted cross-party support (although not from the SNP's two Members of Parliament). Following a short, cogent speech from Cook, MPs backed the change and thus, on 1 February 1981, same-sex sexual activities were legalised in Scotland. Northern Ireland followed a year later.

Robert Finlayson 'Robin' Cook was born in Bellshill in 1946 and studied at Edinburgh University. After working as a teacher, he became an MP in 1974 and held various front bench posts as well as managing the leadership campaigns of Neil Kinnock (1983) and John Smith (1992). Cook was Foreign Secretary from 1997–2001 and then Leader of the House, but resigned in March 2003 over his opposition to the war in Iraq.

We have tabled the clause because we firmly believe that what happens within the privacy of bedrooms is no concern of ours as Members of Parliament, perhaps mercifully. A minority of men, but a significant minority, is attracted only to other men. It is oppressive and impractical of Parliament to say to that large body of citizens that they must choose between lifelong continence or committing a criminal offence. That choice is unsatisfactory. It obliges many otherwise law-abiding citizens in all parts of the community to choose to commit a criminal offence. The propositions are not particularly controversial. As far back as 1968 the General Assembly of the Church of Scotland went on record demanding the same change in the law. It is instructive to recall why the General Assembly called for the change. It recognised that so long as homosexual acts were a criminal offence homosexual men would inevitably be inhibited from coming forward and seeking the pastoral care of the Church. I understand that the Minister may seek to rebut the new clause on the ground that since there are no prosecutions under the section that I am seeking to delete, no damage is done. However, the fact that no prosecutions are taking place does not mean that no damage arises from the fact that homosexuality is a criminal offence in Scotland. Hon. Members will be familiar with the recent case of the gardener-handyman who was dismissed by his employer on the specific ground that he was a homosexual. His subsequent appeal to an employment tribunal was dismissed on the

I am against Parliament being asked to stand on its head or any hon. Members being asked to stand on theirs.

ground that the decision of the employer was a reasonable one. I do not propose to trench on the merits of that case, because it is subject to further appeal and is therefore *sub judice*, but two general truths emerge. First, no hon. Member could argue that the tribunal was not influenced, perhaps unconsciously, by the knowledge that homosexual acts in Scotland are criminal offences. It has reflected in its judgment the prejudice that is sustained by the present state of the law. Secondly, since that judgment there has been a campaign to end discrimination against homosexuals in employment and other fields. A month ago many hon. Members attended a meeting in this House addressed by the leaders of that campaign. It is illogical and impractical to mount a campaign against discrimination against homosexuals, in employment laws or whatever, so long as it is proscribed in our criminal statutes. We therefore tabled the new clause. I hope that the clause will not be rebutted on the basis of the curious and dangerous constitutional argument that because the Government have decided by executive action that they will not implement the law there is therefore no urgency to change it. We debated the issue when the consolidated Sexual Offences Bill was before the House in 1976. The present Under-Secretary of State for Scotland made vigorous attacks on that argument. He said:

> The basis of my opposition to the clause is that it is totally wrong as a matter of basic constitutional principle that Parliament should be asked to approve a consolidation measure of an activity's continuing to be a

> criminal offence while at the same time the Lord Advocate informs the House that the Crown has not the slightest intention of treating such activity as a criminal offence... Parliament should not be asked to make a fool of itself or to stand on its head.

I am against Parliament being asked to stand on its head or any hon. Members being asked to stand on theirs. I therefore hope that if the hon. Gentleman is replying to the debate he will not stand on his head and reverse the arguments that he put forward when the House last debated the matter. I trust that he will not rebut the new clause on the basis of the arguments that he rejected in 1976.

It is ironic that we should debate the new clause on a day when the papers report in a critical vein the arrest by Soviet policemen of Western journalists who were covering a demonstration in favour of human rights for Russian homosexuals. The House is given to developing a strong line in criticising the neglect of human rights in the Soviet Union. Those criticisms are well deserved. However, in this instance the state of our law is no better than that in the Soviet Union. It would be more constructive to put our own house in order first. I therefore hope that the House will seize the opportunity to expunge from the statute book what has long remained an anomaly in Scottish law.[1]

You came to see a race today.
See someone win.
Happened to be me.

Eric Liddell
1902–45

POST-RACE SPEECH TO A CROWD OF WORKING MEN · EDINBURGH
1981

Chariots of Fire was a 1981 biopic of Eric Liddell, the devout Scottish Christian and Olympic athlete. Famously, having trained for the 100 metres in the 1924 Paris Olympics, when he learned the heats were to take place on a Sunday he switched to the 400-metre competition as he was not prepared to break the Sabbath. The gamble paid off: Liddell won a gold medal for the 400 metres and also a bronze medal for the 200 metres.

Eric Liddell was born in 1902 in China, the second son of two missionaries. He was educated at Eltham College, Blackheath, and then Edinburgh University, where he studied pure science. Athletics and rugby were big passions but Liddell chose to concentrate on running. After the 1924 Paris Olympics he returned to China where he served, like his parents, as a missionary. Having remained in China after the outbreak of war, Liddell was interned in a Japanese camp where he died in 1945.

Produced by David (later Lord) Puttnam, the film's title was inspired by the line 'Bring me my chariot of fire' from the William Blake poem better known as the patriotic hymn 'Jerusalem' (although the phrase 'chariot of fire' originally appeared in 2 Kings 2:11 and 6:17). Puttnam commissioned screenwriter Colin Welland to write the script, while the Scottish actor Ian Charleson played Liddell.

The speech below takes place after the Scotland v. Ireland races, when Liddell addresses a crowd of workingmen in the pouring rain. Charleson (who later died of AIDS aged 40), told the director Hugh Hudson that he felt the scripted version was neither authentic nor inspiring, so Hudson and Welland graciously allowed him to put together a few lines he found personally inspirational. Charleson had studied the Bible intensively for the role.

You came to see a race today. See someone win. Happened to be me. But I want you to do more than just watch a race. I want you to take part in it.

I want to compare faith to running in a race. It's hard. It requires concentration of will, energy of soul. You experience elation when the winner breaks the tape – 'specially if you've got a bet on it. But how long does that last? You go home. Maybe your dinner's burnt. Maybe, maybe you haven't got a job. So who am I to say, "believe," "have faith," in the face of life's realities?

You came to see a race today.
See someone win. Happened to be me.

I would like to give you something more permanent, but I can only point the way. I have no formula for winning the race. Everyone runs in her own way, or his own way.

And where does the power come from to see the race to its end? From within.

Jesus said, "Behold, the kingdom of God is within you. If, with all your hearts ye truly seek Me, ye shall ever surely find Me." If you commit yourself to the love of Christ.

And THAT is how you run the straight race.[1]

... for too long... we in Britain have been... drifting on the ebbing tide of history, slipping inexorably backwards under pressures we somehow felt powerless to resist.

Margaret Thatcher
1925–2013

SPEECH TO SCOTTISH CONSERVATIVE PARTY CONFERENCE · PERTH
14 MAY 1982

Although keenly anticipated by Conservative activists, Margaret Thatcher's annual speeches to the Scottish Tory conference, usually held in Perth, did not usually attract attention beyond the Scottish media. But that in 1982 was an exception, for a few weeks earlier Argentina had invaded the Falkland Islands, then as now sovereign British territory.

Margaret Hilda Thatcher was born in Grantham in 1925, after graduating from Oxford she rose to become Education Secretary, leader of the Conservative Party and from 1979 the first woman to lead a major Western democracy. Thatcher won three successive general elections and served as Prime Minister for more than 11 years (1979–90), a record unmatched in the 20th century. In 1992 she was elevated to the House of Lords as Baroness Thatcher of Kesteven.

Thus conference delegates gathered, as Mrs Thatcher put it, 'in the shadow of great events'. She delivered a barnstorming performance, talking quietly and movingly about the dangers which lay ahead. It was a speech intended for a UK, if not international, audience, and thus Scottish references were kept to a minimum.

The Prime Minister finished her speech to a tremendous ovation, a reaction she later reflected 'gave a great boost to my morale'. Others were less impressed. The Liberal leader David Steel accused Mrs Thatcher of jingoism, while even the Scottish Secretary George Younger later told the journalist Hugo Young that events in Perth brought to mind 'the Nuremberg Rally'. She certainly milked it for all it was worth.

For nearly 150 years now, the United Kingdom has been in peaceful and continuous possession of the Falkland Islands. The administration of the Islands has been British and until the invasion, out of the total population of the Islands, the Argentinians numbered only forty. The rest were British and mainly of Island stock. Families which have been there for four or five generations, longer than the ancestors of some of the Argentinians who came from Spain and Italy. Argentina claims that theirs is an act of decolonisation. Ladies and gentlemen, that simply isn't true. No nation in the world has a longer or prouder record of bringing colonies to true independence than our own. What Argentina wants is not to decolonise the Falklands but in fact to put them again under a different colonial control, and one which has not had the respect for liberty and democracy which the Islanders have come to love...

Of course we will continue to negotiate. We'll go on doing all we humanly can to reach a peaceful settlement. A settlement in which the Argentine leaves the islands they now occupy unlawfully. The government wants a peaceful settlement but your government totally rejects a peaceful sell-out. There would be neither honour nor credibility in our country or our people if we were to do that.

I hope that the negotiations will succeed. I don't want to see one more life lost in the South Atlantic, whether British or Argentinian, if it can be avoided.

No nation in the world has a longer or prouder record of bringing colonies to true independence than our own.

But I should not be doing my duty if I didn't warn you in the simplest and clearest terms that for all our efforts, those of Mr Haig, and those of the Secretary General of the United Nations, a negotiated settlement may prove to be unattainable. Then we should have to turn to the only other course left open to us. And that is why, as I have repeatedly said in the House of Commons, the Government, in its attempts to find a diplomatic solution, has done nothing which forecloses any military action now, or any military option for the future... The difficulties we face are formidable but our determination to secure a just solution is relentless and in that I believe we have the whole country with us.

Mr President, for too long, or so it seems to me, we in Britain have been seen by ourselves and by too many overseas people as drifting on the ebbing tide of history, slipping inexorably backwards under pressures we somehow felt powerless to resist. Yet in truth there was nothing irresistible about them if we had but the resolve to reverse the current and to convince others and ourselves of our sense of purpose. Even since I was given the trust to lead our Government it has been my purpose to set a course that both friend and foe may understand and that we may adhere to. And that purpose is the same at home as it is overseas. To uphold certain principles and values which some had thought that we could live without. And foremost among them has been to restore honest money and sound finance and to make our industries profitable once again. Of course, we knew that the paths we set would need to be adjusted to the unmapped terrain that lay ahead and we didn't hesitate to adjust it, but our goal was not adjusted and it shouldn't be. And it won't be. Steadily but surely we are gaining ground, because ordinary folk understand our sense of purpose. They understand we are going to stick to it and more and more are coming to count upon that.

Mr President, sometimes I had the feeling in these recent anxious days and nights, and they have been particularly anxious for me, and those who bear such responsibility in the Government and in the Forces, the one or two of those who have proclaimed themselves expert at analysing our national character have been feeling something of a culture shock. For years they have tried to tell us and others, who observe us from afar, that the British people had lost the taste for independent action. That Patriotism was outmoded. That the words of the familiar Naval prayer which speaks of our fleet as the defence of all those who pass across the seas upon their lawful occasions, that these things they said belong to the scrapbooks of nostalgia. How wrong they were. What have we seen in these last few weeks? We've seen this ancient country rising as one nation to meet a challenge that it refuses to ignore. Men and women working overtime to see the ships and supplies for our Forces in the South Atlantic delivered, not just on time, but well ahead of time, and it's been their pride to do it. Away went the strikes. People worked overtime and I remember one example told me of some

We've seen this ancient country rising as one nation to meet a challenge that it refuses to ignore.

particular thing, some particular modification, which we had been told would take 32 weeks to do, and those self-same people who quoted 32 weeks did it in two. That's the sense of pride that's been aroused.

Great liners called back into service and turned round to take our reinforcements. And all this done in what has sometimes seemed an impossible schedule. Perhaps we have surprised even ourselves. And I know we have surprised all those who didn't think we had it in us. But in these things Britain still leads the world. The love of liberty in the rule of law and in the character of our people.

So, Mr President, two longs have merged [*sic*], too often denigrated, too easily forgotten, the springs of pride in Britain flow again. And one of our poets said, and I finish with his words, "Dear bought and clear, a thousand years our fathers' title runs. Make we likewise their sacrifice, defrauding not our sons."[1]

The miners' strike was the most heroic and courageous struggle of working people in Britain this century.

Mick McGahey
1925–99

SPEECH AT SCOTTISH MINERS' CONFERENCE · SALUTATION HOTEL · PERTH
12/13 JUNE 1985

Michael 'Mick' McGahey described himself as 'a product of my class and my movement', but although Scottish and a towering figure in the British trade union movement, he actually played a relatively minor role during the 1984–85 miners' strike, largely because he was already nearing retirement.

McGahey had opposed the holding of a nation-wide ballot and favoured letting the 'regions' make their own decision as to whether or not to strike. He also saw the appointment of Ian McGregor as chair of the National Coal Board as a 'declaration of war' and feared privately that a 'bloody' strike was inevitable. And so it proved, perhaps becoming the most divisive symbol of the Thatcher era.

Michael 'Mick' McGahey was born in Shotts, North Lanarkshire, in 1925, the son of a founder member of the Communist Party of Great Britain. After school in Cambuslang, he started work aged 14 at the Gateside Colliery and worked as a miner for the next 25 years. McGahey also rose through the ranks of his local union, becoming president of the Scottish area in 1967. In 1972 he became national vice-president of the NUM.

When the strike was over, McGahey became more critical of Arthur Scargill and argued against the growing concentration of power within the National Union of Mineworkers at the expense of regional areas like Scotland. He also delivered this speech – no doubt in his distinctive gravelly voice – during the June 1985 Scottish miners' conference, in which he tried to combine an uplifting assessment of the struggle with a dose of realism about what had gone wrong.

The miners' strike was the most heroic and courageous struggle of working people in Britain this century. It was one of the greatest struggles of the British working classes ever seen and is of tremendous portence for the future. The Union must record its gratitude and thanks to our members and their families for the courage and devotion to the noble cause that we fought for and are still fighting for. It is sometimes forgotten that the struggle was for a policy of action against pit closures, which was decided democratically at a National Delegate Conference of our Union. The National Executive Committee of this Union fought for that policy from the beginning and our members responded. In this struggle we received great support from millions of ordinary people, sometimes Sections of the Labour Movement fought alongside us, but there were problems in implementing the policies as decided by the TUC.

The miners' strike was the most heroic and courageous struggle of working people in Britain this century.

The problems were not all at leadership level in the TUC and Labour Movement. We have to face the fact that thousands and thousands of rank and file members of Trade Unions have been forced back by the weapon of mass unemployment and have still to be won for action. A massive propaganda campaign could and should have been waged by the Labour Movement to win understanding amongst these workers, who after all also comprise public opinion. In Scotland the STUC mounted the only effective day of action in our support and tribute needs to be paid to the role of the STUC throughout the year-long struggle. We were sustained by tremendous cash collections in the Movement and amongst the general public. Our struggle was never a narrow sectional struggle only interested in miners' jobs and the coal industry. Yes, we fought for our jobs, miners' jobs and the coal industry. Yes, we fought for our jobs, for our pits and we fought for our communities, but basically it was a fight for an alternative economic and political strategy as against the Thatcher Government policies in the interests of the multi-nationals. In that sense it was in the broad interests of everyone in Britain. Far from being a vote loser for the

Yes, we fought for our jobs, miners' jobs and the coal industry.

Labour Party, it was and is a vote winner, and I hope that this will be reflected in the earliest possible General Election and a return of a Labour Government.

The forces raged against us were very strong. The whole power of the State machine, the police and the media was ranged against us. The Government and Coal Board presented it as a fight for law and order and for sound economics in the coal industry. The Government and the Coal Board had clearly learned lessons from the struggles of 1972 and 1974; that is why the Movement must also learn lessons from every struggle. Mass picketing, while still necessary in given circumstances, was effectively controlled by the power of the police in a way not done in 1972/74. An analysis of our historic struggle is absolutely necessary if we are to learn the lessons and go forward in the future... This Union requires to make an analysis, to learn the lessons, not only for the miners, but for the whole of the working class in this country in the future struggles that lie ahead. It is also necessary, because such an analysis will help us face up to the reality of our present position with all its difficulties. To be forced back without a negotiated settlement was a major setback. We did not suffer and defeat but we suffered a set back and that has to be faced up to. In the Scottish coalfield, the Coal Board are riding roughshod over negotiated agreements. We have a fight on our hands to secure the restoration of our Trade Union rights...

Since the strike we have seen the National Coal Board pressing on with closures affecting every coalfield, and here in Scotland we have a mighty task on hand, not only for the defence of the Scottish coalfield, but for an expansionist policy with greater investment in new sinkings to meet the energy requirements of our country...

Let us have confidence to fight back;
let there be no disillusionment.

To carry out this campaign we require the maximum unity at all levels of the Union, in conjunction with the Scottish Labour and Trade Union Movement, giving leadership to the whole nation as we are again defending the vital assets of the people. As I have said before, the Coal Industry does not belong to MacGregor, nor for that matter this Union, but it certainly is the assets of the Scottish people, and it should be harnessed and developed in the interests of the Scottish people.

We require this unity not only to defend our jobs, but also to advance our living standards, to ensure job protection and to campaign for the highest possible safety levels in our industry.

Let us have confidence to fight back; let there be no disillusionment. Our young people, our women's support groups, our mining communities have all demonstrated their courage, tenacity and confidence in the future. This will be best advanced by the election of a Labour Government committed to Left progressive policies that will ensure the ending of the scourge of unemployment; that will implement policies of peace and détente and open up the road for an advance to socialism here in Britain.[1]

... the art of ridicule... can penetrate to the marrow. It can leave a salutary scar.

Muriel Spark
1918–2006

SPEECH TO AMERICAN ACADEMY OF ARTS OF LETTERS

1971

By the early 1970s Muriel Spark was applauded the world over for two decades' worth of fine literature, most famously *The Prime of Miss Jean Brodie*. In 1971 she was invited to give an address to the American Academy of Arts and Letters, and she used it as an opportunity to deliver, in the words of Joseph Hynes, a 'manifesto of such clarity and directness' that it should 'caution any critics or other reader about what to look for in reading Spark's fiction'.

Muriel Spark was born in Edinburgh in 1918, but left Scotland aged 19 to marry in Southern Rhodesia. She returned to the UK in 1944, establishing herself in London as a poet and critic. By the late 1950s Spark had published a series of acclaimed novels including The Comforters and Memento Mori. The Prime of Miss Jean Brodie turned her into an international celebrity, and until her death Spark lived first in New York and latterly Tuscany, where she died in 2006.

Spark basically set out why she had avoided producing the sort of novel typical of the previous two centuries, that which invited the reader to sympathise with the less fortunate and acknowledge the cruelty and injustice of the world. She explains that she resisted writing such books, not because she was hard-hearted but because, in short, she thinks such fiction is a cop out, serving to segregate readers from the facts of life with which they so easily empathise.

Rather she wants a 'desegregated' literature, one that will avoid sentimental self-indulgence. Spark says she practices what she preaches, satire and irony, opening her address by pleading she is not 'a thinker by profession', but for her ideas were 'inseparable from words or from any other material that the artist works with'. She is an artist, Spark concludes, 'a sort of writing animal'.

Literature, of all the arts, is the most penetrable into the human life of the world, for the simple reason that words are our common currency. We don't instinctively, from morning to night, paint pictures to each other, or play music to each other, in order to communicate; we talk, we write to each other.

And so, when I speak of the desegregation of art I begin with the art of letters... the art of literature is a personal expression of ideas which come to influence the minds of people even at second, third and fourth hand. Literature infiltrates and should fertilize our minds. It is not a special department set aside for the entertainment and delight of the sophisticated minority. And if this is true, then ineffective literature must go.

We all know that there is a lot of inferior literature about as there are inferior and boring examples of any other art. It is easy to say bad things must go. The critics, in every field of art, are never done denouncing what they feel to be bad art. They rightly prune and cultivate, they attempt to practice good husbandry. And as we become more articulate, itinerant, knowledgeable, we are more and more agreed on what is bad. And everyone knows we have to give up what is bad – it is a banal moral precept. What is wrong, what is bad, must go...

I'm sure you all remember the silly old saying "The pen is mightier than the sword." Perhaps when swords were the weapons in current use, there was some point in the proverb. Anyway, in our time, the least of our problems is swords.

Literature, of all the arts,
is the most penetrable into the human life of the world,

But the power and influence of the creative arts is not to be belittled. I only say that the art and literature of sentiment and emotion, however beautiful in itself, however striking in its depiction of actuality, has to go. It cheats us into a sense of involvement with life and society, but in reality it is a segregated activity. In its place I advocate the arts of satire and of ridicule. And I see no other living art form for the future.

Ridicule is the only honorable weapon we have left... If someone derides me, I don't like it. But at least I can begin to understand the mentality of the mocker. And I can mock back in such a way that he might understand mine. And so there may be room for a mutual understanding. But if he slides a knife between my ribs I'm unlikely to understand anything at all any more.

I would like to see in all forms of art and letters, ranging from the most sophisticated and high achievements to the placards that the students carry about the street, a less impulsive generosity, a less indignant representation of social injustice, and a more deliberate cunning, a more derisive undermining of what is wrong. I would like to see less emotion and more intelligence in these efforts to impress our minds and hearts.

Crude invective can rouse us for a time, and perhaps only end in physical violence. Solemn appeals to out sentiments of indignation and pity are likely to succeed only for the duration of the show, of the demonstration, or the prayer meeting, or the hours of reading. Then the mood passes, it goes to the four winds and love's labor's lost. But the art of ridicule, if it is on the mark – and if it is not true on the mark it is not art at all – can penetrate to the marrow. It can leave a salutary scar. It is unnerving. It can paralyze its object...

The cult of the victim is the cult of pathos, not tragedy. The art of pathos is pathetic, simply; and it has reached a point of exhaustion, a point where not the subject matter but the art form itself is crying to heaven for vengeance. The art of protest, the art which condemns violence and suffering by pathetic depiction is

Our noble aspirations, our sympathies, our elevated feelings should not be inspired merely by visits to an art gallery

becoming a cult separated from the actions of our life. Our noble aspirations, our sympathies, our elevated feelings should not be inspired merely by visits to an art gallery, a theater, or by reading a book, but rather the rhetoric of our times should persuade us to contemplate the ridiculous nature of the reality before us, and teach us to mock it. We should know ourselves better by now than to be under the illusion that we are all essentially aspiring, affectionate, and loving creatures. We do have these qualities, but we are aggressive too.

And so when I speak of the desegregation of art I mean by this the liberation of our minds from the comfortable cells of lofty sentiment in which they are confined and never really satisfied.

To bring about a mental environment of honesty and self-knowledge, a sense of the absurd and a general looking-lively to defend ourselves from the ridiculous oppressions of our time, and above all to entertain us in the process, has become the special calling of arts and of letters.[1]

We have never until now had a government so determined to unpick the very fabric of Scottish life and make it over into something quite different

William McIlvanney
1936–

CHAIRMAN'S LECTURE AT THE SNP CONFERENCE · DUNDEE
SEPTEMBER 1987

From the 1980s onwards, Scotland's writers and artists were generally more inclined to support the SNP and independence than the electorate as a whole. The author William McIlvanney was a good example of this; from a typically working-class and therefore Labour-supporting background, by the late 1980s the experience of Thatcherism had radicalised him to the extent that voting for independence was no longer considered anathema.

William Angus McIlvanney was born on 25 November 1936 in Kilmarnock, the son of an ex-miner who had taken part in the General Strike of 1926. He was educated at Kilmarnock Academy and studied English at the University of Glasgow, and later his working-class background informed much of his broadcasting, journalism and writing, for example the novel* Docherty *in 1975, and* The Big Man *ten years later.

The annual SNP conference in October of each year usually heard from a guest speaker, and in 1987 it must have been a bit of a coup to secure McIlvanney. His novel *The Big Man* (1985) had recently depicted the masculine culture of Scotland's industrial working class and the threat posed by deindustrialisation, so in his speech – 'Stands Scotland Where It Did?' – he did not pull any punches.

Looking at it a quarter of a century later it appears somewhat overstated, with talk of Mrs Thatcher unpicking the 'fabric of Scottish life' and seemingly intent upon destroying specifically Scottish institutions (it is difficult, however, to list what these actually were). Nevertheless McIlvanney undoubtedly spoke for many Nationalists and indeed a significant chunk of the Scottish electorate.

We can all see where Scotland stands clearly enough in general terms. It has a Government it didn't vote for. It stands among closing factories and decaying industries. It is ravaged by redundancies. It has many young people for whom the prospect of a permanent job seems as distant as a mirage...

We have had bad governments in the past. We have had governments whose awareness of Scotland's problems seemed on a par with their knowledge of the other side of the moon. But we have never, in my lifetime, until now had a government whose basic principles were so utterly against the most essential traditions and aspirations of Scottish life. We have never until now had a government so determined to unpick the very fabric of Scottish life and make it over into something quite different. We have never had a government so glibly convinced of its own rightness that it demands that one of the oldest nations in Europe should give itself a shake and change utterly its sense of itself.

We have had bad governments in the past.

Under this Government it is not only the quality of our individual lives that is threatened. It is our communal sense of our own identity. For this government is out to change it. The complex traditions and attitudes and ways of thought that have emerged from the Scottish people's long argument with their own experience – these things are not to be pushed aside. In favour of what? The abacus morality of monetarism? Henryson, Dunbar, Hume, Burns, the ILP, John Maclean, Hugh MacDiarmid – these are to be drowned in a puddle?

For Margaret Thatcher is not just a perpetrator of bad policies. She is a cultural vandal. She takes the axe of her own simplicity to the complexities of Scottish life. She has no understanding of the hard-earned traditions she is destroying. And if we allow her to continue, she will remove from the word 'Scotland' any meaning other than the geographical.

At such a time, we should at least consider what it is we are in danger of losing. What is distinctive about the word 'Scottish'? What should we be losing? What is Scotland?

...The Scots remain Scottish not principally because of the Gaelic bards or the clan system or because Mary Queen of Scots and Bonnie Prince Charlie were briefly and disastrously among us – but because of the characteristic ways we found of responding to the industrialisation of our country.

We are Scottish because our history has been a distinctive struggle with serious issues the woman in Downing Street doesn't seem to know exist. Scottish history has been for centuries engaged on serious business. But it's obviously not Mrs Thatcher's business. Her type of business is the kind you put a name to and float on the stock market. Ours has been about human matters, like how to go about achieving a just society...

Will we allow that country and that culture to be hijacked by a woman who keeps her intelligence in her purse?

I hope not. I hope we will refuse to go where she is trying to force us to go, with the blunderbuss of her economic policies held to our head. I hope we have the courage to remove ourselves, at least some distance, from the bullying shallowness of her philosophy. I hope we have the wisdom to return to prospecting our own traditions once again...

If we wish to remain Scottish, we will honour that tradition. If we wish to remain Scottish, we will reject from the root the fundamental precepts of the present government in Westminster. If we wish to remain Scottish, we will refuse to be coerced into measuring the worth of one another on the Dow Scale. If we wish to remain Scottish, we will have contempt for judging a man by how much money is in his wallet or a woman by the cheques she writes.

We need to measure people? Do we? We need to judge performance? Do we? We need to assess significant contribution to society? All right, we can do that. But if we wish to remain Scottish, we won't use a system based on some crude scale of economic weights and measures: let's see how much his pockets weigh. We won't measure the floor-space of his house. We won't call in an estate agent to evaluate his acreage. We won't phone his bank manager.

No, we'll use another system – a system long established here; a system developed from the experience and the pain and the long thought and the deep humanity of the Scottish people. And that's not a hard system to apply. Its principles are simple enough. You want a measurement of people? Then, if you wish to remain Scottish, here it is. You will measure them by the extent of their understanding, by the width of their compassion, by the depth of their concern and by the size of their humanity.

There's a *real* system for you. And it has never been under greater threat than it's under now. For this government is trying to convert us, is trying to convert this nation, to another system. The conversion to decimalisation? You found that confusing? Wait till this one hits you. This government is trying to convert our very way of life, the way we think, into a contradiction of itself...

Under this Government it is not only the quality of our individual lives that is threatened. It is our communal sense of our own identity.

I honestly believe that time is running out for us if we are to try and realise anything like our potential as a people who have learned to value the human above the material, who have persistently refused to give up our sense of our own identity. The traditions we have proudly inherited are, for the moment, still ours. But that condition carries no guarantee. If you want to hold on to good traditions, you must re-earn the possession of them. Tradition doesn't survive in a vacuum – it survives on living re-commitment. Put it in the deep-freeze and it doesn't keep...

Stands Scotland where it did? Just about, but not for much longer. A crisis-point has arrived. We will either become more ourselves or less ourselves in the next few years. We cannot much longer maintain the ambiguity of our present situation: that of a people who retain a strong sense of themselves as a nation yet have no effective structure of government within which to develop and give expression to that sense...

If there is one incontrovertible argument in favour of some kind of devolved power for Scotland, this is it. If a country, a group of people recognisably distinctive in its characteristics and aspirations, finds its democratically arrived-at will thwarted by the system of government under which it lives, it should seek to change that system. It must seek to inhabit a political context where that will is no longer paralysed. For Scotland, this can only mean some kind of power structure separate from Westminster.[1]

The lesson of Dundee for all of us,
and certainly for me,
is never, never, never, never again.

Norman Willis
1933–

SPEECH TO TRADES UNION CONGRESS · BOURNEMOUTH
6 SEPTEMBER 1988

Norman Willis's stewardship of the once mighty Trades Union Congress for almost a decade from 1984 coincided with a period of considerable change for the British trade union movement. Membership fell as the UK economy deindustrialised, while Conservative governments led by Margaret Thatcher passed Bill after Bill designed to limit the powers of trade unions.

Despite that unpromising context, in the autumn of 1987 the Scottish Development Agency announced, following 18 months of secret negotiations, that the Ford Motor Company had agreed to build a £40 million components factory in Dundee, employing up to 950 people. But when several unions failed to agree a single-union deal, Ford pulled out.

Mrs Thatcher was quick to allocate blame. 'What I do not understand is that, in this modern age, some of the trade unions are more concerned with demarcation disputes, restrictive practices and sectional interests than jobs for their fellow citizens.'[1] It was a PR disaster for organised trade unionism in the UK, and Willis articulated his frustration at the 1988 TUC conference in Bournemouth, namechecking a series of high-profile trade unionists of the period.

Norman David Willis was born in 1933 in Ashford, Surrey, and educated at Ashford County Grammar School and Oriel College, Oxford. He worked for the Transport and General Workers' Union between 1949–70, and in 1974 became assistant general secretary of the Trades Union Congress, taking over the reins in 1984 for the next nine years.

That was not as bad as I expected, actually! You see, a dream nearly came true. I dreamed that Gavin Laird had rushed to the rostrum and said, "Norman, I'll do it differently next time." And then Ron Todd followed him and said, "Norman, trust Gavin on this one". And then I dreamed that John Edmonds, Bill Jordan and Ken Gill said, "I refuse to give an interview on this issue." And then I dreamed there was a letter from Tony Benn, saying, "Norman, when I accused you of going to Detroit on your knees to beg for jobs from a multinational, I'd have said exactly the same if those jobs had been coming to my own constituency." And then, President, your speech woke me up.

There has been a bit of sharp action replay of the respective arguments which took place at the TUC. I have plenty of criticisms of Ford Electronic. I think that it did create a difficult position by insisting on secrecy until the deal was signed. That was an issue, the idea of "do the deal or no deal". It badly underestimated the attachment of Ford unions and workers to the terms of the national agreement. That would be a matter for all-round agreement between us all. And it paid insufficient regard to the fact that Dundee would be seen as national agreement busting. Then it pulled out, surprisingly and suddenly and, from what was said to me, most unexpectedly. It may well have had other reasons for the pull out. The original decision to locate in Dundee was always finely balanced, and that was always part of the problem and the challenge.

But I do not think that we can dodge, and I did not see people expecting to be able to dodge, a measure of responsibility across the board for a major setback.

But I do not think that we can dodge, and I did not see people expecting to be able to dodge, a measure of responsibility across the board for a major setback. The reactions of all good trade unionists – and I have said in earlier interviews that I did not see a catalogue of beasts and saints involved in that discussion – except those in Spain where there are some very good trade unionists – must have been feelings of great disappointment. I do not think that any of us have any option but to recognise that, at least in part, it is our responsibility to prevent it happening again.

Single union agreements, Greenfield sites, managements recognising no union at all, all that has to be faced. And you will find no rose gardens in the notification procedure of the SRB report, although I see the chance to do a bit of cultivating of good relationships and much needed jobs. So my dream for the future is that we learn the lessons and we fact the realities – as I think many of us have. That is the way to get support from the public, of course, because we need it in all those areas, and to avoid the disappointment of the unemployed. We need investment. A foot in the door is always better than a kick in the teeth. Jimmy said it, Ron said it, it ran through everything. The lesson of Dundee for all of us, and certainly for me, is never, never, never, never again.[2]

To Scotland, Thatcherism is an alien set of concepts and values

Jim Sillars
1937–

MAIDEN SPEECH IN THE HOUSE OF COMMONS · LONDON
23 NOVEMBER 1988

In the 1970s Jim Sillars was, at first, a rising star on the Labour back benches and, later, one of only two MPs representing the breakaway Scottish Labour Party. Fiery, articulate and a passionate advocate of, at various points in his career, the Union, devolution and finally independence, Sillars had the rare ability of being able to carry people along on the strength of his rhetoric, including a young Alex Salmond.

But after 1979 Sillars found himself outside the House of Commons, and although influential within the SNP (which he joined in the early 1980s), he lacked a national platform. In 1988, however, the former Scottish Secretary Bruce Millan quit Parliament to become a European Commissioner and Sillars stood in the resulting by-election in Glasgow Govan. Following a memorable campaign the SNP emerged triumphant, with Sillars winning on a swing of more than 33 per cent from Labour.

James (Jim) Sillars was born in 1937, the son of an Ayr railwayman. After leaving school he worked as a fireman and was also active in his trade union, eventually winning the Labour nomination in the 1970 South Ayrshire by-election, which he won. Frustrated by his party's lack of enthusiasm for devolution, he established the Scottish Labour Party in 1976, which resulted in him losing his seat in 1979. In 1988 Sillars re-entered Parliament as an SNP MP, by which point he had also married fellow Nationalist politician Margo MacDonald. He lost his seat in 1992 and spent the rest of his career in business and as a newspaper columnist.

Nationalists hoped this victory would represent the beginning of a long-awaited revival for the SNP, and some of this spirit is evident from Sillars' maiden speech (in fact his second), also infused with references to Mrs Thatcher, whom he believed was 'malicious, wicked and quite evil'.[1] The speech was repeatedly interrupted – unusual for a maiden contribution – by Conservative and Labour MPs. When Sillars quoted Robert Burns, for example, the Colne Valley MP Graham Riddick shouted 'speak English'. And when Sillars terms this 'quasi racist', the Cunninghame North MP Brian Wilson yelled 'stupid'. The presence of an additional Nationalist MP in the House of Commons had obviously ruffled a few feathers.

To Scotland, Thatcherism is an alien set of concepts and values. It is a philosophy driven by greed and self-interest, and it is a great tragedy for the people of England that it seems to have taken such root in the south-east, where so much of the political power now lies. I hope—it is a genuine hope—that the Labour party in England will reassess the attitudes that it has adopted in the past four or five years and understand that it has no hope of gaining Tory votes in the south-east of England by advocating a watered down form of Toryism. If Socialism is to advance, in the south-east of England and elsewhere, it must be by the moral conversion of people to its principles. That is the only hope for the Labour party.

To Scotland, Thatcherism is an alien set of concepts and values.

Scotland rejects the values of Thatcherism because our country has a philosophy of egalitarianism. Unlike the Prime Minister, we also believe in the community. We believe that people have a responsibility to the community but also that the community has a responsibility to people. That is perhaps best summed up in the words of Robert Burns:

Then gently scan your brother man,
Still gentler sister woman;
Tho' they may gang a Kennin wrang,
To step aside is human.

... We Scots are in this place only temporarily. Given that we have an entirely different set of values from those of the Prime Minister and her acolytes—a superior set of values—[Interruption.] It is quite easily proven. There is no way that the Scottish community would ever sit back and let young people be treated as they are at present in YTS [Youth Training Scheme] and outside it. The Scottish people would never allow their education system to be attacked and broken up as the Government intend. Our values are better than the values of the Prime Minister, and the proof is that we have a much better society than the society that she has managed to create down here...

Let me deal with the longer term. First, I place on record my party's position on Scottish independence in the European Community. The self-styled governor-general of Scotland—Governor-General Rifkind—told us in a frenetic speech at a Tory party seminar the other day that Scotland is much more influential and politically powerful with the United Kingdom representing its interests in the Community. I do not think that he can tell that to the folk of the highlands and islands who are trying to extricate themselves from a situation that he should never have allowed to arise.

There is a fundamental difference between what Scotland is and what

Scotland would be if it were independent within the Community. The Secretary of State for Scotland is a placeman. He has no power base in the Tory party in Scotland and he does not command his position from his own power base. Unlike the Home Secretary and one or two other folk in the Cabinet, the Secretary of State for Scotland does not represent a power base inside the Tory party that even the Prime Minister cannot overlook. He is a placeman and he has no power of veto. He can resign only if he does not like certain policies, only to be replaced by the Under-Secretary of State—the chap sitting next to him—who would be much more congenial company for the Prime Minister...

Scotland rejects the values of Thatcherism because our country has a philosophy of egalitarianism.

We should have as much power over our domestic affairs as this Government have over us now. A Scottish Government within the European Community would exercise full control at home. There would be no return to private landlords. No old folks would go cold. No young folk would be cheated on YTS. There would be no privatisation of electricity and the other utilities. There would be no privatisation of the National Health Service. There would be no student loans, and there would be no attack on Scottish education institutions and Scottish universities. In a Scotland that was independent within Europe we should shape our own lives and our social and economic policies at home...

After Govan, the debate has started for real in Scotland. After what happened in 1979, many people thought that Scottish nationalism had reached its peak. It took a long time for the Scottish people to recover from the effects of 1979, but Govan has put that issue clearly back on the agenda...There is a fundamental difference between the Scottish National party—and the other non-Unionist parties, I was going to say, but that is not correct because the Labour party is still a Unionist party. The big difference between the Labour party, the Democrats and our party is that they keep telling the Scottish people what they cannot do. We keep telling the Scottish people what they can do.

I end by quoting from Professor Smout's book, "A Century of the Scottish People." He says: "by the exercise of political will, the people hold their own future in their own hands, and in the last analysis, no one can be blamed for our predicament but ourselves." We can be blamed for our predicament immediately after 1979. We did not do it last time. The Scottish people will do it next time.[2]

You, the people of Glasgow, pledged that you would not relax until I was free to receive this honour in person.

Nelson Mandela
1918–

SPEECH ON BEING GRANTED FREEDOM OF THE CITY
GEORGE SQUARE · GLASGOW
9 OCTOBER 1993

Mandela arrived in Glasgow. Not yet the elected president of South Africa following decades in captivity, he was to receive the Freedom of the City 12 years after it was actually granted by Glasgow (which also named a street after him). That honour, bestowed while he and his ANC comrades were serving life sentences on Robben Island, had never been forgotten by Mandela.

Nelson Rolihlahla Mandela was born in 1918 in Mvezo, Transkei. He became actively involved in the anti-Apartheid movement in his 20s and joined the African National Congress in 1943. For 20 years, he directed a campaign of defiance against the South African government but was arrested in 1962 and imprisoned for the next 27 years. Released in 1990, Mandela served as the first president of South Africa from 1994–99.

Few who met or saw Mandela in Glasgow over the course of a few wet and windy days were immune from his spell. In a scene that was to be repeated time and again across the city, he first arrived at Glasgow's Hilton Hotel from the airport, bringing the place to a virtual standstill. The following day a carnival atmosphere gripped George Square as tens of thousand gathered to see him despite torrential rain.

Moments later, to the delight of the crowd, Mandela could be seen shimmying to a song by the South African singer Mara Louw, who had joined him onstage. It demonstrated, above all, his human touch, an informal charisma that enthused not only veteran anti-Apartheid campaigners, but thousands of ordinary Scots keen to witness a little bit of history.

It is a special privilege to be a guest of this great city of Glasgow, it will always enjoy a distinguished place in the records of the international campaign against apartheid. The people of Glasgow in 1981 were the first in the world to confer on me the freedom of the city at a time when I and my comrades in the ANC were imprisoned on Robben Island, serving life sentences which, in apartheid South Africa, meant imprisonment until death.

Whilst we were physically denied our freedom in the country of our birth, a city, 6,000 miles away, and as renowned as Glasgow, refused to accept the legitimacy of the apartheid system and declared us to be free, and in a real sense we were free, because however cruel the treatment meted out to us in prison, we never lost sight of the vision of the youth of Africa as enshrined in our freedom charter.

a city, 6,000 miles away... refused to accept the legitimacy of the apartheid system and declared us to be free...

The city of Glasgow in granting us the freedom of the city... took upon itself a very clear obligation: it resolved to do everything possible to secure our freedom from the prisons of apartheid. It took up our plight in Britain and internationally... You, the people of Glasgow, pledged that you would not relax until I was free to receive this honour in person. I am deeply grateful to you and the anti-apartheid movement in Scotland for all your efforts to this end...

I hope that you will also take home another message; it's a simple message: today, I and the majority of our people still don't enjoy the most precious freedom, the right to vote. Over the past three-and-a-half years the African National Congress has spared no effort to secure a negotiated settlement which will lead to a genuine end to apartheid, and a new united non-racial, non-sexist and democratic South Africa. This prospect is now clearly on the horizon. April 27 1994 has been set as the date for South Africa's first non-racial election...

However, the road ahead won't be easy. Unprecedented violence has been unleashed in our country by those determined to prevent a democratic change. There are others who cling to the old order or yearn for ethnic privilege. They fear the demonstrated will of our people. Our message today is clear: let democracy triumph; we need your help to make sure that the elections take place as agreed and that they are genuinely free and fair... nobody must underestimate the threat, but I want to assure you that there is no reason for pessimism.

The democratic forces in our country are too powerful to be diverted from

Our message today is clear: let democracy triumph.

their main course of ending our minority role in our country... we have put forward the concept of a government of national unity in which we have declared that all political parties which poll more than five per cent of the total votes cast in an election will be invited to serve in government. We will respect a majority rule and will not allow small parties to undermine the process of redistribution of opportunities to the people of South Africa... the 85 per cent of our population who are denied opportunities, who cannot vote, who can't share in the resources of our country, that is our top priority.

It's for this reason that we respect, admire and, above all, love you all.

But we are not just concerned with blacks, we are building a South Africa where all South Africans should have confidence in their own people, in themselves, and in their country, who should regard themselves as part and parcel of this great transformation. And fortunately we have the men and women even in unexpected quarters, even among those quarters who today have formed the so-called Freedom Alliance, who realise that violence is not in the interest of even their own community...

... but as far as this gathering is concerned I wanted to tell you that this is for me an unforgettable occasion, a moment I will never forget. I will always look back to this occasion with fond memories because I now have the opportunity to thank directly the men and women who have taken interest in the events that have taken place 6,000 miles away, these are the men and women who have made it possible for my comrades and I, both inside prison as well as in exile, to come back to their country to help to build a new South Africa. It's for this reason that we respect, admire and, above all, love you all.[1]

...please give us the opportunity to serve our country. That is all we ask.

John Smith
1938–94

SPEECH AT A EUROPEAN GALA DINNER · LONDON

11 MAY 1994

John Smith's final speech only became famous because of his premature death just hours after he delivered it. Paying tribute in the House of Commons the following day, the acting Labour leader Margaret Beckett, recalled the setting. 'He was in fine fettle and in high spirits', she said. 'He spoke not from a text but from notes, and when he sat down I congratulated him especially on his final sentence – spoken, as it was, off the cuff and from the heart. They were almost the last words I heard him say. He looked at the assembled gathering, and he said: "The opportunity to serve our country – that is all we ask." Let it stand as his epitaph.'

John Smith was born in 1938. After graduating from Glasgow University he worked as a lawyer before entering Parliament in 1970. He was the Secretary of State for Trade from 1978–79, and then Shadow Chancellor of the Exchequer under Neil Kinnock from 1987–92. He was elected leader of the Labour Party following Kinnock's resignation, but died just two years later.

For Brian Brivati, who edited a volume of Smith's speeches after his death, this one 'reflected the growing consensus that Labour would win the general election', not just Smith's 'tone', but 'the number of business people in the audience'. 'Here is the final political statement from a man ready for the top job in British politics,' wrote Brivati, 'its themes, echoed throughout this volume, were of social justice, European social democracy and the need for active government.'

I think there is a great hunger amongst our people. There is a great hunger amongst our people for a return to politics of conviction and idealism. The Thatcher years proved that it was not possible for people to be successful and content simply by being successful on their own part because there were so many that had not been successful and the menace of high unemployment still threatens our society. The mission of the Labour Party must be to get Britain back to work, to get the people who are unemployed now employed in the useful work that needs to be done in building houses for people without homes, in building a new transport infrastructure for this country, and starting regional development on a scale that has never been attempted properly in this country, bringing not only power but economic success back to every region in this country, empowering industry and local authorities by a participating Government, a partnership Government that says that, if you are prepared to commit yourself to the success of your country, your Government will be behind you. That applies at home and it applies abroad – a Government that supports British industry when it fights for orders abroad, supports the investment in technology and science which is desperately needed in our country...

There is a great hunger amongst our people for a return to politics of conviction and idealism.

But it must not be a Government which imagines that it can decide everything for business or decide everything for people. It is above all an enabling Government. A Government which seeks to share power, to enable power, to give them the chance to give of their best. I think that is the style of modern society and it ought to be the style of modern Government. I think that Government has to insist on certain important qualifications to business effort. It must say to all our businesses and all our people, you must respect the environment in which we live. You must respect the social rights of our people, but you run your own business. You run them well and you run them successfully and we will be happy

But it must not be a Government which imagines that it can decide everything for business or decide everything for people.

about that. But it will be in your interest to respect our environment and to respect our social rights and to give power to your people, and to clever and intelligent people working in your companies and in your industries. I think that is the message that Britain wants to hear. But there is, perhaps, the most important message of all: no society, no country can ever survive to be successful without a profound sense of social justice and unless we bring social justice back to this country, this country cannot be healthy and cannot be successful.

When I go campaigning round this country and I meet the old age pensioners who are having to pay the VAT on fuel, I see the poor people who are struggling to make ends meet. One understands what social justice means when I meet the people who are dependent on state education for the future of their children, when I meet the vast majority of the people of this country who depend on the National Health Service for the health of their families, and they know – don't they know! – what is happening to our NHS. Ministers can produce statistic after statistic but our people who are connected to the Health Service from the moment they are born until the moment that many of them die, know the truth about our National Health Service and they know one wonderful truth about the Labour Party. If the Labour Party did nothing else in all its history, to have founded the National Health Service and lifted the care and worry from our people and founded a Health Service which was only to do with human need and not to do with money and access, or to do with privilege or anything else, they would know that the Labour Party had achieved a great virtue. But now we have to come back and restore it once again. So when you sum up all the issues we have in this country – social justice, economic justice, conquering unemployment, giving our young people the opportunities they ought to have in modern Europe and a modern world, it adds up to a stunning case for Labour.

There is something fundamental happening in this country now.

I am glad to say that our Party has been reinvigorated in recent years. This is now a confident Labour Party that you see meeting here tonight and can I say to those of our guests who may not be totally committed to our case, thank you for coming to us and thank you for listening to our case tonight. I think we have a strong, powerful and persuasive case. It is one which will be assisted by your contributions here tonight. It is one, I can tell you, which will be persisted in. Because this is a Labour Party that is determined to win. We believe in the idealism of our cause but we also believe it is not enough to be idle idealists who think we should just announce policies and hope that somehow people will come to them. We have to go out, argue fiercely, everywhere and in every town and hamlet and part of this country.

There is something fundamental happening in this country now. I suppose the academics would call it a circular shift in political attitudes. But we all know that it is happening. People who for years have been Conservatives have lost faith and many people who sat on the edge of British politics have realised there is only one way forward for this country: a Government with purpose, pragmatism and economic determination and for social justice. I believe that everything is moving our way. We must never be complacent and must never take anything for granted but I believe the signs are set fairer for the Labour Party than they have been for a very long time.

Thank you all very much for coming here tonight and helping us perhaps partly to achieve that objective. We will do our best to reward your faith in us but please give us the opportunity to serve our country. That is all we ask.'

The people have lost a friend – someone who was on their side and they knew it.

Donald Dewar
1937–2000

SPEECH AT JOHN SMITH'S FUNERAL · CLUNY PARISH CHURCH · EDINBURGH
19 MAY 1994

On the evening of 11 May 1994 the Labour Party leader John Smith made a speech at a fundraising dinner at the Park Lane Hotel, which ended with the line: 'The opportunity to serve our country – that is all we ask.' The following morning, while in his Barbican flat, Smith suffered a massive heart attack, from which he died around an hour later at Saint Bartholomew's Hospital.

Donald Campbell Dewar was born in Glasgow, and studied at the city's university before practicing as a solicitor. He entered Parliament in 1966 as the MP for Aberdeen South but lost his seat four years later. He did not rejoin the House of Commons until 1978, when he won the Glasgow Garscadden by-election. Dewar served as, successively, Shadow Scottish Secretary, Shadow Social Security Secretary, and finally Labour Chief Whip until becoming Secretary of State for Scotland in 1997. He died, in office as First Minister, in 2000.

Stunned MPs paid tribute in the House of Commons. Prime Minister John Major said he and Smith 'would share a drink: sometimes tea, sometimes not tea', while Margaret Beckett, who became acting Labour leader, ended her comments with Smith's own 'opportunity to serve' line from the previous evening. Many MPs were said to be in tears. On 20 May 1994 Smith's funeral was held at Cluny Parish Church in Edinburgh (although he was later buried privately on the island of Iona), attended by 900 people (with 3,000 more lining the streets).

His close friend Donald Dewar acted as one of the pallbearers and was also called upon to give the last of three eulogies. 'Donald rose to the occasion,' wrote Mark Stuart in a biography of Smith, 'stressing John's consistency of purpose, and the face that his principles lasted throughout his life, as well as raising a laugh or two in the audience.'[1] Characteristically, Dewar left preparation to the last minute. The night before the funeral, Elizabeth Munro, a mutual friend, heard him rehearsing the speech at 3 a.m. The ceremony was televised, so millions of people beyond the church witnessed Dewar pay emotional tribute to his friend, as well as colleague, John Smith.

A journalist talking to me recently chose to decry John's consistency as though it were a fault. He was indeed a man consistent of purpose but this was a strength. His principles lasted throughout his life.

At a time of loss, you remember and remember. The other day someone produced the Glasgow University Handbook of 1959. In it John, aged 21, writing on behalf of the Labour Club, proclaimed that "in this Club we think it valuable occasionally to indulge in political activities such as canvassing."

Even in my most Presbyterian moments I would not describe canvassing as an indulgence – a penance perhaps, never an indulgence. Given his work rate then and through the years it must have been a case of breaking the bad news gently.

More importantly, in that article John set out what he described as his "credo". He believed that "the opportunity of each individual to lead a complete and civilised life should be as equal as far as is possible to that of his neighbour" and there followed a plea for a more just distribution of material wealth. He laid out then principles which he argued right to the end.

He would often tell me of individual problems he came across in the constituency or on the stump – cases where the system presses sorely on families already struggling to cope with hard times. John's anger and frustration was something you could almost touch.

He knew that poverty and inequality killed life chances: that for too many failure became a self-fulfilling prophecy.

He knew that poverty and inequality killed life chances: that for too many failure became a self-fulfilling prophecy. John was not interested in the trappings of power. He wanted power not for what it did for him, but for what it might allow him to do for others. There were great causes straddling the years for which, whatever the price, he stood his ground. He was consistent.

I remember John working his guts out in student days to elect Albert Lithuli, Rector of the University at a time when the horror of apartheid was not a universal student cause. We elected Lithuli who then symbolised the struggle in South Africa and could not take office as Rector because of prison bars. I remember John's joy when Mandela was freed and freely elected. I do not object to such consistency of principle and purpose.

There was the need for a positive and constructive approach to Europe, which led John to defy the Whips as a young backbencher – just one example of the courage that marked and made his career.

There was his determination that power should not be a monopoly hoarded in Whitehall and Westminster. It was a principle relevant to every part of this kingdom, but with a special significance for Scotland and for John who made his Parliamentary reputation fighting the Scotland Act onto the Statute Book in 1978. It was this unfinished business to which he intended to return.

There will be many – some here today – who thought he was wrong in these views, but who could deny the sincerity, the tenacity and the true spirit of the man. Consistency was at the core of him. Politics a series of practical problems to be overcome. Square, determined, sometimes thrawn, always probing, pushing for a way forward.

His life and his work, his reassuring presence, were a standing reproach to the easy cynicism that brands politics as a dishonest game. He was, of course, consistent in friendship. Politicians of real stature gather around them friends who are prepared to fight for them even when they are in error. John had that ability. He did not command, he earned respect. I was proud to be one of his friends.

I will remember the good times. Those who saw John as douce, dark suited and safe knew not the man. He could start a party in any empty room – and often did – filling it with good cheer, Gaelic songs and argument. He enjoyed people and loyalty was a prime virtue, and never with John a one-way process. He would walk through walls to help a friend – I can bear witness to that. John was always himself. He was genuine through and through. He told the truth.

What has been striking over the last dark week has not been the tributes of the great and the good – handsome as they have been – but the sadness, the dismay, the sense of loss across the range of our community. The people have lost a friend – someone who was on their side and they knew it.[2]

They may take our lives, but they'll never take our freedom.

Sir William Wallace 1270s–1305

FICTIONAL BATTLE SPEECH · FROM THE FILM *Braveheart*

1995

The Scottish patriot William Wallace was known for his motivational rhetoric, snippets of which survive. In a speech before the Battle of Stirling Bridge in 1297, for example, he said: 'We come here with no peaceful intent, but ready for battle, determined to avenge our wrongs and set our country free. Let your masters come and attack us: we are ready to meet them beard to beard.'

And when Randall Wallace set about adapting Blind Harry's epic poem, *The Actes and Deidis of the Illustre and Vallyeant Campioun Schir William Wallace*, for the big screen, he included a scene in which Sir William rouses the Scots against the English from horseback. The resulting 1995 film, directed by and starring Mel Gibson, was an international hit, nominated for ten Academy Awards and winning five.

The speech takes place before the Battle of Stirling Bridge in 1297, when Wallace sealed his reputation by successfully repelling the English invaders. But unlike that quoted above, this one is entirely fictional.

Sir William Wallace was born in Elderslie in Renfrewshire into a gentry family. He emerged during the rebellion against English rule in May 1297 when he attacked the town of Lanark, killing an English sheriff. Wallace was knighted and appointed 'guardian of the kingdom', but when the English rallied, the Scots were defeated at Falkirk in July 1298. Wallace escaped to France and after returning to Scotland was charged with treason and executed in London in 1305.

William: For presenting yourselves on this battlefield, I give you thanks.

Lochlan: This is our army. To join it you give homage.

William: I give homage to Scotland. And if this is your army, why does it go?

Tall soldier: We didn't come here to fight for them.

Short soldier: Home. The English are too many.

Wallace: Sons of Scotland, I am William Wallace.

Young soldier: William Wallace is seven feet tall.

Wallace: Yes, I've heard. Kills men by the hundreds, and if he were here he'd consume the English with fireballs from his eyes and bolts of lightning from his arse. I AM William Wallace. And I see a whole army of my countrymen here in defiance of tyranny. You have come to fight as free men, and free men you are. What would you do without freedom? Will you fight?

I see a whole army of my countrymen here in defiance of tyranny.

Veteran soldier: Fight? Against that? No, we will run; and we will live.

Wallace: Aye, fight and you may die. Run and you'll live – at least a while. And dying in your beds many years from now, would you be willing to trade all the days from this day to that for one chance, just one chance to come back here and tell our enemies that they may take our lives, but they'll never take our freedom!

Wallace and Soldiers: Alba gu bra! (Scotland forever!)[1]

The Scottish Parliament, which adjourned on 25 March 1707, is hereby reconvened.

Winnie Ewing 1929–

OPENING SPEECH IN THE 'RECONVENED' SCOTTISH PARLIAMENT
EDINBURGH
12 MAY 1999

So many hopes and aspirations had been invested in the creation of a devolved Scottish Parliament that its opening day warranted a fine speech. The veteran Nationalist Winnie Ewing, the victor of the sensational 1967 Hamilton by-election, took the chair as the oldest elected member. She had promised Robert McIntyre, the SNP's first ever MP, that if ever she got the chance to be in the new Scottish Parliament she would draw attention to the fact that the old parliament had never been abolished, merely adjourned.

Of course, historians quibbled that the old Scots parliament was not being reconvened at all, but it did not really matter; Ewing had caught the mood of the moment, and as she rightly observed in her memoirs, it was 'probably the most important and historic speech' she ever made. The following day's *Scotsman* used Ewing's 'hereby reconvened' quote as its headline, while the journalist Ruth Wishart wrote of her speech: 'If she never says another word she has said enough.'

Winifred Margaret Ewing was born in 1929 and worked as a lawyer before taking Scottish (and British) politics by storm on winning the Hamilton by-election in 1967, only the second SNP MP to be returned to the House of Commons. Throughout a long and high-profile career, Ewing also represented Moray and Nairn in Parliament, and the Highlands and Islands region in the European Parliament. She was an MSP for the first term of the new Scottish Parliament, and also president of the SNP from 1987–2005.

I have the opportunity to make a short speech and I want to begin with the words that I have always wanted either to say or to hear someone else say: the Scottish Parliament, which adjourned on 25 March 1707, is hereby reconvened (applause). I could not say those words until all members had been sworn and the Parliament really had been convened.

This is an historic day and, after a long time in politics, I am aware that we owe a debt to many who are not here, who did not live to see the promised land. I would like to mention a few people from across the parties: Arthur Donaldson,

Robert McIntyre, Alick Buchanan-Smith, Johnny Bannerman, Emrys Hughes, John Mackintosh and John Smith – today is the fifth anniversary of his death. I would also like to mention my colleague Allan Macartney, who so nearly lived to see the day. There are many others, but I have been able to mention only the people who have been my friends. Many people are named in the history books; many are not, but all of them have made this moment in history possible. I give my thanks to every one of them...

I have several practical and sincere hopes for the Parliament. The first is that

All of us here can make it work – and make it a showpiece of modern democracy.

we try to follow the more consensual style of the European Parliament and say goodbye to the badgering and backbiting that one associates with Westminster. Secondly, in the House of Commons, I found that there was a Speaker's tradition of being fair to minorities. I am an expert in being a minority – I was alone in the House of Commons for three years and alone in the European Parliament for 19 years – but we are all minorities now, and I hope that the Presiding Officer, whoever that may be, will be fair to each and every one of us.

My next hope is that this Parliament, by its mere existence, will create better relations with England, Wales and Northern Ireland, and I believe that to be in the hearts of the peoples of all of those countries. My last practical hope is that everyone who was born in Scotland, some of whom, like me, could not help it, and everyone who chose Scotland as their country, will live in harmony together, enjoying our cultures but remaining loyal to their own.

On behalf of my party, I pledge to make this Parliament work. All of us here can make it work – and make it a showpiece of modern democracy. It is no secret that, to members of the Scottish National Party, this Parliament is not quite the fulfilment of our dream, but it is a Parliament we can build a dream on. Our dream is for Scotland to be as sovereign as Denmark, Finland or Austria-no more, no less. However, we know that that dream can come true only when there is total consensus among the people of Scotland, and we accept that.

I will end by quoting from the debate of 1707. I have chosen a passage by Lord Belhaven, who was an opponent of the treaty:

> Show me a spurious patriot, a bombastic fire-eater, and I will show you a rascal. Show me a man who loves all countries equally with his own and I will show you a man entirely deficient of a sense of proportion. But show me a man who respects the rights of all nations while ready to defend the rights of his own against them all and I will show you a man who is both a nationalist and an internationalist.

It was said that 1707 was the end of an auld sang. All of us here can begin to write together a new Scottish song, and I urge all of you to sing it in harmony – fortissimo (applause).

Scattered throughout South Africa are Scottish names that attest to the relationship between our peoples...

Thabo Mbeki
1942–

SPEECH TO THE SCOTTISH PARLIAMENT · EDINBURGH

13 JUNE 2001

The visit of the South African president Thabo Mbeki to Scotland was largely the brainchild of Sir David Steel, the Scottish Parliament's first Presiding Officer. He had grown up partly in colonial Kenya and had campaigned against Apartheid in South Africa since his student days. Having Mbeki address Scotland's new devolved Parliament, for which Steel had also campaigned, was personally as well as politically satisfying.

Mbeki was, of course, a controversial figure, not least because of his unorthodox views on HIV/AIDS, but nevertheless he was given the full works. Having flown into Scotland that morning as part of a four-day State Visit to the UK, the President, accompanied by HRH the Duke of York, arrived at the Mound in Edinburgh and was greeted by the city's Lord Provost Eric Milligan.

Thabo Mvuyelwa Mbeki was born in Transkei in 1942, the son of a prominent anti-Apartheid activist. He joined the African National Congress (ANC) Youth League in 1956 and studied economics in the UK. Nelson Mandela appointed Mbeki deputy president in 1994 and he became South Africa's second president in 1999. He resigned nine years later at the request of the ANC.

MSPs, guests and a packed public gallery gave Mbeki a rousing welcome as he entered the Church of Scotland's Assembly Hall. In a short introduction, Sir David said his links with the President went back more than two decades, and Mbeki then treated Parliamentarians to the history of Scottish-South African links and latterly his hope the 21st century would be the 'African century'.

Scattered throughout South Africa are Scottish names that attest to the relationship between our peoples, in an earlier epoch. For example, many of the roads through our world-famous mountain passes were designed and constructed by a Scot, Andrew Geddes Baines, more than a century and a half ago.

Yet the impact of Scotland on South Africa goes far deeper than simply the physical manifestations of a Scottish presence. When in 1795, the London

Missionary Society started its work in South Africa, no one would have anticipated that it would contribute indelibly to a non-racial tradition in South Africa which would finally come to fruition with our 1993 and 1996 constitutions...

Despite the best resolve of our people, our achievements have not been without problems and setbacks.

In more recent years, the Scottish link was more directly political, and I want specially to recall the very influential role of the Scottish Anti-Apartheid Movement, now called Action for Southern Africa, Scotland (ACTSA, Scotland), which upheld Scotland's tradition of commitment to our liberty. We shall not forget the pioneering role played by Aberdeen when the city imposed sanctions against apartheid South Africa as early as 1964...

Thanks, among other things, to the support of the Scottish people, by 1994 we were able to hold our first democratic elections. In 1996 a democratically elected Assembly drew up our final Constitution of which we are justly proud. Our Bill of Rights entrenches all the freedoms that are an essential part of any genuine democracy.

The overwhelming majority of MPs who entered Parliament in 1994 had never voted before. Our own experience of democracy was restricted to democratic practices developed and entrenched within the liberation movement and struggle. Yet, in the past seven years we have held two national and two local government elections which have all been characterised by robust political engagement, debate and contestation. Moreover they have all been free and fair...

Despite the best resolve of our people, our achievements have not been without problems and setbacks. Nevertheless, we can never forget that these achievements were rendered possible, to a great degree through the support from the international community, friendly governments, institutions and political parties, not least among which has been the support from people and organisations in Scotland.

As we enter the 21st century, we do so alive to the fact that there are many challenges. We are well aware that for Africa, the last four decades have been turbulent ones. We have seen the hopes of many African people dashed after the celebration of independence as they observed the frustration of their democratic hopes in waves of military coups, conflicts, greed and corruption. We have no doubt that these have contributed to the current condition of African indebtedness, poverty and underdevelopment.

Yet, we closed the last century on a note of hope, since we are convinced that we are at the start of a different stage in the history of the African Continent. It is and will be a period during which the process of democratisation will spread relentlessly and inexorably across the continent. At this moment, as we meet at the beginning of what we have designated as the African Century, we look forward to the future with confidence, knowing that we have the support of friends and allies who have sustained us through the darkest days of our history.

A new generation of African leaders has acknowledged the mistakes we have made as a continent, noted the obstacles and assessed the setbacks. We have recognised the need to establish, nurture and consolidate democracy, to prevent and to resolve conflict, and to focus our efforts on the true rewards of democracy, on the eradication of poverty, and the upliftment and development of Africa.

There is no doubt that Africa's democratic Parliaments are central to our success, as they are no doubt to yours. As the elected representatives of our

Our great hope is that the 21st century will be the African century.

people, Parliaments are not only the custodians of democracy and the guardians of a human rights culture, but as important, we are the vanguard of the forces that must ensure the realisation of the aspirations of our people...

However, legitimacy is the basis of all institutions of governance, and so it must be within the international order. We recognise the need to democratise decision-making in the international arena. This includes as a priority, the restructuring of key multi-lateral organisations such as the UN, the international financial institutions and international trade organisations.

So while Parliaments are the custodians and promoters of democracy, human rights and human development in their own countries, they have to play a role in promoting this agenda in the international institutions of governance as well. The imperatives of globalisation oblige us to do this. Our great hope is that the 21st century will be the African century. We are certain that the Scottish people and the Scottish Parliament will help us realise this historic objective.

I thank you.[1]

look: hey,
you're a memorial lecture now and look:
hey, stranger still: I'm giving it.

Tilda Swinton
(1960 –)

'IN THE SPIRIT OF DEREK JARMAN'
EDINBURGH INTERNATIONAL FILM FESTIVAL
17 AUGUST 2002

Tilda Swinton is one of the UK's best-known actresses. Born in London 1960, she has Scottish ancestry through her father, and in 1986 she made her big-screen debut in Derek Jarman's film *Caravaggio*. She completed two more films for Jarman, *The Last of England* in 1988 and *The Garden* in 1990, becoming one of the director's closest collaborators as well as a good friend.

Katherine Matilda Swinton was born in 1960 in London, the daughter of a major general in the Scots Guards. On leaving Cambridge she performed with the Royal Shakespeare Company before turning to film, mixing art house projects with more mainstream roles. In 2007 Swinton won a Best Supporting Actress for her role in the thriller Michael Clayton. Until 2003 she was married to the Scottish artist John Byrne.

During the making of *The Garden*, Jarman became seriously ill and by the time of his 1993 film *Blue*, he was losing his sight and dying of AIDS-relation complications. He died the following year. Eight years later Swinton was asked to give a speech at the Edinburgh International Film Festival, which she memorably framed as a 'letter to Derek' and even reflected his narrative style in its content.

Several years later an adapted version of Swinton's speech provided Isaac Julien's documentary on the director's life and work, *Derek*, with a counterpoint in the present to Jarman's voice from the past (Swinton also narrated). When *Derek* premiered at the Sundance Film Festival in 2008 Swinton spoke eloquently of the reaction to the 'letter' and its subsequent publication in the *Critical Quarterly*; she was besieged by letters, phone calls and emails from people who recognised its call for creativity against the dead hand of corporate bureaucracy.

I have always wholeheartedly treasured in your work the whiff of the school play. It tickles me still and I miss it terribly. I forage for it now in the films I make with Lynn Hershman. The antidote it offers to the mirrorball of the marketable – the artful without the art, the meaningful devoid of meaning – is meat and drink to so many of us looking for that dodgy wig, that moment of awkward zing, that loose corner: where we might prize up the carpet and uncover the rich slates of something we might recognise as spirit underneath. Something raw and dusty and inarticulate, for heaven's sake. This is what Pasolini knew. What Rossellini knew. What Abbas Kiarostami knows. This is also what Ken Loach knows. What Andrew Kotting knows. What Bill Douglas knew. What Michael Powell and Emeric Pressburger, what William Blake knew. And, for that matter, what Caravaggio knew, painting prostitutes as Madonnas and rent boys as saints; no – Madonnas as prostitutes and saints as rent boys... there's the rub. It's all about rhythm: it's all in the knees. Bring it from home. Bring it out from under your bed. Your own bed. Your own life. That's – eventually – what you did, Derek, and measures your highest contribution as an artist, in my opinion: that you made your work out of the soup kitchen that was your life.

I think that the reason that people wanted to inaugurate this event in your name, the reason that you count for so much, so uniquely, to some people, particularly in this hidebound little place we call home, is that you lived so clearly the life that an artist lives. Your money was where your mouth was always. Your vocation – and here maybe it helped a little that you offered that special combination of utter self obsession with the appearance of the kindest Jesuit classics master in the school – was a spiritual one, even more than it was political, even more than it was artistic. And the clarity with which you offered up your life and the living of it, particularly since the epiphany – I can call it nothing less – of your illness, was a genius stroke, not only of provocation, but of grace. With your gesture of public confessional, both within and without your work – at a time when people talked fairly openly about setting up ostracised HIV island communities and others feared, not only for their lives, but, believe it or not, also for their jobs, their insurance policies, their friendships, their civil rights – was made with such particular, and characteristically inclusive, generosity that it was at that point that you made an impact far outspanning the influence of your work... you made your spirit, your nature, known to us – and the possibility of an artist's fearlessness, a reality. And the truth of it is: by defying it, you may have changed the market as well...

It's all about rhythm: it's all in the knees.

There is a character in *La Dolce Vita* – shall I leave out that he is the suicide? – who describes himself: "too serious to be a dilettante, too much of a dabbler to be a professional". I use it in my own head from time to time to explain to myself, if to no-one else, my peculiar idle ways. Now I look at it again, I think of you and how it might well describe you. Your focus on the ball beyond the crowd. Your amateur's enthusiasm. Your delight in process. Your perennial beginner's mind...

You should have been a Catholic, I sometimes think, Del. All those robes in *Caravaggio*, all those poppies in *War Requiem* and again in *The Last of England* and *The Garden*, to say nothing of all that buggery in the crypt in *Jubilee*... you and Michael Powell have to be the best subscribers to the passionate use of cardinal red in English cinema. The secret language of holy blood in the hands of pagans... longlivethepassion. Why is it that the English never mention that Shakespeare was a Catholic? All those squeaky scrubbed classical columns. The colourfree reformation. Clean up the sweat and blood, if not the tears. Here we go again. Longlivesweat. Longlive secret blood. There's more than one way to organise a clearance...

Maybe it's as bad as you and I used to say it could possibly get, now. Maybe it's worse. But here we are, the rest of us, tilting at the sameold sameold windmills and spooking at the same old ghosts, and keeping company, all the same. It's a rotten mess of a shambles, you could say. It's driving into the curve, at the very least. Some would say you are well out of it. I reckon you would say let me at 'em.

I say bring it on. Bring on the fisticuffs and let's get weaving. And that we could do with you here among us. And I can't be the only one, 'cos look: hey, you're a memorial lecture now and look: hey, stranger still: I'm giving it... Are they tired of the academic view, one wonders, tired of the need to listen to lectures about funding bodies and cultural diversity? What do they want to hear about from me? What can I give them?

Given that it's you who should be the one standing here giving your own Memorial Lecture – not for the first time, your closest friends might cry – and you are presently otherwise engaged, or at least have left the building, I suppose I might as well read them this and let them in on the trick – that the conversation is not done yet... that the company you keep with us, when we care to think of it, is just as strong and empowering as it ever was. That the example you set us is as simple as a logo to sell a sports shoe; less chat, more action, less fiscal reports, more films, less paralysis, more process. Less deference. More dignity. Less money. More work. Less rules. More examples. Less dependence. More love...

I say bring it on. Bring on the fisticuffs and let's get weaving.

This is what I miss, there being no more Derek Jarman films:
the mess
the vulgarity
the cant
the poetry
the edge
the pictures
Simon Fisher Turner's music

the real faces
the intellectualism
the science
the bad temperedness
the good temperedness
the cheek
the standards
the anarchy
the gauchness
the romanticism
the classicism
the optimism
the activism
the challenge
the longeurs
the glee
the playfulness
the bumptiousness
the resistance
the wit
the fight
the colours
the grace
the passion
the goodness
the beauty
Longlivemess
Longlivepassion
Longlivecompany
yr,
Tild.[1]

For those who like to keep count, there are 123 reshuffling days left before dissolution...

David McLetchie
1952–2013

SPEECH IN THE SCOTTISH PARLIAMENT · EDINBURGH
28 NOVEMBER 2002

In late 2002 Richard Simpson, Scotland's deputy justice minister, was forced to resign after describing striking firemen (at a private dinner) as 'fascists' and 'bastards'. Jack McConnell, the then First Minister, moved quickly to plug the gap by moving Hugh Henry sideways to replace Simpson and appointing Des McNulty deputy social justice minister in Henry's place.

David McLetchie was born in Edinburgh in 1952 and educated at George Heriot's and Edinburgh University, where he studied law. He became a solicitor in 1976, becoming a partner in Tods Murray WS four years later. Active in Conservative politics since 1968, McLetchie was elected president of the Scottish Conservative and Unionist Association and, in 1998, leader of the Scottish Tory parliamentary group in the Scottish Parliament. Forced to resign in 2005, he retained his Lothians seat until his death from cancer in 2013.

This mini reshuffle had to be endorsed by the Scottish Parliament, and the resulting debate allowed the Scottish Conservative Party, then led by the Lothians MSP David McLetchie, to repeat its call to reduce the size of the Scottish Executive, having long argued that 22 ministers was too large.

The debate also provided scope for McLetchie, one of the first Scottish Parliament's most talented debaters, to have a bit of fun at the Scottish Executive's expense. He knew the reshuffle would win majority support, so his caustic wit kept MSPs (of all parties) entertained as he speculated when the next game of ministerial musical chairs would take place.

Here we are again—another day, another reshuffle—as the accident-prone Government stumbles towards its date with destiny on 1 May next year. For those who like to keep count, there are 123 reshuffling days left before dissolution and opportunity may yet knock for the mere seven Labour back benchers who have still to be given a job of any description.

It would be remiss of me not to comment on the circumstances that have led to the elevation of Mr McNulty to the dizzy heights of junior minister. Two years ago in this Parliament, Jim Wallace announced proposals to reform family law in Scotland. He said:

> We will end the status of illegitimacy in Scotland.

End? End? Far from ending it, Labour politicians talk of little else. The vulgar and intemperate Dr Simpson is, of course, not the first. Members will recall that infamous taped conversation between Helen Liddell and Henry McLeish in which the parentages and pedigrees of John Reid and Brian Wilson were discussed in less than flattering terms. We know that the Labour party in Scotland struggles with numeracy, but its language is not much better.

With Dr Simpson's departure, Hugh Henry moves to the justice portfolio at a highly opportune time. Thanks to the Scottish Conservatives, the Criminal Justice (Scotland) Bill has been significantly improved. There has been a partial U-turn on the ludicrous proposals to criminalise parents for disciplining their children and a humiliating retreat on the plan to send 16 and 17-year-olds to children's panels. Accordingly, the bill has been shed of some of the higher nonsenses of the Wallace-Simpson era, although little did we know that it would also be followed by an abdication. So I say—[Laughter] Come on. Members will have to be quicker than that. I say to Hugh Henry that if he wishes to prosper in that portfolio and make a real difference to tackling crime in Scotland, he would be well advised to listen to Bill Aitken, James Douglas-Hamilton and others in the chamber who are in touch with reality, rather than to Jim Wallace.

... the truth is that Scotland needs [not] another mini-reshuffle, but a wholesale clear-out.

I turn to Mr McNulty. I hope that he will not take it personally if I say that he should never have been appointed. This was an opportunity missed by the First Minister to make a start on cutting government down to size in Scotland. However, it seems that he and the Liberal Democrats are determined to persist with their overblown Administration, so that we continue to have five times the number of ministers governing Scotland today than was the case only three years ago.

However, as far as Mr McNulty is concerned, I think that his contributions to this Parliament have been considered and measured and that, in his new portfolio, he may prove to be the perfect foil for the more passionate and combative style of Margaret Curran. We all know that we should never underestimate the determination of a quiet man. On a personal level, we wish Mr McNulty well in his few months in ministerial office. However, the truth is that Scotland needs [not] another mini-reshuffle, but a wholesale clear-out. Next May, the people will get their chance.[1]

The war has already claimed its first victim, which is the truth.

George Reid
1939–

SPEECH TO THE SCOTTISH PARLIAMENT · EDINBURGH
13 MARCH 2003

George Reid was precisely the sort of person Scotland's new Parliament was supposed to attract: individuals with a broad hinterland and beyond domestic politics. Reid was one of the few MSPs who could draw on international experience in the course of his Parliamentary duties.

George Newlands Reid was born at Tullibody, near Alloa, in 1939, and was educated at Dollar Academy and the University of St Andrews. He then worked as a broadcast journalist before entering Parliament as the MP for Clackmannan and East Stirlingshire in February 1974. After working for the International Red Cross, Reid re-entered Scottish politics in 1995 and stood for the Scottish Parliament in 1999.

After losing his Westminster seat in 1979, Reid returned to journalism, presenting television programmes for BBC Scotland and producing the famous reportage by Michael Buerk of the Ethiopian famine of 1984. This led to him becoming Director of Public Affairs for the International Red Cross, during which he worked around the world in conflict and disaster zones.

Reid drew on these often harrowing experiences for this speech to the Scottish Parliament during a debate on the impending war in Iraq. There was much debate about whether MSPs ought to be discussing this at all, given that foreign affairs were beyond their remit, but Reid's contribution demonstrated that it was justified. Just a few months after doing so, Reid was re-elected and became the Scottish Parliament's second Presiding Officer.

On September 12 2001, the day after the mass murder in New York and Washington, *Le Monde* carried a banner headline, the translation of which is, "We are all Americans now." That headline encapsulated our feelings of outrage and grief. In London, in a speech of great clarity and compassion, Tony Blair called for justice and mercy, a campaign to extirpate the terrorists from their lairs and a ruthless war on the global poverty that fuels terrorism. I warmly endorsed that speech. Just for a moment, it seemed that good might come out of evil.

Today, the French, the Germans and other old Europeans are openly vilified in the American media. Afghanistan, which has been almost forgotten, is slipping back into anarchy, and some of the poorest countries of the world—Angola, Cameroon and Guinea—are being openly bullied and bribed in the Security Council.

The Executive amendment is right to stress the primacy of the United Nations, but members should look at today's headlines: "Blair's gamble as allies prepare to go to war" without the UN, or "War looms as Prime Minister prepares to bypass United Nations". How can that be? It can be only because the war is not about Iraq. It is about a new world order, it is about the Cold War being over and it is about the world's only superpower being determined to impose its own order of pre-emptive strike and pax Americana. That is a serious argument.

Even though I oppose it, I concede that there is an argument for Britain to be part of that order. Such a case is based on perceptions of British self-interest and realpolitik. However, such a case can never be argued on the grounds of compassion and international law.

Just for a moment, it seemed that good might come out of evil.

In recent weeks, our television studios have seen a stream of pundits unburdening themselves of the pain and agony that they personally experienced before deciding to march unto war. Let me tell members what pain is by providing just one personal flashback from war. Pain is a little boy with what is left of his leg in an Oor Wullie bucket of antiseptic, taking it out, turning it over, looking at it and then looking at me as though I knew the answer. I had no answer then, as I have no answer now, except to keep my mouth open.

The war has already claimed its first victim, which is the truth. The resolution is not a mandate. A mandate must specifically authorise the use of military force, as happened in the Korean War and in the previous gulf war. A mandate must be rooted in compelling evidence. In war these days, the truth is that it is safer to be a soldier than to be a civilian. Nine out of 10 casualties of war are civilians, most of whom are women and children. The allies look for a surgical strike with not many dead. I have my doubts about that, but even if it were true, the killing goes on long after the war is over. Last week, the Scottish Trades Union Congress called on all silent MSPs to say where they stand, and many have done so today. Many in the chamber take the old European view, which was articulated by John McAllion, that there is no case for military action against Iraq. The case has not yet been proven. Perhaps later today, we can rally round that one position across the parties—the Liberals, the SNP, the John McAllions, the members of the Labour party and, indeed, perhaps some members of the Tory party.

What the next generation will... is a settlement that honours the birth of devolution without being hidebound by it.

Wendy Alexander
1963–

'A NEW AGENDA FOR SCOTLAND' LECTURE · EDINBURGH UNIVERSITY
30 NOVEMBER 2007

Wendy Alexander was one of the first Scottish Parliament's more cerebral figures. Intimately involved with the devolution project from campaigning through to inception (she helped draft the 1998 Scotland Act), by the time she became leader of the Scottish Labour Party after the party's 2007 election defeat, she was eager to see Scotland's constitutional settlement move on.

Wendy Alexander was born in Glasgow in 1963 and educated in Erskine, British Columbia and Glasgow. In 1997 she was appointed special adviser to Scottish Secretary Donald Dewar, with whom she worked on the 1998 Scotland Act. In 1999 Alexander was elected an MSP and held various ministerial positions until her resignation in 2002. Briefly leader of the Scottish Labour Party in 2007/08, she retired from politics in 2011.

So on St Andrew's Day in 2007 Alexander made a speech at Edinburgh University in which she set out the case for a wide-ranging, cross-party review of Holyrood's existing powers. After slaying several 'sacred cows', Alexander set out her proposals for 'a more balanced home rule package', including greater financial accountability and new tax powers.

This quickly took tangible form as the Commission on Scottish Devolution chaired by Sir Kenneth Calman, although, to no one's great surprise, the SNP refused to take part. And while the Commission's recommendations, which took legislative form in the 2012 Scotland Act, never really caught the public's imagination, the issues – particularly financial – aired in Alexander's lecture still loomed large in the Scottish constitutional debate several years later.

Throughout my adult life I have always believed in home rule for Scotland. I believe in it in principle because the Scots are a recognisable nation with their own culture, legal system and view of the world. And as a democrat it has always seemed self-evident to me that Scotland should have democratic control over its own domestic affairs...

One key issue, which must be part of these efforts, is to strengthen the financial accountability of the Scottish Parliament. In short the financing of the Parliament almost wholly through grant funding does not provide the proper incentives to make the right decisions. Hence strengthening the financial accountability of the Scottish Parliament by moving to a mixture of assigned and devolved taxes and grant is something the Commission should consider... But for those committed to the UK, financial transfers within the UK – the grant element – must continue to ensure that areas with greater spending needs have the resources to fund them. Such equalisation systems are commonplace in all modern democracies...

Throughout my adult life I have always believed in home rule for Scotland.

I believe it is for the Commission to consider the proper balance between devolved, reserved and assigned taxes if the accountability of the Parliament is to be strengthened and relative need still respected... Most British citizens want to see the Union continue. It is always vital to reassess what we have in common – the glue that holds us together. We are held together by a shared identity, shared interests and shared citizenship. Our shared identity is based on common history, family ties, values and culture. England is not just any other country for most Scots. We have important shared interests. The UK is indeed stronger together and we benefit economically, from being part of the world's largest economies as well as globally in terms of international standing. And as we respond to global challenges such as migration, terrorism, climate change, flooding – the reality is they require common responses.

We also share a common citizenship. This has familiar political and legal dimensions – but also social and economic dimensions too. Risk, revenues and resources are shared across the UK to deliver common services and benefits – access to the main elements of the welfare state – social security and pensions, access to healthcare free at the point of need and free schooling.

The Union is something for all its constituent nations: the devolved nations of Scotland, Wales and Northern Ireland – but for England too. It is not for me, as leader of Scottish Labour, to suggest changes there, but I do say to Scots that we should support and welcome greater local and regional decentralisation in England, allowing voices in different parts of England to be heard on their issues just as we have sought that for ourselves. Looking to the future the so-called English question is properly for UK colleagues to consider. We must resist nationalists of whatever provenance fanning English resentment for partisan reasons.

These are exciting times. Scots do want to walk taller within the UK, taking more responsibility. It comes with growing self-confidence. What the next generation will demand of the current generation, is a settlement that honours the birth of devolution without being hidebound by it. In any work we do, we

It is always vital to reassess what we have in common – the glue that holds us together.

must keep sight of the one driving goal – how to make Scotland and the UK better places to live and work.

I do not favour constitutional discussions for their own sake, rather because it is right to re-examine how we work to consider if improvements can be made. The priorities of the people of Scotland remain the same as others in countries across the world – health, education, law-and-order, housing. But if the only reform alternative people can see is one of separatism they can be forgiven for assuming that this is their only choice. It is up to us to offer a better alternative. A new Scottish Constitutional Commission will allow us to do just that.[1]

As the chamber knows,
I have a degenerative condition.

Margo MacDonald
1943–

SPEECH IN THE SCOTTISH PARLIAMENT · HOLYROOD
26 MARCH 2008

The charismatic SNP politician Margo MacDonald – dubbed the 'blonde bombshell' in the 1970s – was understandably shocked on being diagnosed with Parkinson's disease in 1995. With few outward signs she was unwell, she chose not to make it public, although the media eventually learned of MacDonald's illness a few years after she was elected to the Scottish Parliament in 1999.

Only in 2008, however, did MacDonald campaign on the issue publicly, intervening during a Holyrood debate on a motion from Liberal Democrat MSP Jeremy Purvis about Terminal Illness (Patient Choice). The SNP MSP Roseanna Cunningham had just argued that the issue of assisted suicide was not at the forefront of public consciousness, and in a moving speech, MacDonald argued the contrary.

Drawing upon her own experience, she told MSPs she did not want to be a burden to her family if – and when – her condition deteriorated. It was a short speech, but MacDonald was inundated with letters and emails supporting her call for a proper debate about the issue. Later, she introduced her own Member's Bill to legalise assisted suicide but political, if not public, opinion was not yet in her favour.

Margo MacDonald was born in Hamilton in 1943 and educated at Hamilton Academy. She worked as a physical education teacher and, aged only 30, won the Govan by-election for the SNP in 1973. An MP for a matter of months, MacDonald was then deputy leader of the SNP and thereafter worked as a broadcaster and journalist before being elected a SNP (and subsequently Independent) list MSP for the Lothians.

It is very healthy for all of us to consider the value of our life. In fact, it should be mandatory for the human condition. We should all concern ourselves with the contribution that we make to society in general throughout our life, right up to the moment of death.

As the chamber knows, I have a degenerative condition. I would like to have the right to determine by how much my capacity to fulfil my social, familial and personal functions will be truncated. I would like the ability to take that decision. I do not want to burden any doctor, friend or family member; I want to find a way in which I can take the decision to end my life in the event that I am unlucky enough to have the worst form of Parkinson's near the end of my life. From the responses to interventions, we can see that the medical practitioners among us have admitted that palliative care is not as effective in all cases as everyone wants it to be. I am mindful of that. I may be one of the unlucky ones. I apologise for the personal nature of my contribution, but this is not theory for me.

We should all concern ourselves with the contribution that we make to society in general throughout our life

I fully appreciate why Michael Matheson wanted to invoke the law. However, in this case, yet again the law may be an ass. To say that it is illegal for anyone to force themselves to die is to deny the bravery of countless soldiers over the ages. People have taken that decision for one reason or another. It is just that we are now accepting that it is possible for someone to take that decision when they are in sound mind and they can do so in a measured capacity. I am mindful of what the doctors say and how difficult it is for them. However, I have read the personal testimony of doctors and have seen doctors who have admitted in court to assisting a suicide. They are no less doctors in my estimation for having done that.

I congratulate Jeremy Purvis on bringing the debate to the chamber as quickly as he could. Many people have a lot less time than I have.[1]

As you fight for fairness, you will always find in me a friend, a partner and a brother.

Gordon Brown
1951–

SPEECH TO CITIZENS UK · METHODIST CENTRAL HALL · WESTMINSTER

3 MAY 2010

By May 2010 Gordon Brown had served as Prime Minister for exactly three years, but his prospects of victory in that year's general election were widely predicted as slim. Although his response to the 2008 financial crisis had been widely praised, a deep economic recession had damaged his reputation as a prudent manager of the nation's finances.

Gordon Brown was born in Glasgow in 1951, a son of the manse. He was educated in Kirkcaldy and began studying at Edinburgh University aged only 16. After brief careers as an academic and journalist, Brown entered Parliament in 1983, thereafter holding a number of front-bench positions. In 1997 he began a decade-long term as Chancellor, succeeding Tony Blair as Prime Minister in May 2007.

But it went beyond that: Brown was regarded as socially awkward and inauthentic, particularly in contrast to his charismatic predecessor. So when he rose to speak to Citizens UK – a coalition of civil society organisations – at Methodist Central Hall shortly before polling day, expectations were not high. Instead, as the *Guardian* reported, Brown 'appeared to find an emotional range and vocabulary previously unheard from him'.

In a performance that resembled more of a sermon than a regular political speech (indeed at one point Brown name-checked his minister father), Brown was greeted with several standing ovations, not something he was used to. His speech, reckoned the *Guardian*, 'may end up having been the most electrifying event of the campaign'.[1]

When people say that politics can't make a difference, when people say that people are apathetic and indifferent, when people say that there are no great causes left, let them come to Citizens UK, let them come here. Our shared belief is that wealth must serve more than the wealthy. That prosperity must serve more than the simply prosperous. That good fortune must help more than those who are just fortunate. And your movement is like every other great movement in history, it is built on moral convictions.

First hundreds, then thousands, then hundreds of thousands of people they say. Inequality should not be woven into the fabric of our lives. People of compassion and good will should never journey without hope. And no injustice should endure forever.

Do you know what taught me more than any book ever taught me? It was a video, it was a video created for the Make Poverty History campaign, and it's a video that sums up for me the strength of a movement. It encompasses the great campaigns of our time; it's a video that shows the abolitionist movement, the civil rights movement, the votes for women movement, the anti-apartheid movement. And every time it shows that movement it passes by the leaders who spoke on the stage and zooms in on the faces of the crowds like the crowd here today.

Our shared belief is that wealth must serve more than the wealthy.

The people who gathered to hear Wilberforce speak about slavery, the men and women on the march to Washington with Martin Luther King. And the point of zooming in on the crowds is that nobody was a spectator. That the people in the crowd, the people whose names are not recorded in the books of history are the real change makers, the people who made history by being there and demanding change.

And so when we saw Barack Obama place his hand on that Bible to take the presidential oath on Capitol Hill on that Washington day, we saw not just one man, we saw all who fought and campaigned to end slavery, to win the vote, to go back to Lincoln and beyond and we know that for all the great leaders of history there are millions of other unnamed men and women who are heroes who make our history happen.

And you know from one person, one candle, can be lit thousands of candles. And then tens of thousands of candles, all lit from that one flame. And think of the change that your movement can create. Once you have learnt something, nobody can unteach it. You cannot ever again humiliate the person who has got pride. You cannot suppress men and women who are afraid no more.

Inequality should not be woven into the fabric of our lives.

And so it is with Citizens UK. Each of you hear will know that your work may not always make the headlines, but you can always make the difference. And I know that in your work as community organisers you share testimony with each other. So please allow me to testify today to what I believe and to tell you who I am. I'm a son of a Church of Scotland minister. He taught me, my father, that life was about more than self-interest, that work is about more than self-advancement. That service is about more than self-service. That happiness is about more than what you earn and own. My parents taught me the fundamental values of taking responsibility, doing your duty, being honest, looking out for others and that is the right way, it is your way and it is my way.

And when I was a student the two causes I worked for most were to force my university to disinvest in apartheid and sell all its shares in South Africa. And I also ran a campaign for decent pay for university cleaners. And across the years I feel my life has come full circle, because when I became Chancellor of the Exchequer the first thing I was able to do was to create the minimum wage for the first time in 100 years. Justice for the low paid...

And your campaign has shown something even bigger, that a community is more than its buildings; more than its institutions, more than its fabric. A community is thousands of acts of friendship and service and compassion

A community is more than its buildings.

to each other. And you've shown something else that the public services, your hospitals, your schools, your children's centres on which communities are built are not things that we can just do on our own, they are what we choose to do together, and that's what a good society is about. Building together, investing in good schools, good hospitals, good public buildings, good community centres and yes, good banks for the future...

The motto of that policy is not God helps those who help themselves, the motto is God helps those whom he has already helped, and that is not acceptable to me... I have said throughout this campaign that the sixth of May is fundamentally about choices. Nations need not be ruled by blind fate. Nations must choose their own history. And so I stand before you proud that Labour chooses to support the living wage, the interest rate cap, the community land trust and a return to community banking. These are your choices and these are our choices too.

And let the word go out that as you fight for fairness you will always find in me a friend, a partner and a brother. When Cicero spoke to crowds in ancient Rome people turned to each other after hearing the speech and said "great speech". But when Demosthenes spoke to the crowds in ancient Greece and people turned to each other they said, "let's march". Let's march for justice, dignity, fairness. That's what we've all got to march for, and let's march for it together.[2]

... we are driven forward, in vigilance and in the spirit of exploration, by the constant, exciting possibility that we are wrong.

Christopher Brookmyre 1968–

SPEECH AT THE 'MARCH TO ENLIGHTENMENT'

23 APRIL 2011

The Glaswegian writer Christopher Brookmyre was raised a Catholic in Barrhead in the west of Scotland but even as a boy he began to doubt the certainties of his faith. 'My wife and I would spend all our time discussing how we couldn't accept what was being taught us, yet we still kept going,' he reflected in 2008. 'But the more I thought about it, the more I realised I don't believe this. So it was not just liberating to give it up, but a sudden realisation of it all making sense.' It was, he added, 'closer to a spiritual experience than anything I'd had.'[1] Instead Brookmyre turned his attention to the Humanist Society of Scotland, becoming its president in April 2008. This, in effect, seeks a secular Scotland in which no 'belief system (religious or not) should have, nor expect, privilege in the democratic process'.[2]

Christopher Brookmyre was born in 1968. He was educated in Barrhead and at the University of Glasgow before working for the film magazine Screen International and as sub-editor on the Scotsman and Edinburgh Evening News. His first novel, Quite Ugly One Morning, was published in 1996, the first of a series of novels to feature the investigative journalist Jack Parlabane. Brookmyre lives in Glasgow.

Brookmyre gave his speech at a rally staged by the Scottish Humanist Society to mark the 300th anniversary of the birth of the philosopher David Hume. A play was staged at the Scottish Parliament, pipers marched up the Royal Mile, then he spoke in front of Hume's statue, which had been decorated with flowers and balloons.

Well, here we all are, gathered to participate in Think for Yourself day. It shouldn't really need a day, should it? International Talk Like a Pirate day, fair enough. Give it a try. National No Smoking Day: yeah, if you're a smoker, you can see where that's coming from. Think For Yourself Day? Kind of like "Wash our hands after you've been to the lavatory" day. We shouldn't need to be encouraged, but unfortunately, it would appear, many people do...

I'm a novelist: I'm not a scholar or a philosopher, so I am not qualified to address the mighty sweep of David Hume's work, but I believe that the principles he evoked, the empiricism embraced by Hume, as by the likes of Hunter, Watt, Boyle and Kelvin, can be distilled down to a simple question: Is this a good idea?

But it's not enough merely to ask that question, because there are, to my mind, three ways of proceeding from there. One is to decide that yes, it is a good idea, and then have an enduring faith in it, no matter what obstacles the world may present. A second is to try, with all your resources and all your imagination, to prove that it is a good idea, and to garner enough evidence in its support in order to convince yourself, should you begin to have some doubts. And still a third, the

The most exciting thing to me is the possibility that I might discover tomorrow that what I believe today is wrong.

empirical procedure, is to try, with all your resources and all your imagination, to prove that it is not a good idea. Because having thrown all of that at it, without bias or expectation, if it remains standing, then, temporarily at least, you can declare that, yes, it is a good idea.

And there is the key-word: temporarily. Because the most important practice is that the next day, and every day, you come back and ask: is this still a good idea? Have the circumstances changed? Is there new evidence?

The most exciting thing to me is the possibility that I might discover tomorrow that what I believe today is wrong. It's the process of constant re-evaluation that opens up this possibility, but also strengthens one's convictions in those ideas that continually withstand such scrutiny. Ideas such as empiricism itself.

When we don't keep asking is this still a good idea, when we don't practice on-going re-evaluation, that is when we cultivate what I would call cultural inertia, whereby we keep doing things because we've always done them; whereby we cease to question things because they've always been that way; and whereby we cease to see absurdities in our midst because we have been looking at them for so long.

We do not have to search hard or far for examples... But undoubtedly the greatest cultural inertia in modern-day Scotland is the on-going tendency to privilege religious beliefs above others: to afford, in fact, greater respect to beliefs that have no rational basis, on the grounds that they have no rational basis. This is precisely as insane as it sounds, but I am not exaggerating. We frequently hear it said of someone, as grounds for according that person reverence and respect, "he is a man of deep faith". And how many times are we told "you need to respect people's religious beliefs". As HL Mencken had it, "We must respect the other fellow's religion, but only in the same sense and to the same extent that we respect his theory that his wife is beautiful and his children smart"...

When a Catholic bishop or someone from the Church of Scotland's Board of Social Responsibility is invited to contribute to the debate on an issue, it is seldom because they are highly qualified to comment on that particular subject, but because of their religious beliefs: because as a society we still consider that there is something to be revered about holding steadfast convictions that are unsupported by any evidence. Maybe they have a point: because let's face it, anybody can have a strong belief in something when the evidence supports it. Anybody can believe in gravity, or in mathematics. But clearly you have to be made of special stuff to be able to hold tight to a belief in the face of overwhelming evidence to the contrary...

The antidote to cultural inertia is constant re-evaluation, asking is this still a good idea: thinking for yourself.

The antidote to cultural inertia is constant re-evaluation, asking is this still a good idea: thinking for yourself. Thinking for yourself can be scary. There's security in going along with what everyone else thinks. Nobody is going to give you a dressing down for it. There is security from the fear of being wrong. You have the reassurance that if you're wrong, then at least you won't be alone.

But for me, the most exciting idea in the world is that I could be wrong, completely wrong; that new evidence could emerge, or a new perspective afforded me, that changes how I think, changes what I believe. That's not a thrill enjoyed by those "men of deep faith". And I can imagine them protesting: "Of course we entertain doubt. We struggle with doubt every day." But their response to that doubt is to believe harder. They make an explicit virtue of overcoming doubt through deeper faith. It's there in the Bible: 'Blessed is he who has not seen and yet believes'.

I think blessed is he who says "further data required". That is why on our march to enlightenment today and all days, we are not walking shoulder to shoulder, unified by a shared steadfast faith that we are right. Instead we are driven forward, in vigilance and in the spirit of exploration, by the constant, exciting possibility that we are wrong.[3]

*For Scotland,
for this Parliament,
this can be a good season
and a good time.*

Alex Salmond
1954–

SPEECH ON OFFICIAL OPENING OF THE FOURTH SCOTTISH PARLIAMENT
EDINBURGH
1 JULY 2011

The Scottish Parliament election of May 2011 gave rise to an array of superlatives, many of which did not quite catch the historic nature of the result: not only were the SNP re-elected, but returned with an overall majority, something the Parliament's founding fathers (and mothers) had sought to avoid any party achieving.

Alex Salmond, who had fought a flawless campaign, was the sole nominee for First Minister when Parliament first met two weeks later and on 1 July he also spoke in response to a short speech from the Queen, who as usual had made a point of opening the new Holyrood session. Delivering her speech to politicians and dignitaries in the Parliament's sun-drenched main chamber, Her Majesty jokingly observed that no one 'would ever argue that Scottish politics is the business of the meek, the passive or the faint-hearted'.

'Now, in its second decade,' she added, 'the Scottish Parliament is firmly established as an integral part of Scottish public life.'[1] The First Minister's reply was eloquent, packed with literary and historical references, and also quite daring politically. He spoke openly of his plans for an independence referendum, but also took care to reassure the Monarch that no matter how a majority of Scots voted, her position as head of state would remain undisturbed.

Alexander Elliot Anderson Salmond was born in Linlithgow on Hogmanay 1954. After attending St Andrews University he worked for the Royal Bank of Scotland as an economist before entering the House of Commons in 1987. He was elected leader of the Scottish National Party in 1990 and served until 2000, returning four years later. Salmond was first elected First Minister of a minority Scottish Government in 2007 and re-elected on gaining an overall majority at the 2011 Holyrood.

Your Majesty, on behalf of the people of Scotland, can I thank you for declaring this fourth session of the reconvened Scottish Parliament open... Your Majesty has been the firmest of friends of this Parliament, particularly in some of our early and difficult years, and you now return to demonstrate that confidence as we move into a different age.

Scotland, and Parliament, have changed since you first came to congratulate our newly-democratised nation in 1999. We have grown in esteem and ambition and we wish to grow more. Since May, a whole clamour of voices have been scrambled to debate the road ahead. Some urge us to ignore Edwin Morgan's call – repeated by our new Makar – to be "bold". But the "nest of fearties" approach is for another time and place.

Scotland, and Parliament, have changed since you first came to congratulate our newly-democratised nation in 1999.

This is a country increasingly comfortable in its own skin. We aspire to be more successful, more dynamic, fairer and greener. We want to uphold the values of the Commonweal – to protect the vulnerable and nurture the young. We want to emerge from current economic difficulties into better times.

Your Majesty, can I quote from a recent speech which you made to another nation of these islands, and one that was received with great praise and warmth. At a banquet in Dublin Castle – after an impressive opening in the Irish language that I will not attempt to emulate – you said:

> Together we have much to celebrate: the ties between our people, the shared values, and the economic, business and cultural links that make us so much more than just neighbours, that make us firm friends and equal partners.

Scotland, Ireland, England and Wales – together we do have much to celebrate – the English language of Shakespeare, James Joyce, Dylan Thomas and Edwin Morgan himself. One of the greatest works in that language of course is the King James Bible, which is 400 years old this very year.

The translation was first suggested – not at Hampton Court as is often claimed – but at the General Assembly of the Church of Scotland in Burntisland, Fife, in 1601. It was driven by Scottish egalitarianism and commitment to education – the

This is a country increasingly comfortable in its own skin.

desire that everyone should be able to read and understand scripture. The idea travelled south with King James VI of Scots when he accepted the English Crown two years later – and it was brought then to life by scholars in Cambridge, Oxford and Westminster...

So there is much we share, that is a given. But the nations of these islands are also distinctive, with our own unique history and culture, our own economic challenges and our own opportunities. Some of us believe the best way to articulate that uniqueness and tackle those challenges lies within ourselves – and should be fully expressed within the work of this Parliament.

However, whatever constitutional path that the people of Scotland choose – and it is their choice to make – we will aspire to be, in your words, "firm friends and equal partners".

It gave me great pleasure recently to represent Scotland at the wedding of your grandson in Westminster Abbey. And we look forward, as you do, to another wedding, that of your grand-daughter Zara, in the Canongate Kirk – a holy place which you first visited in the first day of your first visit to Scotland as our Queen.

Some of us believe the best way to articulate that uniqueness and tackle those challenges lies within ourselves

It is worth remembering that the Canongate was commissioned in 1688 by James VII, King of both Scotland and England when these two countries had their own parliaments in Edinburgh and London. From 1603, until this Parliament entered a rather long adjournment in 1707, your predecessors reigned over two sovereign nations – and there was nothing particularly unusual in that arrangement.

And today, Your Majesty, you come here as Queen of Scots but also as head of state of 16 different realms – and leader of a Commonwealth comprising 54 nations. It is a role which you have always taken seriously and discharged flawlessly...

We are a proud people, keen to contribute to the global Commonweal, and that marvellous egalitarian principle which inspires the modern Commonwealth. Or as the King James Bible would have it: "To everything there is a season and a time." For Scotland, for this Parliament, this can be a good season and a good time.[2]

As Einstein said, insanity is doing the same thing over and over again and expecting different results.

Murdo Fraser
1965–

SPEECH LAUNCHING SCOTTISH CONSERVATIVE LEADERSHIP CAMPAIGN
DOVECOT STUDIOS · EDINBURGH
5 SEPTEMBER 2011

The Holyrood elections of May 2011 were traumatic for all Scotland's Unionist parties, all of whom lost seats and votes as the SNP romped home with an unprecedented (and apparently impossible) overall majority. Within weeks all three opposition party leaders had resigned, and in September the Scottish Conservative Party prepared to elect a successor to the popular Annabel Goldie.

Murdo Fraser was born in 1965 and educated at Inverness Royal Academy and Aberdeen University, where he studied law. Chairman of the Scottish Young Conservatives from 1989-92, he worked as a solicitor before entering the Scottish Parliament in 2001. Re-elected in 2003, 2007 and 2011, Fraser stood for the Scottish Conservative leadership in the autumn of 2011 but was defeated by Ruth Davidson.

Further electoral decline had prompted something of an existential crisis in Scotland's oldest party of the Union, and one of the candidates, the party's deputy leader Murdo Fraser, argued that the recent election ought to be seen as 'a line in the sand'. 'We should not look for excuses,' he said in the speech that launched his campaign. 'We should not use the SNP landslide as a shield to protect us from our own shortcomings.'

But Fraser also went much further. Initially nervous, once he got into his stride at the Dovecot Studios in Edinburgh (a converted Victorian swimming pool), he set out a lucid case for abolishing the Scottish Tory Party and starting all over again. Lucid, but not successful, for Fraser lost to Ruth Davidson when the votes were counted. It seemed the party grassroots was content to keep things as they were, at least for a while longer.

Our supporters and members are deeply disappointed. They are disillusioned. Tired. Fed up. Fed up of fighting. Fed up of losing. I understand their feelings. I share their feelings. They want to start winning. So do I. But we won't start winning until we understand why we keep losing. And the reason is that our party, in its current state, is not fit for purpose. It hasn't changed.

So we must now recognise that change is no longer an option, but a necessity. Now is the time to face the truth. It is a brutal truth. But it is the truth. And it is that the Scottish Conservative and Unionist Party is failing. It is failing as a vehicle for the promotion of the values we stand for. And it will never succeed in its current form. A clear contradiction undermines everything we say and do. We are a party which believes in devolving power to people but we haven't devolved power to ourselves. And make no mistake. This absence of power is putting the Union at risk because it is preventing us from carving out a distinctively Scottish, unionist position.

So, in this leadership campaign, I want to make it absolutely clear in which direction I wish to take the party. That's why today, I am announcing that if I am elected as Leader of the Party, I will build a new and stronger party for Scotland. A new party. A winning party with new supporters from all walks of life. A new belief in devolution. A new name. But, most importantly, a new positive message about the benefits of staying in and strengthening our United Kingdom. A new party. A new Unionism. A new dawn.

For those people who think this is a leap in the dark, let us remember that our most successful electoral period as a party came before 1965. We were not the Conservative Party then. We were a party which had a distinct Scottish identity. And in 1955, we gained the only absolute majority of votes in Scotland in the period of modern democracy. So this new party will take us back to our roots...

We won't start winning
until we understand why we keep losing.

Now, I am under no illusion about the scale of the change I am proposing. Or the fact that this might not be a universally popular proposal within the party. There will be some in the party, perhaps even some of my colleagues, perhaps even some people in this room today who will say this is heresy. Who will say that I am risking the future of the Scottish Conservative and Unionist Party. I say to them with complete clarity and conviction: there is no future for the Scottish Conservative and Unionist Party in its current form. Our vote has continued to slip as we convinced ourselves things would get better. But they didn't. This will be difficult for some people to accept. It is an emotional wrench for us all.

We have all worked for years, decades, for the Scottish Conservative and Unionist Party. But that work will be wasted if we cannot transform ourselves into a winning party. We have not failed as individuals. But our party has. At the minute, we know we are doing precious little to help the UK Conservative Party to form a government at Westminster. Indeed, we are far more of a hindrance than a help....

Of course, there will be a predictable reaction to these proposals from our political opponents. They'll say that we are changing the sign on the office, but inside there are the same people, with the same policies. Same old Tories.

I am under no illusion about the scale of the change I am proposing.

The people of Scotland will see through it, they'll say. I say to them; this time, you're wrong. This is not simply a re-branding exercise. This is not PR or spin. This will be a new party. With a completely new approach. A party which embraces values which many Scots hold dear. A party which offers a home to the many people across Scotland who want a progressive, centre-right party...

Ladies and gentlemen, a new party and new unionism are the political equivalents of a foot in the door. They offer us a fresh opportunity to be heard. A fair hearing, free of preconceptions and negative perceptions. They give us a chance to convince people in Scotland of the value of what we stand for... Too often, we hear defeatist assertions that Scotland is somehow a more left wing country than England. But we know there are thousands of people throughout Scotland who share our desire to see an enterprising economy, strong, safe communities and effective public services. Yet, we have lost thousands of centre-right votes over the last 20 years. If we don't change, we will never get them back.

As Einstein said, insanity is doing the same thing over and over again and expecting different results.

By changing our party, we will put ourselves back in the game. There is everything to play for...

So the choice we face is stark and serious. It is, without exaggeration, adapt or die. My ideas could be rejected. We could adopt the old approach. Disengaged from the evolution of the Scottish Parliament; negative towards our prospects as a country; further alienated from the people of Scotland; an attempt to push back the tide of history; I've seen that movie before. It doesn't have a happy ending.

As Einstein said, insanity is doing the same thing over and over again and expecting different results. It is time to try something different. A bold, new direction. Creating a new party; uniting people of all ages; from all backgrounds; and from all areas; not ashamed to vote for us; saving our United Kingdom. To me, it would be a great honour to lead such a party.[1]

Vote, Jock.
Vote, Sweaty Sock.
Talk properly.

Alan Bissett
1975–

'VOTE BRITAIN' YOUTUBE VIDEO

13 JANUARY 2012

The writer Alan Bissett came up with 'Vote Britain' while on Raasay in January 2012. He had just heard the Prime Minister on the radio discussing his plans to enable the Scottish Parliament to hold a legal referendum on independence subject to certain conditions. 'I was quivering with anger,' recalled Bissett.

He went for a short walk with his laptop, 'feeling heavily pregnant with something', and wrote the poem in about an hour and a half. 'I was literally shaking with excitement as I finished it,' he remembered, 'as I knew I'd written the piece that would pretty much define my career from then on in, but knew also that it articulated something subterranean, defiant and taboo.'

Bissett posted 'Vote Britain' on his website that same day, and after a few days of 'excited attention' also memorised and filmed it for YouTube. It went, in web parlance, viral, and received around 25,000 hits in the space of two days. 'I was from that moment – for better or worse – in the thick of the independence debate.' In September that year Bissett also read the poem to thousands of people at an independence rally in Edinburgh, and remembers a 'colossal roar the like of which I'd never heard for any reading of mine'.[1]

Alan Bissett was born in Falkirk in 1975. He studied English literature and education at Stirling University, before going on to teach English. He returned to Stirling to study for a Masters degree and subsequently lectured in creative writing at the Universities of Leeds and Glasgow before becoming a full-time writer, novelist, playwright and performer. His debut novel,* Boyracers*, was published by Polygon in 2001.

People of Scotland, vote with your heart.
Vote with your love for the Queen who nurtured you, cradle to grave,
Who protects you and cares, her most darling subjects, to whom you gave
the glens she adores to roam freely through, the stags her children dearly
enjoy killing.
First into battle, loyal and true. The enemy's scared of you.

That's why we send you over the top with your och-aye-the-noo Mactivish
there's been a murrrderrr jings! crivvens! Deepfriedfuckinmarsbar wee wee
dram of whisky hoots mon there's a moose loose aboot this smackaddict
Vote, Jock. Vote, Sweaty Sock. Talk properly.
Vote with those notes we scrutinise in our shops
(might be legal tender but looks dodgy to me).
Vote for the Highland Clearances. Baaaaaaaaaa.
Vote for nuclear submarines in your water.
Vote for the Olympic Games you didn't vote for
(but you'll pay for it, you'll pay for it).
Vote Conservative. Vote Lib Dem. Vote Libservative. Vote Condabour.
Vote with the chip on your shoulder.

People of Scotland, vote with your heart.

Vote Labour. New Labour. Old Labour. Scottish Labour.
(Get back in line, Scottish Labour, HQ in Solihull will issue their commands shortly,
just keep the vote coming in from up there thanks goodbye.
Subsidy junkie.)
Vote for any argument you construct in your defence being "anti-English".
Vote for Scots who make their career in Scotland being "unambitious".
Vote for enjoying your own culture being soooooooo parochial.
Vote God Save the Queen and that bit about us crushing you all.
Hush. There there.
Vote for Scotland being refered to as a "region", like, say, Yorkshire? Or East Anglia?
Vote for our voices dominating your media, but in no way telling you what to think.
Take a drink. Go on, son, take a drink.
Vote for oil revenue, which we ensure flows directly from us into you.
Vote for being told you're the only country in the world that could not possibly survive and that without us you'd fall to pieces like children abandoned in the wild, caked in faeces.
Vote Daily Mail and Rupert Murdoch and
illegalimmigrantskilledPrincessDiana and
London London London most exciting city in the world, darling
(Glasgow is a very violent place, is it not. Do you have art?).
Vote with your heart. Vote Empire. Vote tradition.
Vote for our proud shared history of
enslavingothernationsandstealingtheirnaturalresources
Bringing Wealth and Prosperity to the World!
and being on the right side just *once*, and that's only because it was against yer actual fucking Hitler.

Vote for the #ScottishConspiracy at Westminster
(who really runs the show here eh – Blair, Brown – got your own in that time, we aren't allowed to vote in Holyrood but there's Archie McPhee pulling wee strings in our parliament when we wouldn't even *think* about interfering in how you run your own affairs but while we're at it, this referendum eh? A so-called referendum, is it? Have it *now*, make sure it looks like *this*).
Vote for very, very, very rich people patronising you.
Vote for Glasgow having the highest knife-crime and lowest life expectancy in Europe
due to our generosity. You may thank us at your leisure.
Vote for the absence of your history in our schools.
All Brits together.

Vote with the chip on your shoulder.

Vote for our shock at your ingratitude!
Vote for us saying "Eh? Eh?" when you open up your porridge mooth.
Vote for bafflement about why you want the England football team to lose.
We always want the Scots to win (except in referenda).
Vote for psychopathic villains with your accent in a soap opera.
Vote for tuition fees and student loans, ensuring that the brightest of your working class
(since you still insist upon the term, although Our Leaders had it banned)
will one day rise and take their place in this great land.
Vote for us deploying strategic references to Braveheart to dismiss you all.
Vote for Robert Burns being called by Paxman "sentimental doggerel".
Vote for The Iron Lady. Such a *strong* leader, gave this country *backbone*
(you didn't really want those unions, industries or council homes, just made the place look tatty).
Vote for a deregulated banking class, lionising of the
hardworkingwealthgeneratingjobcreatingentrepreneurs
who you will in no way refer to as "greedy, selfish bastards".
Give them your taxes.
Vote for foreign wars.
Yes, sadly, some of you will die. But you will return to a hero's welcome Jock
the Union Jack, proud symbol of integrity and honour, draped across your coffin
while your mother, dabbing at her eyes, recalls the words she learned in school
in Kircudbright
"There is some corner of a foreign field that is forever England."
Vote with your heart.[2]

I'm here to stand up and speak out for what I believe in. I believe in the United Kingdom.

David Cameron
1966–

SPEECH ON A SCOTTISH INDEPENDENCE REFERENDUM · EDINBURGH
16 FEBRUARY 2012

For David Cameron, the Old Etonian leader of a Conservative Party with, as he joked, fewer MPs than there were pandas at Edinburgh Zoo, to make a speech in Scotland and the prospect of independence was obviously like walking a rhetorical tightrope – one false move and the Prime Minister would have killed his Government's chances of keeping the United Kingdom together. History would have written him up as a 21st-century Lord North.

David William Donald Cameron was born in 1966 (his father was Scottish) and educated at Eton and Oxford with the first in politics, philosophy and economics. He worked at the Conservative Research Department and then as a special adviser, to the Chancellor and Home Secretary. Cameron then spent seven years at Carlton Communications before entering Parliament as the MP for Witney in 2001. He held several front-bench posts before being elected Conservative Party leader in 2005. In 2010 Cameron became Prime Minister of a Conservative-Liberal Democrat Coalition.

But that did not happen. Instead, a few weeks after a controversial intervention in which Cameron made it clear he would temporarily equip the Scottish Government with the power to hold a referendum, he delivered a well-crafted speech (with Edinburgh Castle visible behind him) which won plaudits from unlikely quarters; the left-leaning *Scotsman* columnist Joyce Macmillan thought for 'the first time in a decade, [Alex Salmond] has a Unionist opponent who is seriously challenging [his] narrative'.

The Scottish First Minister, however, did not share Macmillan's enthusiasm. He seized upon the Prime Minister's vague commitment to devolve more powers to Holyrood following a 'no' vote, harking back to a similar pledge from another Old Etonian Tory who had promised a better scheme of devolution if Scots voted 'no' in the 1979 devolution referendum. 'The shadow of Sir Alec Douglas-Home I think is cast very large over this,' said Salmond. 'What's the old saying "fool me once, shame on you, fool me twice shame on me". Scotland, I don't believe, will be fooled twice.'

For politicians north and south of the border... there is a danger of living in the past when thinking of Scotland. That is partly because its history is populated so thickly with great men and women who we might want to conscript for our contemporary battles. Those of us on the centre right will pray in aid of Adam Smith and David Hume: economic liberals and philosophical conservatives whose enlightenment thought laid the basis for later political action. On the left, the examples of James Maxton and Keir Hardie can still inspire class strugglers to one more heave...

But proud as that past and present are, I am convinced that both for Scotland and for the United Kingdom, our best days lie ahead of us. And that even though it may be a great historical construct, the United Kingdom is actually even more of an inspiring model for the future... So I come here today with one simple message: I hope and wish that Scotland will vote to remain part of the United

For politicians north and south of the border... there is a danger of living in the past when thinking of Scotland.

Kingdom... I am not here to make a case on behalf of my Party, its interests or its approach to office. I am here to stand up and speak out for what I believe in. I believe in the United Kingdom. I am a Unionist head, heart and soul. I believe that England, Scotland, Wales, Northern Ireland, we are stronger together than we ever would be apart...

Now it is absolutely right that since the SNP won the Scottish elections, they should be able to determine the business of the Scottish Parliament and the agenda of the Scottish Government. They want to put the question of independence to the Scottish people and their ultimate ambition is clear: they want Scotland to leave the United Kingdom. And it is right too that the choice over independence should be for the Scottish people to make. But that choice should not be made – with its consequences for all of us – without explaining why I believe in the United Kingdom, and why it matters to so many of us...

My argument is simple. Of course Scotland could govern itself. So could England. My point is that we do it so much better together. I can – and I will – enumerate a number of practical reasons for our United Kingdom. But the reason I make the case is partly emotional. Because this is a question of the

Of course Scotland could govern itself. So could England.

heart as well as the head. The United Kingdom is not just some sort of deal, to be reduced to the lowest common denominator. It is a precious thing; it is about our history, our values, our shared identity and our joint place in the world. I am not just proud of the Union because it is useful. I am proud because it shapes and strengthens us all...

Just think of what we have achieved together. Scotland has contributed to the greatest political, cultural, and social success story of the last 300 years: the creation and flourishing of a United Kingdom built on freedom and inclusivity. Individual nations can – of course – adhere around ancient myths, blood-soaked memories, and opposition to others. But we have built – in the United Kingdom – something that also coheres around the values embodied in standing up for freedom and democracy around the globe: in free healthcare for all; in a generous welfare system for the poorest; and championing the most vulnerable on the world stage. A United Kingdom which is not monoglot, monochrome, and minimalist but multi-national, multi-cultural, and modern in every way...

Just think of what we have achieved together.

But it is not just about what we have achieved together; it is about who we are together. The ties of blood are actually growing thicker. Far from growing apart, we are growing together. There are now more Scots living in England, and English people living in Scotland, than ever before. And almost half of Scots now have English relatives. I am something of a classic case. My father's father was a Cameron. My mother's mother was a Llewellyn. I was born and have always lived in England: I am proud to be English. But like so many others too, I am proud to be British as well. Proud of the United Kingdom and proud of Scotland's place within it...

But then there are the practical reasons for the Union to stay together. The United Kingdom helps to make Scotland – and all of us – stronger, safer, richer and fairer... And let me say something else about devolution. This does not have to be the end of the road. When the referendum on independence is over, I am open to looking at how the devolved settlement can be improved further. And yes, that does mean considering what further powers could be devolved. But that must be a question for after the referendum, when Scotland has made its choice about the fundamental question of independence or the United Kingdom. When Scotland has settled this question once and for all – and ended the uncertainty that I believe could damage and hold back Scotland's prospects and potential – then is the time for that issue.

So, I believe the strengths that have served us all through the centuries are precisely the ones that we need today. Our United Kingdom is a modern Union: it is one that evolves; one that protects us; one that allows our different nations to grow stronger; because we share the same secure foundations: institutions that celebrate diversity and turn it into a strength. Scotland's greatest poet said we should 'see ourselves as others see us', and that is worth doing, because our

Union is not some antique imposition: it is living; it is free; it is adaptable; it is admired around the world as a source of prosperity, power, and security. Just think for a moment: could you explain to someone in America, or France, or Australia what was so intolerable about Great Britain that we decided to build artificial barriers between our nations?'

This job has taken me in every hole in my fucking body.

Malcolm Tucker

FINAL RANT FROM *the thick of it* SERIES 4

27 OCTOBER 2012

Shortly after *The Thick of It* first appeared on BBC4 in 2005 it became a favourite with the UK's political classes, the *Yes, Prime Minister* of its era. Although obviously exaggerated, its depiction of hapless government ministers, insipid civil servants and aggressive spin-doctors struck a chord at the height of the New Labour era.

Malcolm Tucker was the aggressive and foul-mouthed director of communications for the government depicted in the television series* The Thick of It*, the film* In the Loop *and, during the 2010 general election, a column in the* Guardian *newspaper. Generally considered to be based on the real-life spin doctor Alastair Campbell, after 2010 Tucker also featured as a similarly profane opposition chief spinner.

Written by the Glaswegian satirist Armando Iannucci, the series continued when Gordon Brown became Prime Minister in 2007. Its most popular character was undoubtedly Malcolm Tucker, the menacing Scottish spin doctor played by Peter Capaldi (another Glaswegian). By series 4 the government and opposition have switched places following a general election and a Coalition now governs the UK.

The last few episodes show both parties trying to cover their tracks after a public healthcare bill leads to the suicide of Douglas Tickel, a nurse with a history of mental illness. 'The Gooding Inquiry' is launched after Tickel's medical records are leaked, and this Tucker rant (not so much a speech) takes place after his evidence session. Aware his political career is over, he lets rip to Ollie, his likely replacement.

I'm gonna leave the stage with my head held fucking high. What you're gonna see is a master class in fucking dignity, son. The audience will be on their feet. "There he goes!", they'll say. No friends – no *real* friends. No children, no glory, no memoirs. Well, fuck them...

You know Jackie fucking Chan about me. You know fuck all about me! I am totally beyond the realms of your fuckin' tousle-haired, fuckin' dim-witted compre-fucking-hension. I don't just take this fucking job home, you know!

I take this job home, it fucking ties me to the bed, and it fuckin' fucks me from arsehole to breakfast! Then it wakes me up in the morning with a cup full of piss slammed in my face, slaps me about the chops to make sure I'm awake enough so

I'm gonna leave the stage with my head held fucking high.

it can kick me in the fucking bollocks! This job has taken me in every hole in my fucking body. "Malcolm!", it's gone, you can't know Malcolm because Malcolm is not here! Malcolm fucking left the building fucking years ago! This is a fucking husk, I am a fucking host for this fucking job. Do you want this job? Yes? You do fucking want this job? Then you're gonna have to swallow this whole fucking life and let it grow inside you like a parasite, getting bigger and bigger and bigger until it fucking eats your insides alive and it stares out of your eyes and tells you what to do.[1]

... a nation that knows itself, perhaps for the first time.

Nicola Sturgeon
1970–

'BRINGING THE POWERS HOME TO BUILD A BETTER NATION'
UNIVERSITY OF STRATHCLYDE
3 DECEMBER 2012

In October 2012, following months of negotiation, representatives of the Scottish and UK Governments put their signatures to what became known as the Edinburgh Agreement, an inter-governmental understanding that a referendum on Scottish independence would be conducted under certain conditions and a spirit of mutual goodwill.

Nicola Sturgeon was born in Irvine in 1970 and educated at Greenwood Academy. She also studied law at the University of Glasgow and worked as a solicitor in Glasgow before entering the Scottish Parliament in 1999. In 2007 she was appointed Deputy First Minister and Health Secretary, while in September 2012 Sturgeon became Cabinet Secretary for Infrastructure, Investment and Cities.

Nicola Sturgeon, Deputy First Minister of Scotland since 2007, was one of the Scottish Government's signatories, for she had successfully concluded talks with her Westminster counterparts a few days before. A month or so later Sturgeon consciously tried to raise the level of an often fractious debate with a thoughtful speech at the University of Strathclyde.

From its opening lines by the (very English) poet T.S. Eliot, to its 'Kirsty' motif, Sturgeon's speech was unusually deep, eloquent and layered. Although it said little new, it worked because as the *Daily Telegraph*'s Alan Cochrane put it, she 'delivered what was essentially a personal manifesto',[1] drawing on her family background and early life to explain why she believed in independence.

"We shall not cease from exploration and the end of all our exploring will be to arrive where we started and know the place for the first time". That wonderful T.S. Eliot quotation always makes me think of Scotland.

As a nation, we have done a lot of exploring – we were a sovereign, independent country, and then gave our independence away. We helped to build an empire, and saw it decay. We transformed a rural economy into the workshop of the world – and then watched as the work left. We discovered oil and stood by as the revenues were spent by others. And today – with more oil,

We transformed a rural economy into the workshop of the world

in value, still in the North Sea than has already been extracted – we stand on the brink of a renewable energy revolution. Politically, we have been a Liberal stronghold. We have voted Tory in huge numbers – hard though it is to believe that now. We have been a bastion for the Labour party. We have argued over our best form of government for centuries and after three hundred years without it now have our own parliament. A parliament that was intended to kill demand for independence stone dead, but is now governed by a pro-independence majority. And in 2014, we will decide if we want to complete our Parliament's powers and restore our nation's sovereignty. And that is when Scotland will have the chance to bring home the powers we need to build a better country.

Today I want to talk, as a Scottish Government Minister, about the Scottish Government's case for independence and our vision for an independent Scotland...A country with a stable economy that works for the many and not just the few; one that knows it must create the wealth it needs to support the strong public services we value; a country that manages our vast resources responsibly, with an eye to the future; a country that gets the government it votes for; a country that has fairness at its core and allows all of us as individuals to reach our full potential. That is the destination of our journey – Scotland. The Scotland we want to be. A nation like any other, a nation bound in the grasp of other nations as we are all united in a globalised world, but a nation that knows itself, perhaps for the first time...

Down the years, many people have asked me why I ended up in the SNP and not the Labour Party. Why did a young girl, growing up in a working class family in the west of Scotland – a part of the country where in those days, they would joke that the Labour vote was weighed rather than counted; someone who was, just like Labour was in those days, anti-Trident and pro-social justice and went on to work as a social justice lawyer in Drumchapel – why does that person end up in the SNP instead of Labour.

The reason is simple. I joined the SNP because it was obvious to me then – as it still is today – that you cannot guarantee social justice unless you are in control of the delivery. And that is my central argument to you today. Not just

We have argued over our best form of government for centuries and after three hundred years without it now have our own parliament.

that independence is more than an end in itself. But that it is only by bringing the powers home, by being independent, that we can build the better nation we all want. And I ask you, as you make up your minds over these next two years, to base your decision, not on how Scottish or British you feel, but on what kind of country you want Scotland to be and how best you think that can be achieved...

When I think of the why of independence, I think of a child. Let's call her Kirsty. She is part of the new generation in this land. According to where Kirsty is born, and what her parents will do, much of her life will be pre-determined. If we let Kirsty down in the first months of her life, then the chances are that all the welfare, free education, and state intervention that we can provide, will never

I believe we do live in the early days of a better nation.

quite make up for that. If we fail her when she is young, then we have failed her for life.

Not only that – but by denying Kirsty proper support we have switched her from being an asset – to herself, her community and Scotland – and turned her into a demand – for money, services and help. Every time we fail Kirsty, we fail our own future. Because Kirsty will be the carer to tomorrow's pensioners and the Chief Executive of tomorrow's companies. She will be the inheritor of our mistakes. Fail her now, and we fail her again and again and again, until she is just another figure shuffling through our welfare statistics, set to die a decade or so earlier than her richer neighbours.

I think of Kirsty because none of us in the movement to bring powers home are doing it just for the here and now. We are doing it for Kirsty, for our own version of that child, for the thousands of children right now growing up in poverty, for the disabled person facing welfare cuts, for our friends who can't get a job or who are worrying about how to pay the mortgage, for the single mother slaving away at two jobs but still struggling to put food on the table...

I started with a quote from T.S. Eliot. Let me end with Alasdair Gray. He urged us to work as if we live in the early years of a better nation. I believe we do live in the early days of a better nation. The journey towards a better Scotland has started. The duty of our generation is to ensure that the next generation has the ability to complete that journey.[2]

Appeasement has never worked to further the cause of peace in the past, and it will not now, and it will not in the future.

Dr Liam Fox
1961–

SPEECH DURING DEBATE ON MILITARY ACTION IN SYRIA
HOUSE OF COMMONS
29 AUGUST 2013

When, in the summer of 2013, reports emerged of a chemical weapons attack on the outskirts of Syria, the Coalition Government led by David Cameron resolved that Bashar al-Assad had crossed a line. Denouncing the attack as a 'war crime', even before United Nations weapons inspectors had finished their investigations, Westminster was on a war footing.

The Prime Minister also decided to recall Parliament, which met on Thursday 29 August to debate the proposed military intervention in the Middle East, chiefly targeted missile strikes intended to discourage future chemical attacks. Crucially, Cameron believed the Labour Party intended to vote with the Government. On the eve of the debate, however, matters had taken an unexpected turn and the Prime Minister was forced to water down his proposed motion.

Dr Liam Fox was born in 1961 and studied medicine at the University of Glasgow, working as a GP and Civilian Army Medical Officer before joining the House of Commons in 1992. He held several ministerial roles in John Major's government, and thereafter in opposition. Fox stood unsuccessfully in the 2005 Conservative leadership election, but in 2010 was appointed Defence Secretary. He resigned in October 2011 following a lobbying scandal.

Several Conservative MPs, including the former Defence Secretary Liam Fox, did their best to convince the House to back the Government. Dr Fox said he shared public 'scepticism' about military intervention, but also spoke movingly of the consequences of doing nothing. It was not enough. When MPs voted on the main motion late that evening, they defeated the Government by just 13 votes, killing any prospect of UK involvement.

There are a number of things on which the House will be generally agreed. The first is that, for whatever reason, there is widespread scepticism among the British public about any further military involvement overseas. A number of questions need to be answered before we become involved in any form of military action. The first is what a good outcome looks like, the second is whether such an outcome can be engineered, the third is whether we will be part of engineering such an outcome, and the fourth is how much of the eventual outcome we want to have ownership of.

I do not believe that we can answer any of those questions to our satisfaction with regard to the civil war in Syria. I believe that that is why the British public are deeply sceptical about our being involved in that civil war in any way, shape or form. I share that scepticism. I also believe that there is no national interest for the United Kingdom in taking a side in that civil war. To exchange an Iran-friendly and Hezbollah-friendly Assad regime for an anti-west, anti-Christian and anti-Israel al-Qaeda regime does not seem to offer us any advantage.

However, that is not the issue before us today. There is a separate issue on which we need to have great clarity, which is how we respond to a regime that has used chemical weapons against its civilian population—something that is against international law and is a war crime. The pictures we have seen in recent days have shocked us, even in our desensitised age. The pictures of toddlers laid out in rows were, and should be, deeply disturbing to all of us. The question is whether we are willing to tolerate more such pictures and, if not, how we go about minimising the risk of such pictures coming to our screens in the future.

The pictures we have seen in recent days have shocked us, even in our desensitised age.

It is true that if we take action against the Assad regime we cannot guarantee that it will not do something, or similar things, again in the future, but I believe it will minimise the risk and show the people of Syria that we are on their side and that the rest of the world is serious about its obligations in enforcing the existing law about the use of chemical weapons.

Much of the debate has focused on the consequences of taking action, but we must also focus on the consequences of not taking action. Will it make the Syrian people more or less safe from the use of such weapons in the future? On the implications for the Syrian regime, will it make it feel that it is more or less secure in taking such actions again in the future? On regimes in other parts of the world that might decide to use chemical weapons against their domestic populations, what signal would we send them about the international community's willingness to stop such use in future if we do nothing? Let us also not forget the onlookers in this—Iran—who have their own nuclear intentions and are intent on testing the will of the international community...

As the Prime Minister said, it is a judgment call. It is incumbent on those who take these decisions ultimately to determine whether they think it is more likely that we will be drawn into such a conflict or whether we will achieve the objectives without that happening. That is a matter for legitimate debate in the House. I believe that if we do not take action—and that probably means military action—the credibility of the international community will be greatly damaged. What value would red lines have in the future if we are unwilling to implement those that already exist?

What value would red lines have in the future if we are unwilling to implement those that already exist?

... Let me say briefly one other thing. The Government should be commended for taking the United Nations route. It is right and proper that we do so and that the appropriate amount of time is given to consideration, but that comes with a caveat. It is clear that Russia has military interests in the port of Tartus and that it still feels very sore about its belief that it was sold a pup over Libya. We are not likely to get Russian support in the Security Council, nor are we likely to get Chinese support there, either. We cannot allow a situation whereby the international community's ability to implement international law is thwarted by a constant veto by Russia and China. Therefore, I think we should be deeply grateful to the Attorney-General for the clarity of the advice that he has set out on how we can carry forward our international humanitarian obligations were such a situation to present itself.

Let us be very clear that to do nothing will be interpreted in Damascus as appeasement of a dreadful regime and the dreadful actions it has carried out. Appeasement has never worked to further the cause of peace in the past, and it will not now, and it will not in the future.[1]

Endnotes

JOHN KNOX

1 http://www.applesofgold.co.uk/john_knox.htm

FOLLY

1 http://www.stagingthescottishcourt.org/texts/jamie-reid-baxter-on-a-satire-of-the-three-estates/

2 Sir David Lindsay and Roderick Lyall, *Ane Satyre Of The Thrie Estaitis* (Edinburgh, 2008), pp. 252–55 (iBooks edition).

3 http://books.google.co.uk/books?id=lkwJAAAAQAAJ&pg=PA541&source=gbs_toc_r&cad=4#v=onepage&q&f=false

MICHAEL CAMERON

1 http://www.thereformation.info/sanquhardec.htm

THOMAS MUIR

1 Thomas Jones Howell (ed), *A Complete Collection of State Trials and Proceedings for High Treason and Other Crimes and Misdemeanors* (London, 1817) pp. 227–28.

MARY QUEEN OF SCOTS

1 http://www.gutenberg.org/files/6791/6791-h/6791-h.htm#link2H_4_0025

DAVID LIVINGSTONE

1 George Seaver, *David Livingstone: His Life and Letters* (London, 1957), pp. 286–87.

2 http://davidlivingstone2013.blogspot.co.uk/2012/05/cambridge-speech-of-december-1857.html

ALEXANDER 'GREEK' THOMSON

1 *Glasgow Herald*, 23 February 1859.

SIR JOHN A MACDONALD

1 William Jennings Brian (ed), *The World's Famous Orations Vol V: Great Britain* (New York, 1906), pp. 3–16.

THOMAS CARLYLE

1 William Jennings Brian (ed), *The World's Famous Orations Vol V: Great Britain* (New York, 1906), pp. 17–30.

SHERIFF ALEXANDER NICHOLSON

1 *The Inverness Courier*, 25 April 1882.

WILLIAM EWART GLADSTONE

1 *HC Deb 7 June 1886 vol 306* cc. 1215–40.

KEIR HARDIE

1 Emrys Hughes, *Keir Hardie* (London, 1956), pp. 60–61.

2 HC Deb, 7 February 1893, vol 8, cc. 724–32.

ANDREW CARNEGIE

1 http://historymatters.gmu.edu/d/5766

WINSTON CHURCHILL

1 http://www.winstonchurchill.org/learn/speeches/speeches-of-winston-churchill/99-liberalism-and-socialism

ARTHUR JAMES BALFOUR

1 HC Deb, 13 June 1910, vol 17, cc. 1141–45

ANDREW BONAR LAW

1 Robert Blake, *The Unknown Prime Minister: The Life and Times of Andrew Bonar Law 1858–1923* (London 1955), p. 130.

JOHN BUCHAN

1 HC Deb 6 July 1927 vol 208 cc. 1310–17.

JENNIE LEE

1 HC Deb, 25 April 1929, vol 227, cc. 1114–19.

WILLIE GALLACHER

1 HC Deb, 4 December 1935, vol 307, cc. 200–07.

SIR DAVID MAXWELL FYFE

1 http://www.loc.gov/rr/frd/Military_Law/pdf/NT_Vol-XXII.pdf

HAMISH HENDERSON

1 Courtesy of Timothy Neat.

BARONESS ELLIOT OF HARWOOD

1 http://www.parliament.uk/about/living-heritage/evolutionofparliament/houseoflords/house-of-lords-reform/from-the-collections/from-the-parliamentary-collections-lords-reform/background-life-peerages/introducing-the-bill/
2 HL Deb, 4 November 1958, vol 212, cc. 160–67.

JUDITH HART

1 HC Deb, 3 November 1959, vol 612, cc. 894–98.

WILLIE ROSS

1 STUC minutes were typically recorded in the third person.
2 Records of the Scottish Trades Union Congress (Glasgow Caledonian University Archives), 71st STUC Annual Report, 1968, pp. 412–18.

PASTOR JACK GLASS

1 http://www.pastorjackglass.com/articles.html

JOHN CLEESE

1 http://montypythonline.tumblr.com/post/6698437544/the-pythonline-internet-lecture-on-cowardice

RUSSELL JOHNSTON

1 Russell Johnston, *Scottish Liberal Party Conference Speeches* 1971–1978 (Bookmag, 1979), pp. 55–63.

QUEEN ELIZABETH II

1 http://www.royal.gov.uk/ImagesandBroadcasts/Historic%20speeches%20and%20broadcasts/SilverJubileeaddresstoParliament4May1977.aspx

DUKE OF EDINBURGH

1 *Prince Philip Speaks: Selected Speeches* 1956–1959 (London 1960), p. 3.
2 'Intellectual Dissent and the Reversal of Trends', in Seddon, Arthur, ed., The Coming Confrontation (IEA 1978), pp. 208–17.

MALCOLM RIFKIND

1 HC Deb, 20 June 1979, vol 968, cc. 1453–58.

ROBIN COOK

1 HC Deb, 22 July 1980, vol 989, cc. 285–88.

ERIC LIDDELL

1 http://www.imdb.com/title/tt0082158/quotes

MARGARET THATCHER

1 http://www.margaretthatcher.org/document/104936

MICK MCGAHEY

1 Minutes of Scottish miners' conference, June 1985, courtesy of Nicky Wilson, NUM Scotland.

MURIEL SPARK

1 Joseph Hynes (ed), *Critical Essays on Muriel Spark* (New York, 1992), pp. 33–37.

WILLIAM MCILVANNEY

1 William McIlvanney, 'Stands Scotland Where It Did?' in *Surviving the Shipwreck* (Mainstream, 1991), p. 246.

NORMAN WILLIS

1 *The Times*, 31 March 1988.
2 1988 TUC Congress report, pp. 441–42.

JIM SILLARS

1 *Scotsman* 15/11/1988.
2 HC Deb, 23 November 1988, vol 142, cc. 121–217.

NELSON MANDELA

1 Tape B13078, STV (Scottish Television) archives.

DONALD DEWAR

1 Mark Stuart, *John Smith: A Life* (Politico's, 2005), ???
2 *Scotsman*, 20 May 1994

WILLIAM WALLACE

1 http://www.awesomefilm.com/script/braveheart_transcript.txt

THABO MBEKI

1 http://www.gov.za/search97cgi/s97_

TILDA SWINTON

1 http://www.closeupfilmcentre.com/vertigo_magazine/volume-2-issue-4-spring-2003/tilda-swinton-in-the-spirit-of-derek-jarman/

DAVID MCLETCHIE

1 Scottish Parliament Official Report, 28 November 2002.

WENDY ALEXANDER

1 http://www.institute-of-governance.org/news-events/news/2007/wendy_alexander_presents_a_new_agenda_for_scotland

MARGO MACDONALD

1 http://www.scottish.parliament.uk/parliamentarybusiness/28862.aspx?r=4785&mode=html

GORDON BROWN

1 *Guardian*, 4 May 2010.
2 http://www.totalpolitics.com/print/speeches/35363/gordon-brown-prime-minister-and-the-leader-of-the-labour-party-speaks-at-citizens-uk.thtml

CHRISTOPHER BROOKMYRE

1 *Scotsman*, 24 May 2008.
2 http://www.humanism-scotland.org.uk/content/about_society/
3 http://old.richarddawkins.net/discussions/619092-edinburgh-s-march-to-enlightenment-event-23-04-11

ALEX SALMOND

1 http://www.royal.gov.uk/LatestNewsandDiary/Speechesandarticles/2011/TheQueensAddresstotheScottishParliament1July2011.aspx
2 http://www.scotland.gov.uk/News/Speeches/scotparlopngJuly1-2011

MURDO FRASER

1 MURDO2011 Media Release, 5 September 2011.

ALAN BISSETT

1 Alan Bissett to the author, 21 July 2013.
2 http://www.youtube.com/watch?v=Z-znkbMzi4A

MALCOLM TUCKER

1 *The Thick of It*, Series 4, Episode 7, http://www.imdb.com/title/tt2469726/quotes

NICOLA STURGEON

1 *Daily Telegraph*, 4 December 2012.
2 http://www.scotland.gov.uk/News/Speeches/better-nation-031212

DR LIAM FOX

1 HC Deb, 29 August 2013, cc. 1452–54.

Luath Press Limited

committed to publishing well written books worth reading

LUATH PRESS takes its name from Robert Burns, whose little collie Luath (*Gael.*, swift or nimble) tripped up Jean Armour at a wedding and gave him the chance to speak to the woman who was to be his wife and the abiding love of his life. Burns called one of 'The Twa Dogs' Luath after Cuchullin's hunting dog in Ossian's *Fingal*. Luath Press was established in 1981 in the heart of Burns country, and now resides a few steps up the road from Burns' first lodgings on Edinburgh's Royal Mile.

Luath offers you distinctive writing with a hint of unexpected pleasures.

Most bookshops in the UK, the US, Canada, Australia, New Zealand and parts of Europe either carry our books in stock or can order them for you. To order direct from us, please send a £sterling cheque, postal order, international money order or your credit card details (number, address of cardholder and expiry date) to us at the address below. Please add post and packing as follows: UK – £1.00 per delivery address; overseas surface mail – £2.50 per delivery address; overseas airmail – £3.50 for the first book to each delivery address, plus £1.00 for each additional book by airmail to the same address. If your order is a gift, we will happily enclose your card or message at no extra charge.

ILLUSTRATION: IAN KELLAS

Luath Press Limited
543/2 Castlehill
The Royal Mile
Edinburgh EH1 2ND
Scotland

Telephone: 0131 225 4326 (24 hours)
Fax: 0131 225 4324
email: sales@luath.co.uk
Website: www.luath.co.uk